THE NEW AGE IN GLASTONBURY

The New Age in Glastonbury

The Construction of Religious Movements

Ruth Prince and David Riches

Berghahn Books
New York • Oxford

First published in 2000 by **Berghahn Books**

www.berghahnbooks.com

Library of Congress Cataloging-in-Publication Data

Prince, Ruth.
    The New Age in Glastonbury : the construction of religious
    movements / Ruth Prince and David Riches.
      p. cm.
    Includes bibliographical references (p.) and index.
    ISBN 1-57181-933-2 – ISBN 1-57181-792-1 (pb.)
    1. New Age movement.   2. Glastonbury (England) – Religion.
    3. England – Religion. I. Riches, David. II. Title.

BP605.N48 P755 2000
299'.93 – dc21   00-045497

British Library Cataloguing in Publication Data

A catalogue record for this book is available from the British
Library.

ISBN 1-57181-933-2 (hardback)
ISBN 1-57181-792-1 (paperback)

Contents

v

List of illustrations

Preface

The Harmonic Convergence was a fortuitous moment to start anthropological work on the New Age movement. Ruth Prince had gone to Glastonbury during summer 1987 to conduct a pilot study, and she straight away got caught up with preparations for the 'World Healing Event', a period of global New Age consciousness; it was a time when the New Age in the town was very much on show. The World Healing Event concerned the Mayan prophecy, repeated by José Argüelles in recent times (1987), that the earth heads towards a point of total annihilation, and that a group of people, some 144,000 strong, will come forward to begin the process of healing. Based on the Aztec calendar, a galactic synchronisation (the Harmonic Convergence) timed for 16–17 August 1987 signals the impending new social order (which properly commences in A.D. 2012) (York 1995: 84). In Britain, Glastonbury is a place where the cosmic energies are propitious, and the town had been singled out as one among several world locations for such an historical moment publicly to be acknowledged.

The aim of this book is to analyse how people in the West create social and religious movements, and why such movements take the cultural features that they do. The ethnographic focus is the New Age movement, both as a late twentieth century socio-cultural phenomenon in the Western world, and more especially as it appears in Glastonbury, which is the New Age mecca in Britain. We consider that by deliberating on the New Age in Glastonbury one can expose the social processes by which, in general, non-mainstream social and cosmological worlds are generated and sustained.

In writing the book we admit to many responsibilities. First, we have a duty to social anthropology, our academic discipline. Social anthropology examines the many and varying ways of life practised by humankind and interprets them systematically. This it especially achieves by focusing on the community level of human social existence – the level where real people live out real lives.

vii

Thus in the present study we make sense of the broader New Age movement by attending in the first instance to New Agers in Glastonbury, a specific locality. Second, we have an obligation to a lay readership. Their interest in our work likely arises from the fact that, in the West these days, New Age dimensions are drawn increasingly into many areas of mainstream practice and belief – from health and healing, right through to business strategy. Finally, there is our debt to people in Glastonbury; calling themselves the Alternative Community, the 700 or so New Agers in and around the town comprise just a small proportion of the estimated 100,000 people in 1990s' Britain who may be said wholly or partially to be committed to New Age lifestyles (Sjoo 1994: 22; York 1995: 43). We have set our task to say something original – anthropologically original – about social and religious movements in general, and the New Age way of life in particular. Yet we wish to offer our explanations in language with which readers unfamiliar with the concepts of present-day social science may feel comfortable. It is in the spirit of such intentions that we hope both professional colleagues and a more general audience will judge this book.

Already, in order to give a feel for the New Age as a distinctive way of life, we have used several labels that need clarification – religion, movement, mainstream society. Later on we shall invoke the term, tribal society. There is also the label New Age itself. Assurances may now be given that in appropriate places in this book we shall elaborate on and justify the concepts that the labels depict. However, in the case of three of them it is proper to offer some preliminary comment, for the impression might otherwise be given that the phenomena to which they refer are homogeneous, monolithic and uncontextualised. Firstly, 'New Age' covers a very broad body of often contrasting doctrines, practices and individuals: there may exist a core New Age vision, but in different contexts this is elaborated as quite varying cosmological knowledge, and by quite different types of people. Moreover, New Agers vary a good deal in the extent New Age practices pervade their lives: for example, some people uphold New Age values in a quite restricted way, such as just in the domain of health and healing. Secondly, 'mainstream society' embraces an enormous range of social groups, classes and ethnicities. As a label it is not ideal, yet we shall use it to convey the broad social world of urban-industrial Western society to which New Agers see themselves as counterposed. Finally, 'tribal society', with its unfortunate connotations of the primitive and of an unchanging traditional world, is another imperfect term.

It is a label to refer to certain kinds of small-scale societies in the non-industrial (or developing) world, where the population is relatively small and social organisation is marked by a relative lack of complexity and hierarchy. When it comes to analysing the nature of the New Age movement, such societies as among the North American Indians, which New Agers themselves frequently laud, turn out to be extremely instructive.

Ruth Prince carried out the main fieldwork for this study in Glastonbury from October 1989 through to December 1990. For her, this was a profound experience. We should like her to introduce it in her own words, starting off in a letter from the field to a friend.

> Imagine yourself suddenly set down ... at a desk in an old manor house in Somerset. The house is filled with plants, and Tibetan gods and goddesses decorate the walls. A chime sounds from the room below and seems to hit a ray of sunlight arching into the room. As the daffodils in the field outside turn in the wind, a small group perform Tai Chi. A twirl of smoke from burning incense escapes through the seventeenth-century windows, spiralling into the cold air.

'Imagine yourself suddenly set down': Malinowski's immortal words are about anthropological work in the southwest Pacific, but in the letter I transposed them to southwest England (Malinowski 1922: 4). Grass hut on the Trobriand Islands as against manor house near Glastonbury. The former stereotypes the people under study as 'other': in the Western mind it evokes 'foreign' and 'exotic'. The latter supplies an image of 'back home', the place to which the anthropologist eventually returns, settling down in a leather armchair with strange tales of lands far away.

Among a growing band of anthropologists for whom the place of research is one's own native land, I was to be confronted by issues and dilemmas that then were not very usual in the discipline. Thousands of miles from the developing countries, the anthropologist's more common stamping ground, my field location was not only in England's pastures green but, more than this, just a few miles from the village where I spent my childhood, and with a group of people whose way of life arrived in Glastonbury, in the late 1960s, around the time I was born. This is not all. My own personal beliefs and attitudes were not so far removed from the Alternative Community; I had been a vegetarian for a number of years, and was interested in environmental issues and in experimental forms of lifestyle. Yet as the bumpy country bus brought me once again to the town in October 1989, my conceptualisations changed completely: the familiar became the 'other'. In anthropology, there is an assumption, which is much debated, that when the anthropologist personally shares the same broad culture of the 'group' under study, this enables clearer understanding. Whether or not this assumption holds, nonetheless one's role as analyst comes to supersede one's former role as native. As Marilyn Strathern writes,

> It is clear that simply being a 'member' of the overarching culture or society in question does not mean that the anthropologist will adopt appropriate local cultural genres. On the contrary he/she may well produce something quite unrecognisable. Commonsense descriptions [must be] set aside. Indigenous reflection [must be] incorporated as part of the data to be explained, and cannot itself be taken as the framing of it, so there is always the discontinuity between indigenous understandings and the analytical concepts which frame the ethnography itself. (1987a: 18)

Similarity and difference, familiar and strange, foreign and home: the 'professionally induced schizophrenia' (Mascarenhas-Keyes 1987: 180) that these oppositions imply informed a large part of my fieldwork experience. 'Similarity' made access to the place of study quite easy. I knew the geographical area well, and had a good idea of the various social groups in the locality. As I grew up, New Age festivals, appearances and lifestyles were a constant source of debate in pubs, town halls and council offices. The vicar of the village where I lived described an astrology camp as 'black magic', and warned people to keep their children away. My own parents, though 'straights', took a more liberal and sympathetic attitude to the colourful incomers.

In 1987, doing the pilot study, my local knowledge had been very helpful. I was already familiar with the terms 'Glastonians' and 'Glastafarians', by which 'mainstream' locals and 'alternative' New Agers were then known, and I had a good idea of the social focal points, as well as a few contacts in the community. Returning to Glastonbury in October 1989, this similarity in background, between myself and the people I was studying, continued to be helpful, principally by enabling me rapidly to adopt the appropriate behaviour, at least to the extent that the Alternative Community would make me welcome. I made a point of telling people I was an anthropologist, but as a young woman in her twenties I passed for a New Ager at a superficial glance. Unlike what anthropologists more normally face, my presence as intruder was not immediately apparent through language barriers or obvious physical differences. I tried to reinforce this by taking an empathetic role vis-à-vis my respondents. As much as possible I avoided formal interviewing, and I used a tape-recorder only twice, on two occasions when I visited a healing centre where I felt they expected to see formal research techniques. Sometimes when talking to people I would use a notebook, but mostly I tried to participate and to simply 'observe' conversations – waiting till later to scribble them down. I would ask leading questions, but I tried not to direct conversations into data-gathering sessions, and instead endeavoured to get included in them and to let the information evolve as they went along. I restricted the use of a camera largely to what could pass for tourist snaps. In all, the aim was to emulate the lifestyle of my respondents, and my method, in true New Age style, was to 'go with the flow'. I attempted to be an 'observing participant', more than a 'participant observer' (Holy 1984: 22).

Upon arrival in Glastonbury the first challenge was to find somewhere to live and some means of meeting people. I put up a notice in *The Glastonbury Experience* saying I was looking for accommodation and soon received a phone call describing an enticing manor house outside Glastonbury which put on retreats and ran Tai Chi classes. Unlike Malinowski's Trobriand Islands village, my field arena was not geographically tight-knit and I was anxious that my living situation would be directly within a 'New Age' environment, so a few days later we were moving in. For most of the period of the following year, my partner Anthony was with me; an American, a philosopher and a good friend, he provided not only support and company but countless insights and a punchball for ideas.

My next, and the hardest, task, was to 'reach' further into the Alternative Community. There was a limit to the amount of time I could sit in cafés hoping to meet people, so through a contact where I was living I got a job serving and washing dishes in a vegan restaurant. Then I got involved in producing an 'alternative' newspaper, which gave me a reason for being in town every day, as well as an extremely useful position in the centre of the information nexus. The Alternative Community in Glastonbury is very fluid, and many people come and stay for a few months only, so it assimilates outsiders easily. The immediate prerequisite for membership is 'attitude'. Before long I was attending a women's group, yoga, crystal workshops, spiritual healing, full moon meditations and weekend-long spiritual retreats.

At this point the tension began to be evident, between myself, the anthropologist, and the New Age, the topic of study. My appearance, and my basic familiarity with New Age lifestyle and culture, had helped in gaining access. However, whilst I attempted totally to immerse myself in New Age culture, both my role as an analyst, and my personal values and beliefs, which depart from the New Age in many respects, separated me from it. Much of my time was spent participating in rituals and conversations with New Agers, and reading literature about the New Age. The culture places high value upon self-expression; it is also an evangelistic culture. Many of the workshops, rituals and even general conversations put me in a position where I was expected to express my most private emotions. To answer honestly, and yet also retain a degree of detachment and a private identity, was sometimes awkward. As the months passed, I learnt the subtleties of the New Age 'language' and was able to express myself correctly. However, in situations where closer relationships developed, but where I could not conceal opinions that sometimes were basically mainstream, people would get frustrated with me, and unpleasant feelings of alienation would develop.

I always saw myself as being 'different' from the New Age, but this is not to say that my own values and worldview did not change during the course of the fieldwork. Being in an atmosphere which places so much emphasis upon the spiritual, the emotional, the intuitive and the magical, it is not difficult to start seeing new meanings, hidden coincidences and novel ways of interpreting events. Tanya Luhrmann (1989), in her ethnography on witchcraft in present-day England, refers to this as interpretive drift, explaining how from involvement in magical practices people brought up in a rational scientific milieu come to incorporate mystical ideas into their worldview. Looking back, I remember private conversations with Anthony during the fieldwork period where the ideas we exchanged employed New Age terminology and called on New Age associations, and were framed, for example, by saying 'I had an intuition', instead of 'it occurred to me' or 'I thought that'.

My personal experiences above all reflect confrontation between similarity and difference. I had intended to build upon similarities in order to construct a bridge between myself and those whom I was studying. On occasion, unlike the white anthropologist in a developing country, I was able to become fully a 'part of the furniture'. Yet for all this, and not least on behalf of my own psychological well-being, I remained apart. Thus, for me, the familiar remained foreign.

We are grateful for the financial support of the Economic and Social Research Council (UK), which funded the main field research and a prior year of preparation. We are also indebted to our many friends in Glastonbury for being frank about their intentions and beliefs. With their penchant for approaching matters holistically we fear they will recoil against the dismembering and reassembling of their society and culture which for us is the stuff of anthropological inquiry. We can only say that we have tried to be sympathetic in this regard, and as far as possible reason analytically with their perspective in mind. We hope New Agers will be intrigued by our opinion that, in Glastonbury, they sustain a mode of social organisation and a body of beliefs and ideas whose features in many crucial respects display striking similarities with the social and cultural forms of 'original human society' – that is to say, human society in its evolutionarily basic form. Finally, we should note that in the descriptions of life in Glastonbury in this book, even as we consider that we have done justice to the quality of the New Age scene in the town, we have changed people's names and also altered a little some of the events and personal details relating to our respondents' lives.

We are indebted to many colleagues, friends and university seminars for comment on earlier versions of our argument. In particular we would like to thank Kay Milton and Roy Dilley for detailed observations on the interpretation of the Glastonbury ethnography. The analytical argument in Chapters 10–13 has received a good deal of critical attention, including from Hastings Donnan and the late Ladislav Holy, and from several seminar presentations. Parts of Chapter 10 were presented to the Anthropology seminar at the University of East London, and Chapter 11 both to the Indigenous Amerindian Studies seminar (University of St Andrews) and to the 'Traditional Cosmology Society' seminar (University of Edinburgh). Chapter 12 was presented to a St Andrews University anthropology seminar. Anthony Tappe drew the pictorial map of Glastonbury enclosed in Chapter 3. Our grateful thanks to all.

Part One

The Argument

1

Representations and Creations

The Theoretical Challenges

Religious movements, both those which are historically of long standing and those which have emerged recently, are deceptive phenomena. Their ethnographic character is plain enough at first glance. They declare themselves in the name of a doctrine that they uphold as coherent and intellectually complete. They lay claim to a way of life morally superior to any other (either in the mainstream world or among rival movements). And to anyone prepared to share in their philosophy of being, they warmly extend a welcome. Yet these features' standing is problematic. These are the images a religious movement supplies: this is the way a movement represents itself to the world.

Theoretical caution is therefore required when a religious movement is the topic of study. One should not succumb to the movement's representation of itself: anthropological analysis is not immune to a movement's charismatic lure, nor to its seductive procedures for drawing followers in. A movement's self-images merit explanation, but these are not its fundamental elements. The challenge must be to elucidate the deeper social currents which bring the movement, in its entirety (including its self-images), into being.

Participants in religious movements uphold representations as well. For example, in the case of recently emerged religious movements, such as the New Age movement, the people involved once fully lived their lives in the mainstream world. Their self-images will refer to personal dissatisfaction with mainstream values and practices, and to the fact that the movement with which they now identify offers something profound which the mainstream failed to provide.

Whilst the opposition between mainstream and movement may be critical, theoretical caution is necessary here as well. One should resist the supposition that the particular cultural character of the religious movement is determined by the background mainstream experiences of those presently associating with it. People's involvement in the religious movement amounts to a fresh start with respect to all or part of their lives, and this should be the point of departure for anthropological analysis as well. Of course, the people who forge the religious movement bring to bear considerable mainstream knowledge, which implies the facility, on their part, once committed to the movement, to reflect back on the areas of mainstream life that they have now rejected. But turning away from the mainstream means that such knowledge becomes wedded to entirely new understandings and meanings. Such new understandings and meanings, which constitute the religious movement, emanate from the circumstance of 'fresh start'. For the explanation of the religious movement, this implies an analytical position where the way people used to experience things in the mainstream is of conditional relevance. With respect to the movement's basis in 'deeper social currents', the challenge must be to define the sociological nature of 'fresh start', and to establish the social processes which link fresh start to the movement's distinctive understandings and meanings. The opposition between mainstream and movement must be seen in this context.

As concerns the description of the New Age in Glastonbury, the emphasis, by the people in the New Age community in the town, is on New Age beliefs and ideals. This is a third area where there should be caution, for beliefs and ideals evoke both doctrinal perfection, and also the idea that bad mainstream experiences determine the shape of New Age life. We prefer the analytical position that people's experience with practical activities – forging relationships, keeping healthy, engaging in work, educating children – are of more fundamental importance. The challenge, in particular, is to make sense of these latter experiences in the context of fresh start. For New Agers, as will be seen, fresh start implies considerable predicaments and dilemmas in respect of practical activities. Only once these have been explored may the distinctive beliefs and ideals be properly understood.

We elaborate, in the remainder of this chapter, on some dimensions relating to all three of these areas of enquiry. In this regard the theoretical challenges may be brought together. Thus if Glastonbury New Agers' beliefs may be explained in terms of experiences relating to certain practical dilemmas, then this should hold good for religious movements generally; and if the character of newly emerged religious movements should be explained in terms of the experience of fresh start, then this should likewise have a more general import. We shall demonstrate the value of this perspective in Part 3 of this book where, while concentrating on the Glastonbury New Age, we examine the social basis of religious movements more broadly. Meanwhile, in the rest of the book we provide the concepts (Chapter 2) and the Glastonbury ethnography (Chapters 3–9) to help make our case.

The New Age

From the viewpoint of the Western mainstream, the New Age signals a distinctively different – certainly intriguing, possibly inspirational and perhaps subversive – lifestyle. It is not surprising that anthropologists are being drawn to study it in increasing numbers. Yet the subject poses many difficulties. Firstly, the New Age appears in a very wide variety of contexts and circumstances, ranging from holistic health therapies (Burrows 1993) through to Deep Ecology communes (Hendershott 1989), and including the so-called New Age Travellers whose convergence on certain sacred places in Britain each summer has, in recent years, provoked a now-familiar moral panic. Again in Britain, New Age ideas and customs are variously included in witchcraft movements (Luhrmann 1989) and (surely at the other extreme) businessmen's self-transformation courses (Roberts 1994). Some commentators have even linked the New Age to the ideology of the New Right (Sjoo 1994).

A second problem is that New Age is hard to observe as a lifestyle in the round. The New Age upholds a departure from, indeed a radical turning away from, the social values of the Western mainstream; yet in practice New Agers make the break only partially. There are two opposed senses in which this is so. Either, people entertain New Age notions in limited areas of their lives, whilst otherwise they remain engaged in the mainstream; for example, they take up just the holistic health therapies, or, as Wiccans, follow the prescriptions of witchcraft only during selected occasions or periods of the day. Or else, New Agers devote themselves to keeping the mainstream at bay, as when they locate in remote Celtic parts, or gather in communes which outsiders cannot easily penetrate, or, as Travellers, set out to follow the nomadic road. We suspect that if there is such a thing as a New Age culture and society, then approaching it through the lenses of these sorts of circumstances may well introduce considerable complexity.

If there is such a thing; the term 'New Age' is in any event an ambiguous one, so that, for example, some people whom the label seems to fit dislike it, though they may concede that theirs is an 'alternative' way of life. Moreover the array of social and religious doctrine that, during the last thirty or so years, has been entered under the heading of New Age is in its sheer variety quite breath-taking, with Eastern religions and tribal ways of life providing the definition at one end of the spectrum, and Neo-Paganism and occultism at the other – which implies the possibility of all permutations and combinations in between. (For recent discussion, including the dissenting view that Neo-Paganism should be placed outside the New Age, see Pearson 1998; also York 1996.)

This raises the question of a definition. Definitions are sleights of hand. They purport to open up an area of enquiry, yet the analyst who formulates them knows full well where this enquiry will lead and what it will yield. Therefore definitions have a strategic function: to be uncontroversial and non-alienating, and yet hint at the line the analyst will take. The phenomenon at issue should be delineated as inclusively as possible, and the analyst's perspective anticipated more in terms of the form this phenomenon takes than its specific content. The definition may be refined on the strength of further discussion (Hanegraaff 1996: 5). A main aim of this chapter is precisely to effect such a refinement. This book is an enquiry into social innovation relating to the distinctive practices and beliefs of a minority way of life within Western society which commentators have termed New Age. The New Age celebrates a small scale, egalitarian and spiritually-imbued way of life, and articulates this through a distinctive combination of relatively holistic cosmological ideas and relatively individualistic social practices. 'New Age' implies a rejection of the mainstream and a declaration that New Age ideas and routines are open freely to everyone for the sake of both personal and collective betterment. New Age doctrine includes the rider that people may involve themselves to an extent and in a manner that they see fit.

Our ethnographic data, drawn from Glastonbury, southwest England, is appropriate for this enquiry. The focus of study is the Alternative Community settled around the town. This community is a clearly identifiable, albeit dispersed and largely unorganised, body of people who feel they belong together in pursuing a lifestyle which, as they say, is 'alternative' to the surrounding mainstream society (Bowman 1993). To be sure, the Alternative Community in Glastonbury cannot but be involved with the mainstream, in both the senses mentioned above – participants are inevitably caught up in mainstream institutions (such as the British educational system), even as they also attempt to keep the mainstream at bay (for example, by establishing their own independent primary school). Yet the Community sustains a distinctive way of life, encompassing all life's strands (health, work, relationships, education, religion etc.) in circumstances where relations with the mainstream are comparatively relaxed and open. We consider that to label the particular constellation of social customs, concepts and values that make up this way of life 'New Age' is not unreasonable – and claim that in Glastonbury we glimpse a New Age community in a relatively simple form. In this book we employ strategies from the discipline of social anthropology to examine how these customs, concepts and values interrelate. Social innovation, in this respect, amounts to the social processes in which people in the community setting of Glastonbury create and sustain such social and cultural features.

Doctrine or Practical Experience: the Idea of Social/Religious Movement

Throughout history Western culture has spawned social and religious movements in their thousands, some of them short-lived but others coming to assume considerable prominence and influence in the Western cultural landscape, and very many manifesting themselves in recognisable communities with characteristic social organisations. Thus the Hutterite and Amish colonies, their roots in flight from religious persecution over several centuries in Europe, comprise distinctive Christian enclaved communities on the North American rural scene, well-known for their ascetic lifestyles, relatively authoritarian social and religious organisations, and, in the case of the Old Order Amish, rejection of most modern agricultural technology (e.g. Hostetler 1980).[1] Then again, the kibbutz, the large agricultural commune, has come to encapsulate in practice the socialist ideals held to be valid within the Israeli nation state (Spiro 1968). And, from the 1960s up to the present day, there have emerged numerous 'new religious movements' (Wallis 1984), their social roots in many cases replicating those of the 1960s' Western counter-culture, though their doctrines embrace intellectual ideas associated with much earlier periods of non-conformity.

The New Age movement is an example of a new religious movement. But it is immediately obvious that it subdivides. Thus among the many New Age groupings there is considerable social organisational variation, such that, for example, in Glastonbury seven hundred or so New Agers are scattered throughout the town and the immediately surrounding countryside, whilst in Findhorn, in northern Scotland, two hundred or so New Agers constitute a successful spatially discrete commune. And the doctrinal segmentation is quite striking, taking in (for example) utopian, Pagan, ecological and feminist strands. As a worldwide phenomenon, the New Age 'movement' is, organisationally speaking, more properly a SPIN[2] (York 1995), a loose agglomeration of imperfectly connected centres of activity, such as (in Britain) the Wrekin Trust in the west Midlands, the Findhorn Foundation in Scotland and various semi-official 'centres' in Glastonbury. Both mass transportation and the mass media (including the internet) have crucially made possible the efflorescence of New Age submovements, such that people who share particular doctrinal preferences can keep in touch and spread the word, by pamphleteering and globe-trotting (e.g., Dawson and Hennebry 1999). Yet as they stimulate one another in terms of developing, rejecting and debating ideas, New Agers everywhere definitely experience the sense of an in-common participation in a non-mainstream flow, even as particular individuals conclude that some New Age practices and ideas are more appealing than others.

From Hutterite colonies, to New Age communes, to Wiccan covens: the anthropologist will capitalise on, and not despair over, such variety. Indeed we shall argue that such movements amount to variations (or transformations) of one another, which invites the elucidation of social processes which commonly underpin them all. In this book we shall conceptualise the emergence, and perpetuation, of religious movements in a distinctive manner: by our individualistic approach we shall deliver an unusual account, which the examination of the Glastonbury New Age is intended to exemplify. We offer an interpretation of social and religious movements that concentrates not on matters of doctrine (or ideology) and agenda, but prioritises the social circumstances of the human individuals who make movements possible. Our starting point is the situation, experienced by members of such movements, of 'having abandoned the mainstream', together with the social transactions that this experience implies. This processual approach requires that analytical focus be put on the local community: the body, or network, of people who feel they know one another personally is the primary context within which individuals consummate their social experience. The approach also means that the very notions of social movement and religious movement need to be treated with considerable caution.

'Social movement' (including 'religious movement') refers to the existence of a body of opinion and practice that presents itself as radically different to the mainstream, or the 'establishment', with respect to which people formally opposed (in full or in part) to mainstream/establishment values can find common cause. Common cause means that this body of opinion and practice is linked to a system of beliefs and customs, which implies, to a greater or lesser degree, a distinctively non-mainstream way of life. 'Green movement' or 'Labour movement' therefore refers to more than the pursuit of specific social or political goals; it implies a particular culture which permeates all or part of the adherents' social being.

The notion of social movement or religious movement is helpful in a descriptive sense, for it signals the existence of ways of life in opposition. Thus 'religious movement' implies a distinctive social cum spiritual life which spurns what the mainstream offers. Moreover, the empirical fact is of a two-way transfer of personnel between the movement and the mainstream, and, this being so, people who involve themselves in, say, a religious movement may be presumed to be reasonably knowledgeable about mainstream belief and practice. Thus in Chapter 11 we shall argue that the members' sensitivity to the contrast with the mainstream is centrally reflected in religious movements' belief systems, and plays a large part, indeed, in explaining why such movements are religious in character. People associated with a religious movement continually ask of themselves the existential questions of 'why am I here (as opposed to being in the mainstream)' and 'what have I done (in leaving the mainstream)', and some of the key cultural elements of the movements may be explained as answers to these questions. The variation among religious movements reflects a continuum of circumstances in this regard. Thus, for most New Agers in Glastonbury the existential experience is departure from the mainstream. Meanwhile, for Hutterites, life-long members of their generations-old colonies, it is the decision to resist the mainstream – which, these days, looms increasingly large in Hutterite consciousness, as intriguing, exciting and sinful. As for Westerners who subscribe to the New Age in very restricted domains of life, for them it is a matter of imagining moving away from the mainstream and across to becoming fully-fledged New Agers.

But the idea of social or religious movement is problematic because it connotes matters of doctrine and agenda rather than the witnessing communities where individuals carry these doctrines and agendas out; indeed, to talk in terms of 'social movement' can conceal the fact that such communities exist and are important. We would suggest that, as objective entities, social movements, as spoken about by their coordinators and described in pamphlets and other media pronouncements, merely reinterpret and rationalise ideas and values which ordinary individuals, in shared local predicaments, have worked to produce. With reference to the New Age this may be put slightly differently. The New Age is a particularly striking global phenomenon, yet even striking global phenomena find their rationale in the mundane of everyday community life. The distinction between social movement and religious movement relates to this. We shall offer a considered definition of religion later in the book, but may note immediately that very many social movements are also religious movements. For us, this confirms the basis of social movements in local communities – such that anti-mainstream communities established for purely secular ends commonly and rapidly come to take on a religious ambience.[3]

Academic commentators on the New Age who maintain that the focus should be on ideas, texts and history, rather than on anthropological studies of particular New Age communities, may therefore be profoundly mistaken (Melton 1992; Hess 1993: 180–1). New Age communities are so varied, some protest. But such variation is something to be treasured, both for understanding the New Age and also for an appreciation of social and religious movements more generally (including the Hutterites and the kibbutz). Thus Glastonbury should be treated not as a particular idiosyncratic example of the New Age, but rather as the means by which one may make sense of religious movements in general. However, in this study we shall wear our labels lightly and retain 'movement' as a convenient odd-job word; we shall use the terms 'social movement' and 'religious movement' in accordance with what context and commonsense suggest, and correspondingly speak of 'alternative communities' and 'religious communities'.

Religious movement is certainly a dangerous notion in the context of analysis. It invites reification. The term 'movement' implies an active agent with a life and will of its own – as something qualitatively different from the separate individuals who, by assembling together and sharing certain practices and ideas, go to make it up. Thanks to reification, religious movements as 'things' existing under their own independent momentum, are construed as acting on people. Ours is a quite contrary perspective. The social and cultural content one dubs a religious movement should be viewed, in its entirety, as emanating from the activities of individuals who come to be described as movement members. In short, the doctrines and agendas of religious movements must be seen not as determining forces, but rather as the social product of people who are departed-the-mainstream.

Many prominent institutional features encourage the analyst to sustain the (mistaken) position of treating religious movements as active agents. Thus religious movements typically include striking procedures for the recruitment and retention of followers, such as flirty fishing, love bombing, or promises of altered states of consciousness. The charisma of a movement's founder and of its subsequent inspirers and teachers (gurus, shamans) is another standard element, as also are the movement's seductive rituals and symbols. Moreover, individuals who join the movement from the mainstream are commonly said, in movement parlance, to have experienced a radical change in subjective identity, which is normally considered to bear a distinctively spiritual quality. And so on: much corresponding with this may be found in the New Age movement. For our part, the *explanation* of these institutional features in terms of individualistic premises will clearly be an important matter for this study.

Attention to the level of agenda and doctrine is clearly present in scholarly attempts to capture the essence of the New Age. Thus several definitions elucidate a doctrine of religious individualism, including the definitions offered by scholars who have played the major role in developing the New Age as an area of academic enquiry. Paul Heelas captures the New Age in terms of its ideological stress on liberating the perfect inner, and higher, being (1993: 104; 1996), and Gordon Melton speaks of it as centering on matters of primal personal transformation (1991: xiii). Coupled with New Age preoccupations with eastern religions and the occult, such perspectives uphold the New Age as the post-1960s manifestation of such late nineteenth-century intellectual movements as Theosophy and New Thought (Alexander 1992: 30–5; see also Hanegraaff 1996). Thus, according to some, the New Age movement is just one strand in the transcendent individualism, premised on the moral supremacy of the individual human being, that has infused Western social and philosophical life for decades, if not centuries – a morality that, in the present day in the West, the so-called post-modern era seems to have elevated into the whole purpose in life (Heelas ibid., Hess 1993).

The focus on doctrine is a focus on a religious movement's internal property, and it is, in our opinion, unhelpful. It is blind to the opposition between the Western mainstream and the New Age which bears on crucial areas of New Age life. Such opposition, whereby New Agers, embarked on 'fresh start', are departed-the-mainstream, is critical as a basis to the New Age's distinctive social and cultural character. Also, as Greer points out, to characterise the New Age in terms of personal transformation and the liberation of self downgrades the movement's equal emphasis on Deep (Gaian) Ecology. This latter dimension, which celebrates the human individual's suspension in a transcendent ecological, or universe, system, seems to be decidedly anti-egotistic (Greer 1996).

The construal of religious movements as active agents, and the focus on doctrines, agendas, and techniques of recruitment, rests easily with the idea of the New Age 'movement' as a worldwide phenomenon with auspicious historical credentials. Yet we consider that such an approach is ultimately undesirable in that it damagingly separates doctrinal ideas from participants' experience relating to the situations of ongoing everyday life (Holy and Stuchlik 1983). New Age-type doctrines may intellectually be speculated upon in think-tanks such as the Esalen Institute, in Big Sur, California.[4] But doctrine, in the final analysis, is meaningful only in relation to ordinary practical routines: this is the reason why Glastonbury New Agers who live the New Age are so important. New Age culture exists not because it consists of inherently compelling intellectual ideas, or because it is the end product of some sort of historical, intellectual or social momentum, or because of the influence of modern spirituality in California, but rather because it is reproduced, in a local context, in people's daily activity. Of such activity the most momentous relates to the fact of being departed from the mainstream, which leads in turn to other vitally important matters, such as keeping healthy, making a living, bringing up children and making social contacts. In Part 3 of this book we shall show that New Age doctrine, or ideology, reflects, not determines, the shape of these activities and routines.

Academic study of 'new religious movements' is similarly

anchored in matters of agenda and doctrine. Thus Roy Wallis (1984) distinguishes such movements as respectively 'world affirming' or 'world rejecting' according to whether their agendas rest content with mainstream priorities in life or else condemn and refuse them. ('World accommodating' movements are a third, and less important, category.) Wallis adds that world rejecting movements are disposed to incorporate their followers in authoritarian social organisations, whilst world affirming movements permit high levels of personal autonomy. But there are problems here. First, the distinction does not hold good with regard to the experience of practical activity. In relation to this level, many world affirming movements are world rejecters, for their central platform is that the desired (mainstream-type) goals cannot be delivered through mainstream routines. This is the case with some New Agers, such as those involved in the American firewalking movement, who accept Western priorities of business and monetary success but insist that the means to achieve them will not be reached other than by self-realisation and spiritual growth – which the practical ritual of walking the fire assists (Danforth 1989).[5] Others in the New Age pose a more important problem for Wallis' distinction. Many committed New Agers, people precisely wedded to the hope of release from all mainstream methods and agendas, are, in the Wallis sense, world rejecters, yet they fervently uphold the importance of personal autonomy – making them quite different from other world rejecting movements, such as the Unification Church (Moonies), where authoritarianism is indeed quite marked.

Comparable problems obtain in academic discussion of religious movements in general (i.e. taking in both historical religious movements and the new religious movements). Bryan Wilson (1970, 1973), to make sense of their enormous number and variety, classifies all such movements on the strength of their doctrines in relation to their 'responses to the [mainstream] world', listing seven distinct types. The Hutterites exemplify the 'introversionist type', where the world is seen as 'irredeemably evil and salvation is to be attained only by the fullest possible withdrawal from it' (1973: 23). Meanwhile many New Agers would be regarded as 'utopians' who, precisely in seeking a new age, aim to 'remake the world' in the image of non-mainstream ethical principles (ibid.: 25).[6]

Classification into types inevitably plays up differences among phenomena, which may turn out to be less important than similarities as measured according to entirely different criteria. For example, the Hutterites and the New Agers indeed contrast

markedly in terms of overt doctrine and basic community organisation, yet they are also alike, for both strongly uphold the importance of harmony with nature and the idea of interpersonal love –
which are very significant notions. An opposite approach is therefore preferable. One should discover a relationship between doctrine and other aspects of life (including practical aspects) by first
exploring in depth just a single movement. This provides the foundation for analysing other religious movements. We shall grasp the
social logic of the New Age (especially the Glastonbury New Age),
and then suggest that other movements reflect transformations of
this logic (Chapters 11 and 12).

As between 'doing' a religious movement (New Age practical
experience) and 'thinking' a religious movement (New Age doctrine), it is obvious that there is a mutual, or dialectical, relationship. Thus New Age practical experience will somehow make a
difference to New Age doctrine, and vice versa. Indeed, in the New
Age there is, to an extent, a division of labour here: some New
Agers largely think, whilst others both think and do. We insist,
however, that in analysis priority must go to one side or the other.
Our own particular bias should be evident from our review of other
approaches to religious movements: there would be no 'New Age
to think' if the alternative lifestyle were not being done, and in the
experience of doing producing the customs and beliefs to think
with and about.

Religious Movements: Towards a New Perspective

In analysis, one should resist addressing religious movements via
their observable features. These are the movement's social and
cultural forms that are immediately recognisable and talked about
– they constitute the movement's 'surface appearance'. One should
avoid observable features partly in order to prevent circular reasoning. In analysis, the aim is to discover the social forces that pre-
cipitate a phenomenon, and to understand the processes that
account for the phenomenon's distinctive social and cultural
forms. Circular reasoning occurs when the nature of these social
and cultural forms function as the means to work out what the pre-
cipitating agents are. It is easy to succumb to this in the study of
religious movements. A religious movement's distinctive social
compositions and intriguing rituals and beliefs are normally highly
compelling, so one is tempted to use them as conduits to the

movement's rationale. Another reason to avoid observable features is that their significance is clear only once analysis is complete, so to commence through these features is likely to be misleading. True, specific observable features sometimes echo a particular general theory of the human condition that academic commentators might be prepared to treat as received wisdom. A religious movement's distinctive social class composition could in this way invite a Marxist interpretation. But such a general theory would regard these features as something to be critically inspected, for example by giving them sense in the way they related to other features of the movement; it would not take them at face value.

Two brief illustratations, typical of New Age studies, show these problems occurring, the first where analysis focuses on matters of class composition, the second where it attends to human psychological dispositions. The first case concerns the interpretation of the New Age movement as a rebuff to the urban–industrial way of life, where the point of departure is the movement's objective social composition. It is first noted that New Age communities like Glastonbury mostly have middle class mainstream origins, plus the fact that their members' background educations usually identify them with the non-productive sector of the economy (teachers, social workers). Then it is concluded that the New Age movement constitutes in essence a revolt against mainstream materialism. The difficulty with this interpretation is that the movement's social composition is used to discover what causes the movement – whose features include its composition. Moreover, from among all the New Age movement's observable features, why select social composition as its key? Should social class be the way to characterise such composition? The argument is circular and the ethnographic focus is arbitrary. The second case invites the same conclusion. This is where the point of departure in the explanation of religious movements begins with their charismatic, or ecstatic, dimension. Here a movement is understood in terms of personality types generally existing in the human population. Certain psychologically inspirational types are drawn to initiate such a movement (as gurus, shamans, etc.), whilst other types are especially susceptible (as acolytes) to this type of leader's inspirational lure. But, again, why focus on the charismatic presence from among a movement's many features?

In sum, we worry about circular reasoning in the study of religious movements in much the same way that Wallis was concerned about tautology, whereby (as Wallis put it) the analyst looks to see what a movement offers and then concludes that this is what the members therefore seek (1979: 3–4). One should unpick circularity and tautology. An outcome is that a religious movement's more seductive features, whose ostensible function is to lure followers in, may be seen as having rather different meanings (Chapters 11 and 12). But what would a 'non-circular' strategy involve? It would presume that the social factors responsible for its existence lay outside of (or independent from) the movement under investigation. The strategy would be to *hypothesise* such factors, and then show that from them one may deduce the movement's particular features. This is the strategy that we propose to follow.

In Part 3, we shall elucidate the social processes which are foundational for religious movements. These social processes implicate key social factors lying outside the constellation of social and cultural phenomena that the term 'religious movement' labels, and which at the same time cause these phenomena to emerge. We maintain that the critical factor here is the experience, for the people concerned, of 'no longer being mainstream'. In Victor Turner's terms this is a liminal (or betwixt and between) experience, where for individuals who come to be called movement members, mainstream rules and constraints have no meaning, such that the individuals are socially free-floating and unencumbered (Turner 1969). In this book we shall term this experience 'not-mainstream'. Turner has captured very well the existential situation where people have this experience in common. This is 'communitas', a deep experience where those involved relate to one another as total persons (that is, not in terms of filling particular social roles). But, we shall indicate, communitas is inherently unstable, for it implies the contradictory principles of egalitarianism and autonomy. We shall suggest that people who are not-mainstream instigate religious movements in order to be reconciled with this contradiction.

All told, our approach views religious movements as emanating from the ongoing experience of communitas, and, in such creation, as being 'constructed' by individuals. Two dimensions of this, analysed in Part 3, are worth elaborating on. First the recruitment institutions that figure more or less prominently in religious movements pose a challenge to this approach; such institutions commonly implicate the movement leaders (teachers, gurus, shamans). A correct analytical standpoint is vital here; we see the 'emanation process' as precisely generating such institutions. Clearly recruitment institutions are on a cusp between a movement's representation of itself and its construction by individuals: 'recruitment' resonates with the idea of the movement as a whole, representing itself as perfect and desirable, drawing people in, and also with the idea of individuals departing the mainstream so that the movement may be made. Such institutions are still more challenging in the fact that the movement's representation of itself is probably the immediate cause of their existence: the announcement of a morally sound, coherent and unified way of life logically invites the instigation of mechanisms through which everyone is invited to participate – indeed, the strict meaning of the English word, recruitment, corresponds exactly with such mechanisms. However analytical priority must be accorded to processes of construction; therefore 'recruitment institutions' must sustain other meanings as well. The strict meaning of recruitment will have these other meanings as its precondition: without the possibility of these other meanings the strict meaning could not be implemented. Such other meanings will relate not to the notion of the religious movement as a complete, unified social world, but rather to the assembly, into an eventual social phenomenon, of a multitude of component parts. In Chapter 12, we argue, with regard to both charismatic inspiration and recruitment institutions, that such construction meanings, far from being about a movement obtaining members from the outside, are more about resolving problems relating to the movement's internal organisation and management. Questions regarding the social composition of religious movements' memberships must be addressed with this position in mind.

A second dimension concerning the construction of religious movements is that, for the relevant social processes to occur, the substantive context of community life is necessary. This relates to the question of transformation among the various social and religious movements (New Age, Hutterites, kibbutz, etc) (Chapter 12). The key point is that communities are manifest in different guises in terms of the dimensions of space and time. Some, such as the closed Hutterite colonies, are spatially enclaved within specific geographical areas. At the other extreme would be cyberspace communities, 'imaginary communities' where, capitalising on literacy, the members' sense of belonging is secured through mutual engagement with clearly defined and exclusive cyberspace language (we duck the question as to whether cyberspace communities are religious communities). In between (but inclining towards the imagined pole) are the Glastonbury New Agers who, though confined to a local area, are dispersed among a (larger) main-stream population. In our view, spatial–temporal variation in the community setting that obtains (for example, whether dispersed or enclaved) importantly underlies the transformations among the religious movements. The Glastonbury New Age community is appropriate to grasp the roots of such transformations because, relying on neither enclavement nor literacy, it is arguably the simplest of communities; in analytical terms the Glastonbury New Age is the elemental religious movement.

Concluding Observations

In this book we contest much received wisdom about religious movements, with respect both to the way they are viewed from the outside (by mainstreamers and many academics), and to how such movements represent themselves. We reject, in particular, the presumption that, as entities, religious movements have wills of their own; this, in our view, only goes to legitimise the notion of 'movement' (although one can never escape the term). The idea of 'movement' begs the question of why such a presumption obtains.

We also contest the concept of religious movements as fundamentally intellectual phenomena relating to matters of doctrine, ideals and principles. One grants that in their daily lives Glastonbury New Agers strive to put their chosen principles into practice (Chapter 4), yet we insist that a religious movement's principles emanate from everyday practical experience (keeping up social networks, educating children, and so on). In our view, while people strive to put principles into practice, this is occurring at a level different from the processes by which such principles come into being and are sustained; where people put principles into practice, this is a symbolic statement in which they declare that their principles are good.

Now we can refine our definition. The New Age movement is a not-mainstream, local phenomenon, manifesting relatively holistic cosmological ideas and relatively individualistic social practice. This definition, we maintain, both covers the total content of New Age belief and practice, and also invites key areas of enquiry. The task of this book is to demonstrate this.

Two important methodological procedures help with this enquiry. Firstly, in Part 2 we examine the New Age movement in terms of its surface appearance. We describe the observable features of Glastonbury social and cultural life, including some possible interconnections between them. But in the context of the book as a whole, this ethnography is intended to play a particular role, which relates to what we see as a major difficulty with ethnographic interpretation. Normally, anthropological analysis attends to just a restricted part of a total ethnographic arena (or, at least, one restricted part at a time): it problematises this part and then goes on to make sense of it. The snag is precisely that this restricted part is thus separated out from the total scene, and one can therefore never know what logical priority it enjoys in relation to the overall scheme of things. The present study, whilst certainly not immune to this difficulty, attempts to deal with it by generating an overall scheme of things, as deduced from first principles (Part 3). The chapters in Part 2 look at various aspects of New Age society and culture in Glastonbury, and in each one we raise questions relating to the ethnographic material at hand. But the resolution of these questions, rather than their being dealt with piecemeal, chapter by chapter, awaits Part 3. Thanks to the deductive model, the New Age movement's many social and cultural elements may each be explained *in the context of being systematically related*.

In a second methodological procedure, we draw some parallels between the New Age in the West and certain non-Western societies, particularly hunting and gathering societies, such as the Bushman and Inuit (Eskimo), to which in very many areas of social organisation and culture the New Age displays remarkably similarity.[7] The analysis of Bushman and Inuit culture, focusing particularly on the logic of shamanistic religion, very usefully helps with the analysis of the New Age. Moreover, the parallels between the New Age and these egalitarian societies, together with the salience of such evolutionarily critical ideas as communitas, leads us to conclude that studying the New Age may inspire an understanding of human social life more generally. Thus mainstream social and cultural forms, socially constructed just like New Age social and cultural forms, may have their basis in social processes not dissimilar to those that underpin the New Age.

We began this chapter by issuing warnings about a religious movement's representations of itself. Such representations, by which the movement offers itself as a coherent, globally-relevant whole, obscure the deeper social processes by which individuals, in the context of living in local communities, construct the movement's social and cultural forms, in piecemeal fashion. The

19

implications of this for a novel understanding of religious move-ments are fascinating. A movement's representations, it is appar-ent, themselves occur as a result of construction: representations are produced as individuals (constructively) reflect on the accom-plishment of having constructed a social and cultural universe. In short, the representations, in their entirety, are in such individuals' thrall. Moreover, in terms of processes of construction, such repre-sentations are, so to say, the icing on the cake.

Two broad things follow from this (if we may anticipate analy-sis in Part 3). First, standard definitions and typologies of religious movements are thrown open to question. Such definitions and typologies seem normally to correspond with such movements' (self) representations. A social construction perspective is in this respect a subversive perspective. Thus the distinction between the New Age movement and Neo-Paganism, much discussed in the lit-erature, and vehemently upheld by many adherents (e.g. Sjoo 1992), may be shown to rest on symbolic values, such as gender values, functioning as representations: with regard to more pro-found social processes, New Ageism and Neo-Paganism should be seen as one. Then again, 'Glastonbury', which labels a particular body of New Agers, is a constructed idea (Chapter 11). It is not a place which happens to have certain mystical connotations; rather it has certain mystical connotations because individuals converged there decide that it should (Chapter 12). Again, there is the notion, much stressed by adherents and commentators alike, that a defin-ing marker of the New Age is that it consists of some sort of deep individual Experience.[8] But such Experience does not 'descend' on New Agers thanks to the fact that they participate in New Age life; New Agers construct it (Chapter 11). And finally (and more gener-ally), religious movements, in the context of their construction, specify the desires, be these pain or gain, that people can expect from participation, and how these desires may be realised. Reli-gious movements do not exist in order to satisfy people's desires, because from the individual's commitment to the movement he or she constructs the desires one may have.

Our second point about the constructed nature of representa-tions is that such representations are open to manipulation. We have in mind here that representations amount to a resource. If the construction of religious movements, by individuals, has its basis in local communities, then a movement's self-representation, in compelling institutions and vivid symbols, is highly appropriate as a vehicle to communicate the result to individuals in other communities. 'Movements', by definition, are pan-community entities: it is on the strength of such communicative process that they are so (Chapter 13).

Notes

1. An alternative label for such communities is 'intentional communities', reflecting the fact that (for example) the Hutterite colonies, as spatially closed communities, were deliberately established for very clear purposes (e.g. Shenker 1986). Yet we believe that intentional is an unfortunate label because the concept, intention, more normally refers to general mechanisms of human cognition. By this label the connection between intentionality and community is obscured. Indeed, in Chapter 12 we argue that such communities assume their distinctive social and cultural features in large part because of a very particular type of relationship between spatial closure and intentional action. For the moment, then, 'enclaved' is preferred as a more neutral label.
2. Segmented Polycentric Integrated Network.
3. Interesting examples from Britain come from the radical end of the environmental movement. For example, the women's camps at the Greenham Common air base, objecting during a continuous period of several years about the presence of nuclear weapons, rapidly upheld a feminist spirituality reflecting the 'Goddess as planet' (Hess 1993: 88; Sjoo 1992). The Earthfirst!ers and Dongas tribe, well known for their environmental protests especially relating to road construction, would be another instance (Taylor 1991).
4. The Esalen Institute is well-known as the forum where New Age and mainstream academic ideas, notably transpersonal psychology, were encouraged to intertwine; the intellectual genesis of the New Age movement is commonly traced to it (see Alexander 1992: 36–46).
5. New Age 'world affirmers' fall into the same bracket as the number of less obviously religious Human Potential Movements, such as est (Erhard Seminar Training) (Rupert 1992). For many commentators the historical Human Potential Movement was highly influential in the development of the New Age movement (e.g. Alexander 1992).
6. Wilson's full list of religious movements reads: revolutionists, introversionists, reformists, utopians, conversionists, manipulationists and thaumaturgists (1973: 27).
7. Dentan (1994) has usefully demonstrated similarities between the historically enclaved religious communities in the West, such as the Hutterites, and 'refugee communities' in the non-Western world, such as the Semai of Malaysia.
8. 'Experience' is capitalised here to distinguish it, as a cultural component of the New Age, from 'experience', which is a theoretical concept referring to people's understandings and meanings in an ongoing social situation.

2

Key Concepts

The intention in this book is as much analytical as ethnographic. The book aims to reveal the layers of meaning that exist in any one religious movement. And it demonstrates, especially with respect to their social organisations, that different religious movements can be understood as transformations of one another. The Glastonbury ethnography is interesting its own right, but more than this it is intriguing. Our model of religious movements, which depicts layers of meaning and describes transformations in social organisation, depends upon having asked the right questions about this ethnography.

The model, which is detailed in Chapter 11 and 12, supposes that religious movements are constructed, and that it is individuals who do this construction. It presumes that the mainstream/non-mainstream divide is crucial as the context for such construction. At the same time, it imagines that the social and cultural meanings that result should be explained as if they were generated *ex nihilo* theorising this latter state of 'no meaning' as a profoundly egalitarian experience, labelled communitas. It finally calls upon the concepts of individualism and holism to organise the Glastonbury ethnography, treating these concepts as complementary, in contradistinction to Dumont (1980), who regards holism as 'encompassing'. 'Construction', 'mainstream/non-mainstream', 'communitas', 'individualism/holism' – these are the concepts that in this book frame the analytical model and direct the questions of the ethnography. We met these concepts briefly in the previous chapter. In this chapter we shall justify them, and indicate why they are suggestive. As we proceed there will be more glimpses of the New Age as an ethnographic phenomenon.

The Construction of Religious Movements

No anthropological analysis can avoid conveying its perspective through metaphors, and ours is no exception. Yet the 'building' metaphors that inform this study may be misunderstood. First of all, when we talk about the 'construction' of religious movements we have in mind not so much to capture the creation of a religious movement at the moment of its first historical appearance; rather we are saying that the social and cultural phenomena relating to the movement (continue to) exist because work continues to be done to keep them in existence. In short, religious movements are evident at any one time because they are being reproduced. Thus the notion of construction refers to the processes relating to such social reproduction as this is accomplished by human individuals. In this accomplishment individuals *keep in being* particular social and cultural phenomena in relation to the particular goals they establish in their lives, and to the way they understand the activities of people around them as opportunities or impediments. As to the matter of a religious movement's 'first historical appearance', one notes that some sociologists, through interview and documentary evidence, have precisely pieced together an empirical picture of a particular movement's initial moments, focusing on the activities of a small group of individuals. It is a moot point whether the processes corresponding to the movement's (present-day) reproduction will actually be the same as the social forces which prompted certain original members to usher the movement onto the scene. Ours, in any case, is not an historical study. Also it may be that the analysis of present-day reproduction will help discern certain relevant historical factors that might otherwise have remained hidden.

The notion that 'individuals construct' is a second point that needs to be clarified. This implies, for all human beings, a life totally dominated by decision making and deliberation. But again, this notion is a metaphor, not what is literally the case. In this study of religious movements we assume that individuals are the determining force of the respective social and cultural features, and that, in the context of normal human activity, decision making is part of this determination. Metaphorically to express this as 'individuals construct' does not deny that habitual routine informs most daily life. What the metaphor conveys is that human deliberation may relate in some way to habitual routine, and that, when one models such deliberation, fascinating insights about religious movements are forthcoming.

The reproduction of a religious movement implicates several simultaneous processes, and for us the problem is how to present this most effectively. For example, the analytical model of New Age culture (Chapter 11) reveals three basic levels of knowledge, namely, cultural foundation, cultural vision, and cultural representation, with the first logically prior to the second, and the second to the third. This conveys the fact that New Age culture is experienced, by New Agers, in different ways corresponding to the different levels, with some such ways or levels dependent on others. (Indeed, one may additionally discern sublevels within the levels.) To talk of the reproduction of a religious movement means, in effect, the reproduction of these levels in a systematic way, and building metaphors are helpful to put this across. Thus the analytical model pictures individuals piecing together the religious movement, level by level. Once again, the risk with such metaphors is that they evoke historical 'first moments' in a spurious way, as if there occurred some sort of literal chronological assembly of the movement at issue – first the individuals made this bit of the movement, then after some more thought they went on to make that. The correct scenario relating to a movement's levels sees each level's social and cultural content as being continuously and contemporaneously recreated, with 'logically prior' levels constituting knowledge relevant to the construction of logically subsequent levels – functioning, in effect, as preconditions of the subsequent levels. For example, in New Age culture, the holistic person is logically prior to the holistic universe (Chapter 11).

The key point to make at this juncture is that a religious movement's overall appearance – its surface manifestation – says little about the social processes by which it is constructed. This is quite apart from the fact that how a movement 'appears' to the observer may strongly be influenced by how movement members choose to represent it (Chapter 1). As noted in Chapter 1, such representation is itself 'constructed', and thereby constitutes an aspect of the movement at hand that, along with all its other social and cultural aspects, needs to be investigated as the outcome of construction processes. The methodological question as to how the analyst may discern the relevant social processes is thrown into relief by these sorts of problem.

The solution to this methodological question is the procedure adopted in Chapter 11, where we generate New Age culture from a few basic first principles and assumptions. This is the deductive procedure that we mentioned in the previous chapter. By this procedure, one is systematically able, with respect to a religious movement, to imagine the construction of its various levels, including its (cultural) 'representation'. It will be seen that our model embraces as a key principle the notion that the fundamental goals relating to the construction of religious movements pertain to the experience of ordinary people who place themselves in a predicament that we call 'not-mainstream'. This implies an opposition between mainstream and non-mainstream, and indicates that, for people associated with a religious movement, there is a definite experience corresponding to 'separation from the mainstream'. But is this experience born out by the facts?

Mainstream versus Non-Mainstream

Many interpretations of the new religious movements see them as part and parcel of broad historical and cultural trends in the wider Western society. For example, some authors focus on transcendent individualism, which they note is upheld alike by ordinary Westerners and by many religious movements, including the New Age movement. Other authors point to the fact that in the West these days, cultural orthodoxy is generally much in retreat: Western society at the beginning of the twenty-first century is marked by very considerable cultural fragmentation, which the new religious movements no more than exemplify. However, there is also an opposite point of view, which sees the new religious movements as in some way counterposed to the wider Western society (normally represented as urban industrial middle class), and as implicitly or explicitly comprising some sort of cultural or political opposition.

These contrasting interpretations, their scale pitched at the level of Western society at large, amount to two broad macro-perspectives. They will be discussed in some detail in Chapter 10. What needs to be considered here is how the distinction between religious movement and Western mainstream is construed at the local level. The local level is the level where those who construct religious movements live out their lives. Moreover, from the perspective of the local level, whether or not the movement/mainstream distinction is marked will be absolutely fundamental for social existence. The two macro-perspectives inspire alternate possibilities.

The starting point for this discussion is the fact that, in the context of the West, what one calls mainstream society is objectively not culturally homogeneous. It consists of people differentiated according to class, age, wealth, gender, neighbourhood, ethnicity (and so on), where corresponding to their position with respect to such categories people uphold subtly (and not so subtly) distinctive cultural poses. With reference to the local level, the question one asks is whether religious movements amount to just yet another cultural pose? Or are they something radically different? For example, is it valid to talk of religious movements as 'counter-cultures', or 'subcultures', when the culture to which they are counterposed (i.e., the mainstream) is itself not at all monolithic?

Anthropological discussion on the idea of subculture provides an interesting slant on these questions. Probably where class, age, wealth etc. are concerned the prevailing opinion is that to describe the social categories which they imply (working class and middle class, elders and youth, and so on) as distinctive subcultures is misleading since 'subculture' implies a culturally discrete entity. In fact within the broader society (for example British society) there is more in common culturally between the different classes, ages, genders, and so on, than there is difference, such that, within the local community, virtually all sectors of society effectively subscribe to the same basic values – for example, the values of gainful employment, of material accumulation, of male dominance. What is occurring is that, with respect to any particular individual (or groupings of individuals with similar fortunes) personal circumstances, especially economic ones, mean that they are less or more able to achieve these values in daily life; people in different circumstances consequently come to take on their own distinctive cultural profile (e.g., working class profile, middle class profile). Therefore analytical emphasis may be better put on the in-common values that transcend such various profiles, not least since these profiles inevitably shade imperceptibly into one another.[1] Turning to the distinction between (Western) mainstream and non-mainstream (religious movement), this intimates that, at the local level, what is dubbed non-mainstream may have many significant social values in common with the mainstream: therefore, given their oppositional connotations, the very notions of mainstream and non-mainstream are misleading.

However, we shall not be following this intimation. In the case of religious movements, with respect to the local level the experience of a mainstream/non-mainstream divide is fundamental. We shall proceed on the assumption that against the putative in-commonness among British society's many groupings (classes, ethnicities, etc.), religious movements stand apart – that it is indeed in their rationale that they do so. Thus, at a deep-rooted level of knowledge such movements' members experience a world outside (i.e. the mainstream world) that is not their world. Moreover, in relation to themselves and fellow members they experience this world, to which they oppose themselves, as relatively homogeneous. And because of their particular personal backgrounds they will generally construe this world as urban industrial middle class.

It is not easy to defend this assumption, since the sorts of facts by which to do so are precisely those that this assumption will be mobilised to explain. Moreover, abstracted from the religious movement's surface appearance, it is a moot point whether they can enlighten the movement's fundamental social processes. Maybe it would be wise to leave the assumption as it is – as an assumption. However, with regard to the New Age in Glastonbury one might, with due caution, tentatively adduce two bodies of fact. First, New Age ethical standards, which refer to a complex of key social values which thoroughgoingly inform New Age daily conduct, and which definitely convey the impression of a counter-culture. Perhaps New Agers summon these values in order to represent themselves to the world at large as different, even as they in fact share much in common with this world. Yet we believe that one better appreciates these values as hinting at what underlies them: the profound experience of 'having abandoned the mainstream'. Then, secondly, there are the New Agers' personal biographies, which basically recount personal disillusionment with, or rejection of, the mainstream. Again, perhaps the New Ager's anti-mainstream stories merely rationalise the storyteller's failure to experience success in mainstream terms – success that in the storyteller's heart of hearts is still desired. Yet, at this personal level one should surely allow New Agers their integrity, and accept such stories at face value. In any case there is no evidence that the New Agers' anti-mainstream declarations are in some way phoney.

The New Age ethical standards, through a commitment to which New Agers find a distinctive identity, are (in no particular order): spirituality, environmentalism, communalism, emotionality/intuition, non-aggression, the feminine. These standards will all be discussed at length in chapters to come. Here the key point is that New Agers, in Glastonbury and elsewhere, broadly conceptualise the Western mainstream in terms of the industrial process, notably the ethic of material accumulation, so these 'standards' are rather obviously reversals of what the mainstream holds dear. True, not a few New Agers are themselves engaged in material accumulation (such as by running small businesses), yet this causes them considerable intellectual agony, and they invariably attempt to construe what they are doing in a non-material way (i.e., as not materialistic) (Chapter 7).

To be not-mainstream in the West, material accumulation invites a triple response, and this, one notes, implicates all the distinctive New Age ethical standards. Firstly, anti-material suggests notions of spirituality. Thus the New Age celebrates the incorporeal as generally infusing the world, and New Agers play down the worth of the physical, including physical objects. In Glastonbury, ideas associated with the town being a sacred place, and thus the Alternative Community there a sacred community, provide a unique, local reinforcement of this particular ethical standard. Secondly, the New Age upholds environmentalist values. Unlimited material accumulation implies the domination – the exploitation – of the environment on behalf of distinctively human purposes, and this, New Agers maintain, has brought the world to imminent ecological catastrophe. In New Age ethics environmental purposes should be pre-eminent, whereby humans humbly fashion material needs to that which is ecologically non-disruptive.

Material accumulation thirdly supposes a social ambience of competitiveness, which consists of three basic dimensions. Competitiveness implies winners and losers, and therefore domination and hierarchy. Therefore New Agers uphold broadly communalistic values, instructing minimal differences in wealth and power: a New Age community, albeit that its members enjoy considerable personal autonomy, should be pervaded by distributive justice. Competitiveness also implies the rational calculation of ends and of strategy. Accordingly, New Agers, shunning entrepreneurial ruthlessness, attend to the non-rational in human action: proper values are those relating to the emotional and the intuitive. Competitiveness finally implies violence and aggression, whose pre-eminence in mainstream conduct, in New Age thinking, leaves human beings severely damaged, both physically and psychologically. To overcome fear, and release the human being's inner potential, New Agers celebrate peacefulness and social harmony instead.

A further aspect of mainstream materialism, in the view of New Age criticism, is that it exhibits, indeed results from, inherently masculine tendencies. The male is specifically the gender driven by ruthless calculation, the determination to dominate *his* fellows, and, in the context of the public domain where *he* lives out *his* fantasies, the ardent desire to realise prestige through material wealth. Accordingly, a high point of New Age culture – evident from the domain of religion, right through to the domain of personhood – is the valorisation of the feminine. However, the feminine is different from the other New Age ethical standards for it does not, of itself, imply a distinctive orientation in respect of action. That it is a high point of New Age culture comes from the fact that the feminine functions to symbolically embrace all the other distinctively New Age ethical standards: the female, compared with the male, *is* inherently intuitive, non-aggressive, close to nature (environmental), community-minded, and in touch with the mystical. But note the apparent irony here. The equation of the feminine with these various standards replicates, rather than opposes, mainstream understandings: the mainstream itself also invokes such equivalences. One concludes that, in the context of expressing the New Age as non-mainstream, the key point is the moral judgements which gender expresses: for the mainstream, the standards connoted by the masculine are broadly the preferred values for social (and especially public) living; meanwhile, for the New Age it is the standards associated with the feminine that are good. In Chapter 11, we shall reveal still further twists in the complex story of the New Age and gender.

New Age cosmology includes description of how the various ethical standards, along with the gender rhetoric, are connected. It will be seen, in Chapter 11, that there is marvellous scope for disagreement here, as different interpreters, gurus and teachers elaborate different priorities as between the various elements – yielding, within the New Age movement, 'internal boundaries' (Hess 1993), or, as one commentator, calling on more colourful language, puts it, a 'battlefield' (York 1995: 34). Thus spirituality and intuition are marked in shamanic journeying; the feminine, spirituality and environmentalism are the cornerstones of Neo-Paganism and eco-feminism; communalism and environmentalism denote Deep Ecology. There are potentially vast numbers of combinations, every one of which, it sometimes appears, has its advocate. The resultant discourses are typically tight-knit formulations designed to articulate the respective components in a manner akin to orthodox social theory; for example, Sjoo and Mor's ecofeminism, urging the West to return to a recognition of the Earth Mother, upholds the central role of the female in biological and cultural evolution through detailed comparative discussions of both matriarchal and patriarchal human societies (Sjoo and Mor 1987).

Some such interpreters, determined to mark out their own particular doctrine, refuse the New Age label altogether, pejoratively linking the term with the rival doctrines from which they are keen to detract (e.g. Sjoo 1994).[2] However on the matter of articulating moral ideals relating to the human person, the various doctrines, it seems to us, converge. Pervasive in New Age thinking is that the ideal person incorporates all the various ethical standards. The spiritual, the loving, the intuitive, the environmentally-attuned, the peaceful, the feminine (in balance with the masculine) person is how, in virtually all doctrines, the perfect human being – man and woman – is apprehended. In Chapter 11, we shall elaborate on this conception, particularly the way New Agers express such an ideal in terms of bodily purity. For now, we merely say that, in Glastonbury, New Agers find an identity by subscribing to these various ethical standards, both as internalised within the individual and as providing a raison d'être for action. In terms of these rather abstract ideas, New Agers in the local community differentiate themselves, as moral beings, from mainstream society, and so derive a positive sense of self-worth.

We turn now to individual New Agers and their personal circumstances. These also indicate that, in the local context, New Age and mainstream ways of life are fundamentally in opposition. We may situate other distinctive aspects of New Age cosmological thinking as we proceed. We begin with a methodological point, as to what exactly may be claimed from the ethnography here. Contrasting with people's situations in enclaved religious communities, such as the closed Hutterite or Amish colonies in North America, which are typically long-established, structured quite rigidly and are communities of birth for nearly all members, New Ager biographies invariably tell of someone leaving the mainstream. New Age adults in Glastonbury were, almost without exception, once non-New Agers, and most are readily able to relate how they became disaffected with what they now view as the world outside. But what precisely may be made from these sorts of accounts?

Might one extract from the New Agers' personal reminiscences the sorts of factors which objectively motivate someone to abandon middle class surroundings, and set off for Glastonbury and a life in dramatically different social circumstances? Might one discern, from the stories present-day Glastonbury folk tell, what it is about the mainstream that prompts an alternative community to come into existence? In our opinion, the tales told in present-day Glastonbury do not in fact provide answers to these sorts of questions. An enquiry into what motivated people to set off for Glastonbury, or else what, in the first place, prompted the New Age community in the town to emerge (such that present-day New Agers knew it was there to head towards), would require the appropriate historical or long-term study. This would involve observing Glastonbury residents-to-be in their previous mainstream surroundings, and then objectively tracing their decisions both to reject these surroundings and make for Glastonbury. Or else there would be an examination of the documents of the time, thirty or so years ago, when Glastonbury started to assume prominence as a New Age mecca. Ours, however, is not an enterprise in either of these two senses.

In our view, what present-day New Agers in Glastonbury reveal in their recollections of the mainstream is the meaning of living in the Alternative Community in the present day. Present-day New Ager descriptions of how the mainstream used to be some five, ten or thirty years ago can be expected to be considerably different from how things then actually were – it is a commonplace that, through time, forms of social life (e.g. mainstream society) may remain much the same, the while that the meanings, or experiences, people attach to them drift a very great deal. Thus New Agers' accounts of why, as individuals, they moved to Glastonbury must be understood as serving largely to legitimate their authors' contemporary presence in the town, and so cannot be expected to tally well with how things really were with a particular person on the day they set off. The focus of our study is how, at the time of fieldwork, Glastonbury New Agers sustained their distinctive way of life, including both its practical and reflective sides, in the face of the many constraints that impinged upon them. New Agers thought of, and represented, this way of life as worthwhile, and on behalf of this they would inevitably invoke biographical memories. But, not being objective (both whether to remember and what to remember are things people construct), these biographical memories contain no true history. Indeed, the facts these memories recall, since they are designed to serve the present, can be taken at face value, and need not be matched up against what 'really' happened. And as to what these facts retail, they should be understood as describing, from the New Agers' insider standpoint, the way present-day mainstream society ought to be viewed. Overall, New Ager recollections and representations with regard to being in Glastonbury converge in the central present-day experience, enjoyed by each individual, of 'being departed the mainstream'. (Some actual biographies are provided in Chapter 4.)

Their personal experiences of opposition between New Age and mainstream invite New Agers to reflect on the nature of the mainstream. Thus included in New Age cosmology is an intellectual appreciation of how mainstream society functions. Given the fundamental experience of 'being departed the mainstream', the root of this intellectual appreciation comprises a subversive critique of the mainstream. This critique takes in mainstream routines relating to daily practical activities. Thus New Agers in Glastonbury upbraid the (so-called) freedom and social equality much lauded in the mainstream Western tradition as a sham. Western 'freedom' amounts to a Western hypocrisy since it means freedom in the terms set by bourgeois capitalism.[3]

A crucially important resource with regard to such a critique of the mainstream is the commentaries about the mainstream implicit in non-Western and other patently non-mainstream philosophies (this includes certain contemporary perspectives in psychology and physics, the Gaian ecology of James Lovelock, etc.). The New Age movement enthusiastically embraces these philosophies. These philosophies – eastern philosophies, tribal philosophies, the philosophies of 'rebellious science' – are important in that they independently command respect in the society at large, and so amount to powerful means by which New Agers can submit themselves to the mainstream as worthy of sympathetic attention.[4] The syncretism in New Age thinking about the world – varyingly mixing (for example) the Pagan, the Celtic, the Hindu, psychotherapy, even the Christian – may be accounted for in terms of the function of first clarifying and then elaborating upon a body of social principles patently different from, and not compromised by, the orthodox scientific mainstream. It helps that the people who come to be members of New Age communities are often highly educated (in mainstream terms), and are therefore comfortable with the academic discourse by which these philosophies are brought to the awareness of contemporary Western thinking. On the other hand, how some of these philosophies fit with the tenets of personal independence that, as we shall describe from Glastonbury, New Agers hold dear, is not always clear, and the ground is ripe for debate and disagreement. Tanya Luhrmann in this regard wryly comments that 'most Neopagans disagree on almost everything' (bar the principle of polytheism) (1989: 335).[5]

We have argued that both New Age and New Ager origins

relating to Glastonbury cannot straightforwardly be read off from the biographical accounts that residents volunteer in the present-day. However, the relevance for present-day New Agers of the non-mainstream philosophical thinking just mentioned must surely say something about people's personal circumstances before becoming New Age. Individual New Agers will have abandoned their often middle class mainstream routines for highly idiosyncratic reasons. But the availability of anti-mainstream discussion and literature will, in many cases, have been critical in their justifying that decision in the public domain. Here one notes that the lifestyle that subsequently came to be termed New Age effectively emerged, in different parts of the industrial world, in the late 1960s or very early 1970s. The late 1960s, it is well-known, was politically marked by an explosion of introspection about mainstream industrial capitalism, by academics and other social commentators, and most of the anti-mainstream philosophy available to New Agers today was also available then. Exposure to an environment of scepticism about the mainstream, one concludes, is a necessary condition for people to abandon the mainstream. Such exposure will not determine people's decisions to become New Age; nonetheless the personal circumstances of an individual who makes the choice will be marked by it in an essential way.

Communitas

The way the mainstream/non-mainstream divide is pertinent to people's construction of a religious movement is a key question. Careful logic is necessary here. One is asking how one explains a religious movement's distinctive social and cultural content given that the movement stands as radically opposed to the mainstream. We shall insist upon an important principle. How a movement's members once explained the mainstream (they may well have been mainstreamers at some point in their lives) does not directly influence a movement's particular social and cultural arrangements. This would be to imply that the people who are now movement members carried such mainstream meanings unchanged into their present-day lives, which contradicts the notion that the movement is in radical opposition to the mainstream. One concludes that a movement's particular social patterns, rituals and cosmology, which its members find distinctively meaningful (i.e. as contrasting with the mainstream), must be addressed in terms of factors internal to the movement.

Yet the mainstream/non-mainstream divide remains significant. When people construct religious movements the fact that there is a 'mainstream' out there, about which people hold an opinion, is obviously vitally relevant. But this will be so in perhaps not an obvious way. We would insist on two things. Firstly, what the mainstream exactly consists of, and the sense that a movement's members make of this, will be determined by particular needs relating to the construction of the movement. Secondly, in the construction of a movement, since the movement is constituted in several levels of knowledge, such facts about the mainstream will be 'pieced in' at a particular level – which, again, makes a difference to the sense movement members impute to these facts. In short, as people construct religious movements the mainstream society is not drawn upon as something objectively known about or recalled; rather, as part and parcel of such construction its 'facts' themselves come to be imagined, or produced.

We arrive at a major theoretical point for this study, which again calls upon the mainstream/non-mainstream divide, but in a different, and much more profound, way. This is that a religious movement's distinctive social and cultural arrangements (its content) will be explained in terms of some 'ultimate experience' of participating in the movement. The logic above requires as much. If a specific social institution, or ritual, or aspect of cosmology, is to be addressed by recourse to factors internal to the movement, then how may these latter factors (presumably other institutions or ideas) themselves be addressed, except by reference to yet other factors. Even the way the human individual is conceptualised in the religious movement will need to be addressed by 'other factors'. Chapter 11 provides the exemplification of this with reference to the social and cultural arrangements of the New Age movement. For the moment, we wish merely to spell out the nature of this 'something ultimate', for this helps grasp the infinite regression that this procedure seems to suggest. The infinite regression indicates that at some point, something recognisable relating to the religious movement at hand emerges (by way of human construction) from an experience which is essentially content-free, that is to say, from an experience independent of specific social or cultural arrangement. Thus, the analysis of New Age society and culture in Chapter 11 will demonstrate that one may explain such society and culture as arising *ex nihilo*. The key question is how one may conceptualise this social/cultural 'nothingness'. In our view

Turner's concept of communitas provides the appropriate ideas (Turner 1969, 1974). As we shall put it, the distinctive social and cultural content of religious movements can be understood as arising from the communitas experience. This, it will be seen, offers the more profound relevance for the mainstream/non-mainstream divide.

Turner's crucial insight about human societies was that their varying social structures have a pre-condition that has exactly opposite, i.e. anti-structural, qualities. Social structure implies an integration of an array of social positions, or roles, whereby people are differentiated from one another; such differentiation means that, in human society, relations between people will be coloured by power or authority. Anti-structure expresses the idea that for people thus to relate with one another, there must be acknowledgement, at some deeper level, of their common humanity. In terms of social bonding such common humanity may be represented as interpersonal connections where individuals relate with one another as exactly equivalent total persons. Turner summoned the term 'communitas' to label such bonding. In short, one might conceive of communitas as a sort of primordial social soup which underlies and makes possible the complexes of structural roles by whose patternings actual human societies get described. We broadly accept this model of human social life. With regard to religious movements, we contend that the primordial bonding that members share in common, which implies social life but not specific social or cultural arrangements, is the in-common experience of being 'not-mainstream'. We would also read off the following implications.

First, while a religious movement's distinctive social and cultural features constitute various structural levels of experience, there is, underpinning such levels, a baseline, communitas level whereby people are relating with one another in a profoundly egalitarian way. Second, for people in a religious movement, communitas corresponds with knowledge: it may be that knowledge relating to the movement's distinctive social and cultural features overlays it, but communitas experience is something movement members are aware of at some level of consciousness. Turner's own discussions encourage this perspective. In his studies of human societies his especial concern was with real life situations when structural arrangements are stripped away, leaving the communitas experience exposed by default. The rite of passage, in his view, is the classic instance where communitas is in this way available. As public occasions where individuals are released from one type of role in life and conducted into another, rites of passage crucially include an interim (liminal) period during which the person is symbolically proclaimed as being in no role at all. For example, male youngsters in an African society, during initiation into manhood, might submit themselves to periods of seclusion when, among other things, they are educated in adult social responsibilities. Located away from the village, the initiates are deemed during this period to be 'outside society', as if in a state of socially suspended animation. Communitas conveys the quality of the social ties that this in-common experience implies. Our perspective on religious movements takes this scenario in reverse. For us, communitas describes the fundamental in-common experience (of being not-mainstream), out of which, via human construction, a movement's distinctive features spring up.

Turner's account has its difficulties. But these help us clarify and refine our own perspective. Such difficulties become plain when Turner's view is considered, that there are other ethnographic circumstances where communitas is on show. These are monasteries and the pilgrimage, whose rationale, in different ways, is the primordial in human social existence. According to Turner the social setting of the monastery and of a pilgrimage is one where, released from the workaday world, people's social experience is the obverse of the role allocation in terms of the way the workaday world is organised. As it happens, Turner (with E.Turner) mentions Glastonbury as a pilgrimage centre, noting its peculiar, powerful, magical and peaceful atmosphere where people enjoy experiences not normally available in mundane life elsewhere (Turner and Turner 1978; Bowman 1993: 41; Reader 1993: 227). By implication the Alternative Community in Glastonbury, whose members will say they gravitated to the town precisely because of its famous aura, is a pilgrimage community. If the pilgrimage corresponds with communitas, then, following Turner's line of thinking, neither power nor authority should feature in the way Glastonbury New Agers relate with one another.

The snag is, so that their smooth running may be ensured, both monasteries and the pilgrimage incorporate distinctive social organisations, and, in the case of pilgrimages, the respective social experience may replicate much by way of the social frictions that its participants bear in everyday life (Sallnow 1981). Social organisation implies power, authority and social differentiation. Thus, in Glastonbury, though social life is markedly egalitarian, it is not – as will be seen – absolutely so. Turner recognises the point, but insists that in monasteries and in the pilgrimage communitas nonetheless remains people's intention. Accordingly, he coins the labels 'normative communitas' and 'ideological communitas', which describe circumstances respectively where people organise themselves so as to reproduce communitas in everyday living, or where they subscribe to deeply held beliefs that communitas in daily living ought to be occurring. Reader, in his review of pilgrimages, alludes to the latter when he points out that for the individual pilgrim there is generally the sense that, along with others, everyone is involved in the same, very fundamental thing, despite their varying motives (Reader 1993: 242–3). We shall rejoin this discussion when we discuss social relationships in Glastonbury in Chapter 6.

However, Turner's original conception of communitas, which he now labels 'existential communitas', is compromised by these emendations. Accordingly, with regard to religious movements, we must clarify our own conceptions. Turner's notion is that distinctive social structures, from pilgrimage social organisation right through to the organisation of an industrial state, are in some like manner underpinned by (existential) communitas. But how can actual societies, implying distinctive social and cultural arrangements, be explained in this way when communitas, since it is nonspecific with regard to social and cultural arrangement, is the same in all human societies? How can the variability among religious movements be accounted for if all spring from the same existential circumstance of being not-mainstream? Secondly, all distinctive social structures, again including pilgrimage and monastery social organisation, imply hierarchy, even if just to a small degree, whereas communitas connotes an utterly profound egalitarianism. How can such hierarchy be construed as emanating from circumstances of non-hierarchy? Many religious movements incorporate quite authoritarian social arrangements; how may such arrangements be related to the not-mainstreamness that underpins such arrangements, which implies a fundamental in-commonness? If 'communitas experience' underpins social and cultural arrangements in religious movements, then the notion needs to be refined.

Refinement is forthcoming once one realises that, as originally formulated, (existential) communitas fails to represent social life at all. In Turner's conception communitas connotes a state of being, whereas social life is a state of doing. And a state of doing implies, on the one hand, practical activity and, on the other hand, a situatedness in space and time. We suggest that communitas experience should incorporate, as notions, the idea of practical action and the idea of space–time. Neither practical action nor space–time implies specific social or cultural institutions as such, so communitas's essential meaning is not compromised by their inclusion. Secondly through these ideas hierarchy and variability in actual human societies are reconciled with the profound egality and universality implied by communitas. Practical action mediates between egality and hierarchy because it suggests emerging processes, and space–time mediates between universality and particularity because it suggests social variation. In the analysis of religious movements in Chapters 11 and 12 we shall make a lot of this. When we explain the social and cultural content of the New Age in Glastonbury as stemming from being not-mainstream, we deem *contradictions* relating to communitas to be the key generative factor (Chapter 11). The social and cultural content of the New Age gets constructed because, in the context of the in-commonness of being not-mainstream, practical action (notably practical economic action) results inexorably in predicaments antithetical to such communitas. Then we address social and cultural differences among various religious movements through the fact that differences in space–time mean that not-mainstream can be experienced in different ways (Chapter 12). People's preferences for sharing not-mainstreamness distinctively in terms of space (for example, with associates dispersed in space) and in terms of time (for example, in long-term aggregation) result in religious movements distinctive in terms of social organisation. We shall show that, in space–time terms, Glastonbury New Agers represent the most elementary instance; therefore they are ideal as an exemplar for the explanation of all religious movements.

Individualism and Holism

This is a complicated topic, so some broad definitions will be useful. Individualism is a state where the human being, unfettered by social or cultural prescription, is the root of all social and cultural life.[6] Holism is a state where some broader system, greater than the sum of its elements, controls the social and cultural circumstances of human beings. One way in which the topic is complicated is by different societies having different ideas about what the human being exactly is, and by different cosmologies describing 'broader system' and its 'elements' in different ways. Another, more profound matter is that anthropologists have to cope with several, completely different perspectives relating to individualism and holism. Firstly, anthropologists themselves employ the terms as tools to describe different societies and cultures objectively. Secondly, anthropologists employ the terms to label different theoretical approaches in the study of human society. And thirdly, the people anthropologists study may employ the terms (or something very similar) to represent their ways of life to outsiders. In the study of New Age society and culture all three perspectives are in evidence, and it is the purpose of this section to sort them out. We shall also consider an area where all three perspectives come together, namely Dumont's controversial thesis on holism's 'encompassment' of individualism (e.g. Dumont 1986).

Describing Societies and Cultures

We asserted in Chapter 1 that New Age social organisation is relatively individualistic, whilst New Age cosmology is relatively holistic. The term, 'relatively', suggests that in the case of any given society or any given culture both individualistic and holistic tendencies are present, at least to some degree. Individualistic societies are those where, in social organisation, social rules and conventions have limited jurisdiction in daily life, leaving people largely free to direct their affairs as they decide. Thus, in Glastonbury, New Age health practice emphasises 'personal responsibility', New Age relationships 'autonomy', New Age work practice 'self-reliance', New Age education 'self-determination', and New Age religious practice 'acceptance'. Holistic societies are those where, in social organisation, transcendent values, relevant to all strands of social life (economic, political, religious, family, etc.), seem to impinge upon people's every daily action. Holistic tendencies, notably communality and mutuality, are clearly evident in Glastonbury – Glastonbury New Agers say that 'being in the whole allows one to breathe'. Yet, though significant, such holism functions more as background social principle than as a direct determinant of daily process. Accordingly, New Age society is relatively individualistic.

As to culture, holistic ideals importantly inform much by way of what New Agers say and believe. A holistic cosmolgy offers an image of the world where some wider whole incorporates all individual human beings (and other living entities as well), subsuming them as mere parts and entirely determining their destinies. New

Age cosmology, focused around a spiritually animated, encompassing universe (Gaia), is clearly marked by holistic ideas. Cosmological individualism is present as well, particularly in the emphasis on the individual's quest for self-transformation. But, as will be seen in Chapter 11, in New Age thinking, such self-transformation has as its precondition New Age notions of transcendent ethical standards. Accordingly, New Age culture is relatively holistic.

But the New Age also celebrates the idea of an holistic person. This extremely important notion is not difficult to describe. The New Age construes the many dimensions of the human being – body, mind, spirit, emotion, the social – as indissolubly one, such that any one particular dimension is subsumed by the totality. This is very different from mainstream concepts, in which the human being is reduced to independent fragments, most notably in the dualistic separation of mind and body. The New Age holistic person, however, poses problems for analysis, as we shall indicate.

Analysing New Age Society and Culture

Analysis in the social sciences is, for the most part, informed by hard philosophical thinking about the nature of the human social world. One's philosophical conclusions will direct that each society one examines should be inspected in a particular way. Individualistic conclusions insist that all that is social and cultural in all human societies must be explained in terms of situations and predicaments that individual human beings experience. This would be the case even when the society under inspection had been described as a relatively holistic one (thus Indian caste society, where hierarchical social values seem to subsume individual human beings in all their doings, would be explained individualistically). By contrast, holistic conclusions insist that structural or cultural parameters independent of the human individual transcend people's daily conduct. This would be the case even when the society concerned had been described as relatively individualistic (therefore, Western society, where individualism seems to capture daily life best, would be explained holistically) (Dumont 1986).

Debates and disagreements in the social sciences, both about how to describe particular societies and cultures, and about how to go about analysing human society in general, commonly invoke the notions of individualism and holism, not least because describing and analysing refer to two quite separate dimensions of the social scientific task. Sometimes the way a society has been described is invoked to justify the perspective by which it is analysed; other times, the perspective for analysis influences how the society gets described. As to the latter, some philosophical holists are reluctant to concede that there are empirically any individualistic societies. Especially in societies outside the Western world, the human being, as a holistic person, is generally construed as somehow not separate from his or her fellows (Carrithers et al. 1985). We should declare our own position on all this. As the 'construction model' makes it evident, this is an individualistic position, which celebrates the human being – every human being – as master of his or her thought and action. Thus all that is New Age society and culture may be understood in terms of endeavours of the human individual, save only that communitas, as a primordial mutuality, makes it possible that human individuals engage with one another. The New Age 'holistic person' constitutes an aspect of New Age culture to be explained in individualistic terms.

New Age Representations

New Age rhetoric, about themselves and about the outside world, identifies a distinctively New Age way of life. There is a dialectical process occurring in this representation because New Age self-stereotypes build in knowledge relating to how New Agers think they are thought of by the mainstream (generally speaking, the mainstreamer's stereotype of the New Ager is not very flattering). The very words, individualism and, especially, holism, are mobilised in this process.

Holism is the dominant symbol of New Age identity in relation to the world outside. Suffused with spirituality, holism connotes a moral and ethical superiority, and a justification for rejecting material accumulation, hard-nosed rationality and the human domination of nature that, for New Agers, are the defining features of contemporary industrial society. New Agers speak proudly of 'the holistic vision', holistic health', and 'holistic living'. In Glastonbury, holism's salience links in to the rhetoric of community building, which in turn plays on the experience of communitas.

Individualism is less appropriate for New Age self-representation. This is because of the way the New Age movement is stigmatised by the outside world, notwithstanding the fact that in Glastonbury practical action is largely determined by individualistic principles, and ideas of individual self-transformation are important in New Age cosmology. Mainstream sceptics seize critically on New Age individualism when they refer to New Age 'self-indulgence', and when they declare that New Agers are blind to the fact that if one really wants a radically different social world then the means to bring it about is political change in the broader social fabric. Moreover, some of the schisms which seem inevitably to characterise any counter-mainstream thinking clearly revolve around this area of argument. Thus Deep Ecologists, natural ideological allies of the New Age who emphasise spiritual holism relating to the biological environment, sometimes line up with the mainstream critics in insisting that, in alternative society, communal needs should outrank in importance the attention given to personal self-transformation.[7] Stung by such criticism, New Agers respond that such personal transformation is precisely on behalf of desperately needed change in the wider world: along the 'hundredth monkey' principle, once a critical mass of individuals have experienced the paradigm shift in personal consciousness, the desired societal revolution *will* have occurred (e.g. Ferguson 1980). Mark Satin, a key New Age commentator, has effectively expressed the New Age view on the precedence of personal transformation: 'a non-aware self is a raging self' (Satin 1978: 222).

But there is another reason why New Agers downplay individualism, and this is that the mainstream society is itself commonly represented, by academic scholars and ordinary people alike, as individualistic. We shall see in Chapters 6 and 7 that New Age individualism and the entrepreneurial individualism of Western mainstream society are actually rather different. Yet this difference is quite subtle, and likely to be lost on many people: to distinguish themselves from the mainstream, New Agers appropriately stress holism.

Holism in Relation to Individualism

In anthropology general theories are available that attempt to grasp the relationship between holistic and individualistic phenomena when they appear in a particular society or culture. Behind these theories is the idea that whilst holism and individualism are opposites, in fact one or other is primary. Logically this is true, since for opposites to come into being one side (the primary) must trigger the other off. Dumont (1980) has famously discussed this directly with reference to holism and individualism, with the conclusion that holism (the primary factor) 'encompasses' individualism: that is to say, at the primary level holism exists unto itself, whilst at a secondary, dependent level there exists the opposition between holism and individualism. This concords with Dumont's belief that a precondition for individuals being able to interact with one another is that something transcendent (holistic) incorporates them – as Dumont puts it, 'the individual lives on social ideas' (1980: 44). Dumont calls upon Indian society to illustrate, putting his famous view that in this society transcendent ideas relating to purity and pollution encompass (individual) practices of power.

The case of India offers an argument opposite to that of Dumont. We can all agree that at the level of communitas something transcendent incorporates individuals, but when Dumont advances the case for holism as primary he seems to have something more concrete in mind. The problem with Dumont's position is that the holistic ideas then become unavailable for explanation: such ideas, which make the system possible, must be treated as 'givens', for if one tried to explain them, one would be putting oneself outside the system that one is trying to give an account of, and which these ideas define (also Sahlins 1976). In the case of India this means that ideas of purity and pollution cannot then be explicated in the context of Indian daily life, which is quite unsatisfying. For us, if we were to examine the Indian system, these particular ideas would be amongst the first we would address – and we would look to the circumstances of individuals for the answer. In Chapter 10, where we develop a framework for analysing New Age society and culture, we precisely consider holistic ideas in hunter–gatherer society as being determined in this way by individualistic strategy.

New Agers, when they address the relation between holism and individualism, seem content with ideas of balance. This is illustrated in the following poem:

> On the backs of a million, million lives
> From where did I come?
> Out of the prehistoric slime
> I oozed into amoebic life.
> Thence into fish with budding limb
> On, on, on through aeons and oceans
> Then up, up, up I was thrown
> Sliding, helpless, scorched and starved
> I died, died, died and died again
> Until those feet emerged to crawl

Through mating, birthing, suckling, dying,
Evolving, changing, ceaselessly,
'Til I emerged a two-legged creature
Erect and cunning, unknowing, free,
Brighter and broader grew my reason
Warmer and deeper felt my heart.[8]

The evolution of species, in the poem, is a metaphor for the development of the individual. *Out of the universal* – the prehistoric
slime – the individual arises: the (holistic) universe subsumes the
human person even as he or she becomes a distinct entity. But the
entire process is (individualistically) delivered *out of the actions of
separate beings* – on the backs of a million, million lives.

In Glastonbury, there is similar thinking in meditation meetings.
People, in deep, shared contemplation, draw on the powers beyond
. . . yet are thought to combine their 'energy' to form 'light' in
order to create a unified power to be spread around the world.

The New Age also celebrates the simultaneity of holism and
individualism:

I see the New Age phenomena as the visible tip of the iceberg of a mass
movement in which humanity is reasserting its rights to explore spirituality in total freedom. The constraints of religious and intellectual ideology are falling away. (Bloom 1991: xv)

The New Age is a mass movement affecting humanity . . . yet,
unconstrained by religious or intellectual ideology, people are free.

It is a commonplace of anthropology that ordinary people can
live with contradictory ideas, whilst analyst's frameworks cannot.
Set beside the analytical reasoning in this section, these New Age
ideas, celebrating holism and individualism as equivalents, are
contradictory. But there is another commonplace in anthropology,
which is that contradictions in ordinary people's experience are at
the root of the generative processes by which human society and
culture come into being and are sustained. We embrace the latter
commonplace. When we address the construction of New Age
social organisation and cosmology in Chapter 11 and 12, we shall
stipulate the contradiction between communitas and individual
autonomy as the root experience in terms of which New Age society and culture emerge. In those chapters, the task is to apply an
analytical framework which makes sense of what, in this emergence, occurs.

Notes

1. For anthropological work that has established this position, see Jenkins on youth and class in Northern Ireland, Wadel on the unemployed in Newfoundland, and Smith on kinship and class in the West Indies (Jenkins 1983, Wadel 1973, Smith 1985).
2. Thus Sjoo (1994) upbraids the New Age for its 'fascism', declaring herself an eco-feminist . . . which many commentators consider to be an important variety of New Age thinking.
3. Religious movements outside the New Age movement refute Christianity in a similar way. Thus for the Rastafarian, God is, in fact, black. Cargo cultists in Melanesia assert something similar, and accuse missionaries of having removed the pages from bibles where this is described, in order to protect European colonial domination (Worsley 1957).
4. From biology to physics, 'rebellious' thinking is insisting that the essential priority is to reconceptualise the broader systems in which the components of matter (atomic subparticles, genes) are inextricably subsumed, for such systems are conditions for the appearance, and therefore our understanding, of these components (e.g., Ingold 1990). In the case of some of these systems, such as those described in quantum physics, astounding empirical properties have been claimed, to the extent of suggesting the existence of a cosmic plan that is drawing together both matter and human consciousness to some sort of pre-ordained culmination – comparable with what Teilhard de Chardin, in his mystical writings, called the 'omega point' (e.g. Ferguson 1980: 155–83; Zohar and Marshall 1994).
5. As quite a few commentators have noted, most recently Hanegraaff (1996:11), Marxism is not embraced in New Age anti-mainstream thinking. Voicing itself as an orthodox science and focusing most fundamentally on the material realm of life, Marxism was never going to find favour in the New Age movement the while that opposition to the mainstream might equally well be expressed via non-scientific, non-material philosophies (see also Satin 1978: 269). Moreover, as embraced by the New Age, these other philosophies offer scope for radical social change, albeit that the emphasis is not on direct political action (see later in this chapter).
6. See Lukes (1973) for a comprehensive account of the meaning of individualism.
7. For an account of the Deep Ecology movement, see Devall and Sessions (1987). The radical strand in the Green movement, Deep Ecology in ideology shades into the New Age, and some commentators, including ourselves, would include it under the New Age umbrella (also Pepper 1991: 16). Some Deep Ecology 'communities', most famously Findhorn in northern Scotland, definitely incorporate New Age ideas (Hendershott 1989).
8. Poem by Phillippa Bowers. Handout at sculpture exhibition in Glastonbury Experience, 1987.

Part Two

Glastonbury: The Surface Appearance

2

The Glastonbury Scene

The New Age

An umbrella term for any idiosyncratic body of religious beliefs? A Western movement for social change? A paradise gained? In fact, a succinct characterisation of the 'New Age' is impossible. The familiar casual enquiry asks, 'So what exactly is this New Age movement?' – and expects a one-line answer, which is impossible. A simple and essential description is in any event prevented by the fact that New Agers themselves offer diversely individual interpretations. People's accounts of the New Age may also vary with circumstance and company. To go to Glastonbury armed with an *a priori* definition of the New Age as a discrete cultural category would be foolish indeed.

We shall illuminate the New Age movement in Glastonbury as an ethnographic phenomenon by listening to Ruth Prince's respondents, and also by noting extracts from their various pamphlets, newsletters and books. To give a feel for the New Age as a religious movement we shall also slip in some remarks from both scholars and sceptics. But in the end we shall say that this approach only takes us so far.

Sally, owner of hotel:

> We are just on the initial stage of the New Age. The end will be totally unrecognisable. Politically things are beginning to change very fast; Sai Baba teaches us that there will be bloodshed in the Middle East and modified nuclear war yet to come.

Robin, student:

> It's just a personal philosophy, not a movement leading to change.

Sir George Trevelyan, philosopher of the New Age and sometime resident of Glastonbury (in his *Summons to a High Crusade*):

> If, however, we can wake up to our relationship to the wholeness of life and the fact that the universe is a vast living organism shot through and through with creative being, and if we can then channel and co-operate with the energies and forces from that living universe, there is molecular change, which could de-pollute the planet. (1986: 41)

Self-identified New Ager:

> The New Age is hope.

John, local music teacher:

> People get involved with the New Age for a number of different reasons; resentment for example. You get a lot of women involved who have got divorced and feel very bitter about life. Some people get involved as a form of rebellion and others as a genuine quest. The Alternative scene is something you take what you want from.

Doug, retreat leader:

> Sometimes I think the New Age is a mythic representation, a projection or a fantasy in people, resulting from a disenchanted generation who realised that they weren't going to change the world, or at least that the world won't change in their lifetime. So they put those feelings on a fantasy level.

Alan, counsellor in Glastonbury:

> I associate it with the time following the Harmonic Convergence. Before, everyone was dreaming death and now we are dreaming life. There is a new ecological vision where we are suffering from an environmental sickness or cancer. I see the New Age and environmental movement closely associated. They disagree when Deep Ecologists focus on the outer rather than on the inner. Change needs to come from the inside to the outer. Generally society believes we can solve problems rationally but the rational is only part of our processing.

Rosalind Coward, academic commentator:

> The New Age is a mixture of spiritualism, self-development and environmentalism. People are more receptive to the forces of nature and

nature is seen as something intrinsically good. (From a lecture at 'The Watershed', Bristol, 6 February 1990)

Rosalind Coward, again:

> I first became attracted to writing about the New Age as an increasing number of friends became interested in it and suddenly started to embrace a completely new philosophy. They seemed to take on board a lot of very indistinct woolly beliefs which came under the umbrella term of spirituality. The more one looks at them, the more woolly a lot of them become. It has an evangelistic aspect to it, it is 'an experience'. (personal communication)

Joan, resident in Glastonbury:

> The New Age is here. All you have to do is look around you in the town and you can see people living it.

Frank Natale, healer and teacher of New Age ideas (in *The Age of Consciousness*):

> The word 'new' seems to push a lot of buttons, because it gets everybody locked into space-time which we have all become slaves to despite the fact that it is an illusion. Maybe it is best that we do not call it the New Age, but rather the age of consciousness and talk about what is new within this new dimension of consciousness. (1990:20)

George, New Age event facilitator:

> Much of what people are caught up in [in the New Age] is the trappings and this is what the older religions have been warning people to stay away from for a long time.

Shirley MacLaine (in her book, *Dancing in the Light*):

> A new age of awareness. An awareness that includes the knowledge that there is indeed a level of dimension that operates in harmony and with perfection, waiting for us to understand that being alive on earth is only a limited aspect of what we truly are. (1985: 117)

William Bloom (New Age interpreter, in his anthology, *The New Age*):

> I see the New Age phenomenon as the visible tip of the iceberg of a mass movement in which humanity is reasserting its right to explore

spirituality in total freedom. The constraints of religious and intellectual ideology are fading away. (1991: xv)

Rosamund, event organiser:

> We [New Agers] have a new philosophy of life that is spreading with love. Human beings are such sensitive creatures that our thoughts can cause vibrations which, in turn, affect other things, and so the new ideas and way of being is spreading.

What, then, of New Ager, the *social* category? 'New Age' provides terms for people to label themselves, so 'New Ager' might literally be someone who invokes a 'new age'. But matters are not so straightforward. The category, New Ager, incorporates considerable complexity. Thus not everybody in the Alternative Community in Glastonbury would permit themselves to be described by the term – around one in ten seemed definitely to spurn such a self-definition. Since 'New Age' as a body of practices and beliefs is definitively articulated in neither creed nor text this made things difficult during fieldwork, for to build up an understanding of the New Age Ruth was relying on people's statements and comments. People would say, 'no I'm not a New Ager, that's all new fangled American commercialised stuff. No, my guru has been around for ten years, and the spiritual tradition I follow comes from ancient Hindu sources'. Or, 'No, I'm not a New Ager, I don't believe in putting things off into some futuristic vision, we have to change things now'. Some would go so far as to echo Bertolt Brecht and comment that every generation believes itself to be a New Age.

Many people in Glastonbury were clearly ambivalent about the notion, New Age, and particularly towards identifying themselves with it. This can be traced to a number of factors, including the diversity of New Age doctrines and the fact that circumstances can mediate a person's declaration of beliefs. Let us take a group of people sitting round a table in the courtyard of The Glastonbury Experience, one of the focal meeting points in the town. They are discussing different spiritual practices, and Ruth (having just arrived in town) has raised the subject of 'What is the New Age'. At first the people are perplexed at what seems such a strange and naive question, and somewhat out of context as well, but then they begin to discuss the issue. One of them, Lisa, is an artist who practices rebirthing, and has great faith in the powers of crystals; she has just told the group that she sleeps every night with a

crystal under her pillow. Another, Doug, is a bereavement counsellor who runs retreats helping people develop a positive attitude
to death. He also teaches Tai Chi and meditation. Doug has a
degree in philosophy and has a highly analytical worldview.

Lisa: For me, being in Glastonbury is really important. I feel this
        place to be a high energy point for the global change in con-
        sciousness that is happening. I feel like I am on a shamanic
        journey to the New Age.
Doug: You see for you, you are a New Ager, you feel a sense of a
        growing towards. For me, I look around and sometimes I see
        a lot of disharmony amongst people in Glastonbury. For me,
        it's just a personal transformation and the more people it
        happens to the better. But no, I don't feel a New Ager, I
        don't use crystals.

Doug felt uncomfortable with the notion, New Age movement,
in Lisa's company, for her beliefs, and her reasons for being in
Glastonbury, centred around ideas with which he found it hard to
identify. But later on, speaking alone, Doug declared himself to be
part of an 'alternative spiritual scene'. He subscribed to New Age
newspapers and even described his home as a New Age centre. In
short, versus the mainstream Doug seemed content to affiliate with
the New Age, even as in a conversation 'on the inside' he anx-
iously distanced himself from the whole notion, which, he insisted,
was associated with California, the Big Sur and crystals.

Academic studies on linguistic relativity come to mind here. For
example, Nigel Rapport, invoking Wittgenstein, warns:

> language ought to be treated as a spatial and temporal phenomenon, an
> instrument used with intention, a form of action. This calls for a shift
> in focus from the dictionary and the book of grammar to situations of
> linguistic performance, for it is here that the significant properties of
> language are to be discovered (1987: 150).

The discussion between Lisa and Doug illustrates the fact that
'New Ager' incorporates complexity because, just as any other
social category, it is not merely a label to be attached to a body of
people; it is also a resource in terms of which people, with different preferences as to belief and practice, manoeuvre themselves in
relation to one another. Inherent in 'New Ager', as a concept, is the
notion that it may be discarded or picked up, and amplified or
restricted, in accordance with people's interests and strategy.

A pervasively individualistic ethos underscores the ambiguity and ambivalence relating to 'New Age' and 'New Ager'. In Glastonbury there was a 'you are how you are' attitude to life, which squares with the diversity and disagreement in respondents' opinions as to the sorts of practices and beliefs that might be taken in under the New Age heading. In the case of the New Age Travellers, Glastonbury's temporary New Age residents, this is taken virtually to its logical conclusion. Clustered in their vehicles around the outskirts of town, the Travellers would aver that they are but a collectivity of individuals, and that no one Traveller might speak for the group, nor for anyone else. The settled New Agers were not so different: the notion of individualism will dominate the descriptions of their daily lives in the chapters to come.

For the anthropologist the contextual and flexible use of New Age as both a cultural phenomenon and social label is a problem because it makes it hard, probably impossible, to delineate the people under discussion in their own terms. Perhaps one could impose homogeneous definitions (of New Age and New Ager) from without, circumventing awkward borderline instances; yet to do so would be to ignore the whole subtlety of the matter. All the same, wishing to embrace everyone in Glastonbury who, to the fieldworker, was not mainstream, and who, on the face of it, seemed to participate in an alternative cultural lifestyle, some sort of analytical rendering is inevitable. To allow for the cultural diversity and situational self-identity within the Glastonbury alternative scene, we follow Wittgenstein and the Soviet psychologist Vygotsky and suggest a polythetic method. The advantage of polythetic classification is precisely that it builds in diversity. For a given social phenomenon (the New Age) several criteria are laid down, only some of which a given candidate (a particular complex of practices or beliefs, in Glastonbury or elsewhere) need fulfil in order to qualify as a member. Moreover if one were to look closely one would find that not a single one of these criteria would be common among all the qualifying instances. In other words, New Age does not so much specify a single, definitive body of beliefs and activities, as connote a rather large variety of complexes of beliefs and activities which manifest but 'family resemblance'.

Rodney Needham introduced the idea of polythetic classification into anthropology by reference to the diversity of social structures in human societies. He argued that attempts to delineate a particular type of social structure in terms of essential features leads to intractable problems, such as rigid borderlines, not to mention why these particular features have been selected in the first place. Recommending the polythetic method, Needham comments:

> An important aspect of this procedure is that an insufficiently discriminative taxonomic concept [i.e. implying a rigid list of necessary features] is replaced by a set of criteria which might be matched only sporadically, and in highly various combinations, by the [qualifying] jural institutions of real societies. (1975: 351)

Martin Southwold likewise called on the polythetic procedure to consider the notion of religion, arguing that such an approach is consistent with the fact that 'religion is not a homogeneous system responding to any single need or inclination' (1978: 371). Accordingly, he lists twelve attributes (including 'belief in godlike beings', the 'presence of the sacred–profane dichotomy', a 'priesthood'), and proposes that 'anything we would call religion must have at least some of [them]' (ibid.: 370).

Thus we suggest the following polythetic definition of the New Age, which accommodates the flexibility and individualism central to the movement as a whole. This definition includes five rather different criteria relating to beliefs and activities – at least some, perhaps the bulk, of which any complex of practice and belief that qualifies as New Age may be expected to fulfil (note that polythetic borderlines are indistinct, so some criteria will be satisfied by doctrines outside the New Age movement as well). The formulation of the definition has the Glastonbury scene specifically in mind.

1. A prophetic belief in a current or approaching 'new age'. This is most commonly expressed as an age of harmony and tranquillity replacing an age of duality and conquest, and is most famously linked to the impending stellar shift in zodiacal constellations whereby the 'age of Aquarius' supplants the 'age of Pisces'. The 'Aquarian Age', indeed, has become, for many, virtually synonymous with the New Age. Not dissimilar calendrical prophecies were much in vogue in the late 1980s when Mayan and Aztec projections were celebrated at the time of the Harmonic Convergence.

2. In Western Europe and America, the practice of a spiritual lifestyle outside the Christian church. The Christian church is described as 'patriarchal' or 'old age', while the church, for its part, often pejoratively refers to New Agers as 'Paganists' or 'Satanists'.

3. Spiritual practice drawing upon a number of traditions, both historical and contemporary, and not excluding Christianity. Such practice implies personal empowerment, arising from transformation in individual consciousness (also Danforth 1989).
4. A strong emphasis upon the spiritual relationship of humans to nature, in the context of concern for environmental issues.
5. Practices and beliefs relating to the incorporation of spiritual ideas into the way people lead their everyday lives, bring up their children, conduct their relationships, clean the house, and so on.

One notes that through defining 'New Age' polythetically, one reduces considerably the ambiguity relating to the social category, 'New Agers'. A New Ager can reasonably objectively be defined as anyone who carries out or professes (some of) the above practices and beliefs. Thus in the remainder of this book, New Age can comfortably stand both for doctrine and for adherents.

Glastonbury, the Town

Glastonbury is a market town with a population of some 7,500 people, in central Somerset in the southwest part of England. The 1980s saw many mainstreamers moving into the town from southeast England, to buy property, and work or retire, thereby increasing house prices and adding more cars to the roads; yet the town and the general area is still predominantly rural, where mixed agricultural and dairy farming remains extremely important. The main industry was, and still is, leather products. With warm summers, a hazy humidity, apple orchards and winding country roads, Somerset is often described as sleepy.

Looking down from the Mendip Hills into the green and flat moorlands that surround Glastonbury, a Tolkein-esque hill topped with an indistinct tower stands out on the landscape. Often a layer of mist lies low on the ground, adding a sense of mystery both to the hill as it seemingly looms up like an island, and to the surrounding area, which is sometimes referred to as Avalon. The hill, known as the Tor, has at its summit the remains of a fourteenth-century church, and is one of the most famous landmarks in the area as a whole. For many sorts of people it is integral to one's identity as being a part of Glastonbury: for some the summit tower is a sacred monument, for others it is a significant historical relic, while yet others associate it with the burgeoning tourist industry. Variety and difference of perspective are the hallmarks of being involved with the Glastonbury area. The following remarks, from a wide range of sources, serve as an introduction to Glastonbury, and particularly to the diversity of views as to 'what it is all about'.

John, writer and physical immortalist:

> Glastonbury is the heart chakra.

Jane, mainstream mother:

> Glastonbury is full of weirdoes. I say that partly because that's how most of the people I know describe it.

Geoffrey Ashe, writer and historian;

> Glastonbury is a beautiful and peaceful place.

New Ager:

> Glastonbury is like a stage set.

non-New Ager:

> I've lived here all my life, why haven't I felt the vibes?

Local businessman and Quaker:

> I've lived here all my life, and I don't feel there is any particular spiritual power to the place. People come here and impose it, there aren't any vibes on the Tor.

Tom, musician:

> Glastonbury is a place where people come to live out their fantasies.

Marion Bradley (in *The Mists of Avalon*):

> For as I say, the world itself has changed. There was a time when a traveller, if he had the will and knew only a few of the secrets, could send his barge out into the Summer Sea and arrive not at Glastonbury

of the monks, but at the Holy Isle of Avalon; for at that time the gates between the worlds drifted within the mists, and were open, one to another, as the traveller thought and willed. For this is the great secret, which was known to all educated men in our day: that by what men think, we create the world around us, daily new. (1984: ix)

Local Methodist minister:

I don't think Glastonbury is particularly special as an area at all. What is powerful is people's mental associations with the place.

New Ager:

Glastonbury is a form of anarchy with people trying to reorganise/restructure society. As there are no rules it is open to different people's power games.

Dion Fortune (in *Glastonbury, Avalon of the Heart*):

Glastonbury is a gateway to the Unseen. It has been a holy place and pilgrim-way from time immemorial, and to this day it sends its ancient call into the heart of the race it guards, and still we answer to the inner voice. (1986: 2)

New Age Glastonbury

Glastonbury is a town with a strong historical past that revolves firmly around religion and myth. As 'legendary Avalon' it is where King Arthur is said to be buried. In the presence of Glastonbury Abbey, the oldest Christian religious foundation in the British Isles, it also has close connections with the Christian church. Joseph of Arimathea reputedly visited the town and brought with him the cup of the Last Supper, which he buried on Chalice Hill (hence the hill's name). Nearby, on Wearyall Hill, Joseph is supposed to have stopped to rest, and there driven his staff into the ground. Legend tells that it blossomed into a thorn tree. Blake's poem, *Jerusalem*, famously evokes these particular historical associations:

> And did those feet in ancient time
> Walk upon England's mountains green!
> And was the Holy Lamb of God
> On England's pleasant pastures seen?

Glastonbury's historical identity is consciously upheld by Christians and non-Christians alike. Separate Roman Catholic and Anglican pilgrimages take place each year, and much of the developing 'alternative' tourist industry rests upon the perpetuation of the legend of Avalon. New Agers, too, read historical meaning into the town, which one can glean from leaflets and booklets produced and sold locally; these indicate very well the elements of history that New Agers emphasise, and how these elements relate, as may be seen:

1. The Tor. The Tor stands out as a prominent landmark on the horizon. It serves as a site for pilgrimage, group ritual and (on a daily basis) individual contemplation; only on the coldest or stormiest days of winter may one look up and not see people scattered on its slopes like sheep. The hill is imbued with sacred properties. Among Pagans it is often described as the door to the underworld, where souls enter at death before re-emerging in a new life-time:

> Guarding the entrance to Annwn/Avalon was Gwynn ap Nudd – Gwynn, son of Nudd, lord of the Otherworld. An ancient local tradition locates his palace on the Tor. Here he is known as 'the King of Faery'; and periodically he rides out with other members of the 'Wild Hunt', taking the souls of the deceased back into the Otherworld on his return. Accompanying him is Art-thwr, a mythical ancestor of Arthur . . . a link which solidly locates him with Avalon. (Mann 1985: 6)

For others, the Tor's slopes represent the Goddess. At first glance, the hill, with its tower and being surrounded by flat moorland, appears blatantly phallic, but to Goddess-worshippers the rolling sides and rounded shape are indicative of the female form:

> From a distance the most noticeable feature on the Isle of Avalon is the Tor as she rises out of the flat Summerlands. She sits like a Great Goddess, a huge bounteous female figure in the middle of a landscape bowl or Cauldron. To see her is to love her. (Jones 1990: 42)

To still others the Tor's sculpted outline suggests that the sides have been artificially shaped in the form of a maze, in the Cretan style. The maze spirals round the outside of the hill seven times in seven continuous terraces with vertical connections between them. Its function?

It is a ritual maze and needs to be walked with awareness and reverence. It is a sacred rite of passage. (ibid.: 46)

2. The Chalice Well. This is the second main place of 'legendary interpretation and reinterpretation'. Sited near the foot of the Tor, the Well, dating at least from the twelfth century, is fed by a spring which rises from Chalice Hill. Since 1958 a charitable trust has cared for the Chalice Well, preserving the spring and developing around it a small, but voluptuous garden where, for a small price, visitors can come in to drink the waters and sit in the gardens. A sacred space, it is a popular place for meditation and individual contemplation. The spring inside the garden (outside there is another, with a tap) is called the 'Blood Spring', due to an iron-red deposit left on the stones it passes over. This particularly evokes meaning:

> There is the difficult question of menstrual blood to consider. Was the Earth bleeding between two hills – both closely resembling human anatomy – suggestive of the menstrual cycle to the Celts? If it was, was it seen as a sign of life and fertility, or as the final phase in the cycle of a woman which prepared her for her power? Destructive in its power of Renewal? (ibid.: 12)

Something about historical accounts in general is illustrated by such interpretations. Just as the values of the adult world may be glimpsed in the education of children, so cultural priorities in communities in the present-day are evident in particular constructions of the past. The New Age history of Glastonbury may certainly be summed in these terms: it is moulded to contemporary New Age preoccupations and values. For example, the historical sacredness attributed to the Tor and the Chalice Well justifies the present-day notion that the sites incorporate an enhanced spiritual energy that sensitive 1990s' folk can both feel and tap into. And the 1990s' stress on the feminine and on the Goddess has led to the town's historical past, more usually described in terms of the development of Christianity and by reference to male figures such as Joseph of Arimathea, to be re-invented by some people, and re-told with a stress upon Pagan and Celtic figures.

The past is present in contemporary Glastonbury in yet another way. In the one main street (High Street) books on the history of Glastonbury from both 'traditional' and 'alternative' perspectives stand out from the shop windows, along with posters of the Tor. The availability of such books reflects a growing retail trade specifically catering for an alternative tourist industry, whose sales also include perfume oils, crystals, trinkets, and more general literature, which notably covers an enormous range of spiritual themes. The shops tend to be concentrated at the bottom of High Street, and particularly around the two main social focal points of the Alternative Community in the town – the Assembly Rooms and the Glastonbury Experience (see the pictorial map of the town).

Firstly, the Assembly Rooms, which are set back one layer of buildings from High Street. Plants surrounding the stone steps, broadly striped cream and brown double doors, the occasional busker as if on sentry duty, and the odd dog lying outside in the sun awaiting its owner: the Assembly Rooms (the name is emblazoned in red letters above the door) is unmistakably part of the Alternative scene. Inside, amidst trailing plants and bright posters, one finds a café, which sells a variety of organic vegetarian foods, and a particularly thick and soup-like coffee. Children run around, chasing one another under the legs of tables, and a few people who have settled themselves in for the morning sit and roll cigarettes. Occasionally the door swings open into the main hall where the resident theatre company may be rehearsing, or people are mounting an exhibition of paintings. When Ruth was in Glastonbury, the Assembly Rooms was the forum for legions of discussions, plays and musical events. However it could also be caught up in dispute. For example, some 'resident' New Agers felt that it was too heavily dominated by (New Age) Travellers who might put off 'straights' (i.e., mainstream people) from coming into the café; the Travellers, in return, resented what they saw as bigotry.

During 1990, the Assembly Rooms was the object of a good deal of factionalism and division. A group of women who wanted to take over the café talked about this with Ruth, and one suggested that the only way to completely change the energy and resolve things would be for the café to be run by the Women's Institute(!). Another said,

> I feel it is a very negative place just now. The people in there are possibly even into black magic. I would like to fill it with lighter, female energies.

The Assembly Rooms building was originally owned by a board of trustees who hoped to pay the mortgage by renting out the various rooms and facilities. One room, for example, was occupied by a small computer facilities business. However in an interesting later development, the trustees sold the building, and it was in the

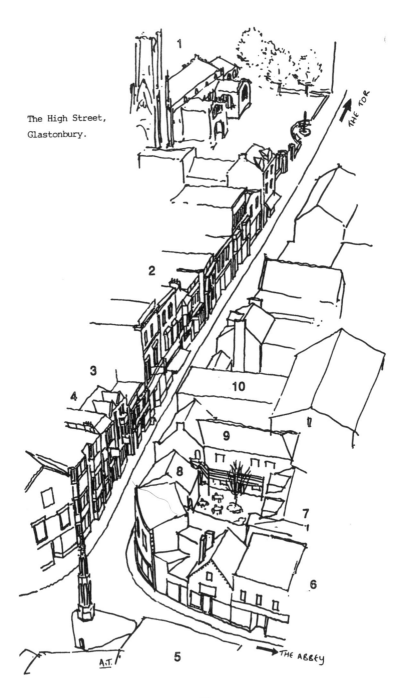

The High Street,
Glastonbury.

process of being re-bought in a system of shared ownership, each share costing £500. An elected steering committee hoped to have enough money to buy back the building and also to refurbish it as a sacred space. This eventually proved to be successful. Overall, the building is described as being central to a sense of community:

> At different times throughout its history the Assembly Rooms has been at the heart of the Avalonian community. It is here we have held community gatherings, danced, sung, listened to music . . .' (Jones 1990: 12)

The second social focal point is just a few premises down from the Assembly Rooms, but it has a very different atmosphere. This is the Glastonbury Experience. The Glastonbury Experience is a courtyard of buildings – whose most significant initial impact is olfactory. With its café and bakery, the smell of baking, herbs and spices fills the courtyard, mixing with the incense that continually burns in the shop selling perfume oils. In 1990 one woman owned all the buildings and rented out the rooms separately to different enterprises. Along the second floor of the courtyard runs a wooden staircase leading to recording studios, storerooms and to a large community space used for workshops, yoga, concerts and therapy groups. There is also an information centre that oversees the activities and books appointments to consult with individual therapists.

The Glastonbury Experience courtyard is a sun trap, and on a hot day one could well close one's eyes and imagine oneself somewhere far away from Britain. Filled with tables and chairs, people sit outside, talk, sell jewellery and old books, and play guitars. There is an ornamental carved wooden seat in the middle, above it a signpost pointing the way to the different enterprises. Exotic smells, a statuette of a woman holding a crystal ball and the range of differing healing therapies, make for a self-conscious tranquillity.

The High Street, Glastonbury (1990)

1. St John's Church
2. Rainbow Café
3. The Gothic Image
4. Isis
5. The Glastonbury Centre for Spiritual Healing
6. Shambhala
7. St. Bridget's Chapel (open for public meditation and prayer)
8. The Glastonbury Experience
9. Ploughshares
10. The Assembly Rooms

This is further emphasised by a chapel, which is left open for individual meditation. A book lies open for people to record their thoughts and prayers to share with the visitor who comes next. Flowers are brought to decorate it. An air of religiosity envelops. It has an entirely different ambience from the Assembly Rooms; and there is no thick black coffee.

Glastonbury: the 'Alternative Community'

The members of the Glastonbury New Age scene are due for introduction. We shall examine the life histories of some of Ruth's respondents in the next chapter, which relate how they see themselves becoming involved in the New Age movement, and we shall also consider some sociological dimensions of the New Age community in the town. For now we offer just a brief impression of the Alternative Community in the Glastonbury area.

In 1990, around five hundred people in Glastonbury fell within the loose category, New Age, extending to seven hundred to include those in outlying communities and nearby villages. These are rough estimations, for the Alternative Community is in a constant state of flux, and to reckon in all the comings and goings the population would have to be recounted almost every month. Also, during the spring and summer a mobile population of Travellers and 'alternative' visitors arrives, particularly around the summer solstice on June 21st when, in most years, Glastonbury swells to three or four times its usual size as people descend on the town for the famous Glastonbury Festival just beyond the outskirts. As the temporary incomers arrive in the area some of the long-term (New Age) residents leave – to travel, to attend courses, or, after a few last minute repairs to an old vehicle-home and painting some stars on the bumper, to go 'back on the road', spending the summer moving around from one music festival to another.

New Agers residing permanently within the town mostly live in council and private flats, and bedsits. Mainstream locals would complain that you could tell a house belongs to a 'Hippy' by its unkempt garden, semi-dressed children, several dogs and the large number of old cars standing outside. Other, more affluent, New Agers have bought larger houses with secluded gardens, stripped wooden floors, hand-made furniture and fitted kitchens. Meanwhile, beyond the immediate area of the town one finds a wider range of living styles. Many occupied small farm cottages, while others (Ruth was one of these) clubbed together to rent a large old farmhouse where they lived communally.

For New Agers living outside town an increasingly usual strategy was to buy a field and set up home on it – much to the anxiety of local councillors who would claim the land was available for agricultural purposes only. In this sort of location varying forms of housing would develop; the most common were caravans, dome structures and tipis, and people occasionally made house in a trailer or else in a bender. The bender is similar to a tent, with tree branches usually forming the basic structure, which is then covered with plastic; benders are often attached to the sides of vehicles or to trees. Many people living this way did so throughout the winter, often with no electricity, and taking fresh water supplies from springs or streams.

To speak of these people as making up the Alternative Community in Glastonbury is misleading if what is suggested is a homogeneous group all involved in an identical lifestyle. We have hinted already, for example, when describing the town's social focal points (the Glastonbury Experience and the Assembly Rooms), that a number of sub-groups are present – with ever-changing memberships as people swap allegiances and tastes. Thus people absorbed in the same or similar spiritual practices or therapies would gravitate to one another, but as the respective practices and therapies altered and evolved, so too would group affiliations. The visual symbolic distinctions between such sub-groups are subtle and not always immediately obvious. In sum, with regard to the Alternative Community in Glastonbury in its entirety, involvement with others lies rather more predominantly in the realm of people's thoughts and ideas, and rather less in the domain of actual communal activity.

4

The Imagined Community

People's perspectives on the social world can be thought of as comprising a large but finite number of social categories or groups, standing in various kinds of relationships with each other: distant/close, above/below, inclusive/exclusive and so on. Usually members of different categories or groups are thought to share certain attributes or characteristics. These are the behavioural, attitudinal and mental characteristics which we usually call stereotypes. (Graham McFarlane, *Shetlanders and Incomers*, 1981, p.89)

'Incomers' they might be, but the members of the Alternative Community in Glastonbury were quick to mention that this does not mean that they represent a recent phenomenon. They would cite the music evenings in the Assembly Rooms in the nineteenth century when Thomas Hardy visited, the music–drama school of Rutland Boughton, and the 1930s' writings of the occultist, Dion Fortune, as examples of the historical presence of music, myth and imagination in the town. For their part, the local (mainstream) people insisted that the New Age presence in this predominantly rural farming region and market town, was entirely recent. According to them it all started in the 1970s with the Worthy Farm festivals, just a few miles outside Glastonbury, where (so it was said) people danced around naked. Now, locals told Ruth Prince, more and more 'Hippies' are coming to the town, are on the roads, and in the shops.

Here are two groups co-existing within the same geographical area who evoke different versions of an historical past, and, as will be seen shortly, attribute distinctive social characteristics to one another. In summer, 1987, when Ruth Prince was in Glastonbury to study the Harmonic Convergence, the Alternative Community, invoking the imagery of Rastafarianism, labelled the groups in a rather amusing way, referring to the traditional (mainstream) locals as 'Glastonians', and themselves, counter-cultural people attracted to the area on the basis of its spiritual powers, as 'Glasta-farians'. At this time there appeared multi-coloured T-shirts and car bumper stickers emblazoned 'Jah Glastafari'. However the bound-ary between the 'alternative' community and the rest of the town is something the Alternative Community has recently come to play down, for reasons to be discussed below; in 1990, New Agers mostly referred to themselves as Avalonians, and local people as 'locals' or 'straights' – and were called 'the Hippies' in return.

As to objective backgrounds, the New Age people in and around Glastonbury are basically those who live in, or have moved to, the area because of the town's mystical associations, while the main-streamers are people who live in, or have moved to, the area for reasons such as work or because of family connections. The Glas-tonbury area, being predominantly rural, has quite a settled and homogeneous indigenous population, but this has always included its own share of incomers, particularly people coming in to work for Clarks Shoes in nearby Street. These incomers turn out to be rather similar to the white collar incomers to whom McFarlane's study of the Shetlands refers (see the quotation at the head of this chapter). They have mostly tried to make a positive effort to become part of the more traditional element in the community, and so have largely been assimilated. McFarlane describes the situation in the Shetlands:

> Many of the first incomers had (and still have) a rather cosy view of life in Shetland, they pursued the meaningful 'community'; as a conse-quence, these individuals tended to establish their closest relations with the bearers of Shetland tradition, the older Shetlanders. These older Shetlanders seemed to create the incomers' links to the commu-nity, in the sense that it was they who helped to forge the reputations attributed to the incomers. Having a reputation, these incomers came to 'belong' to different local communities. (McFarlane 1981: 127)

In Glastonbury, with increased immigration in the past few years the mainstream incomers have become increasingly less absorbed in this way.

But absorption has hardly been on the agenda for the other type of incomer in Glastonbury. Declaring themselves as 'alternative', the New Agers in the town have barely at all sought relationships with the bearers of Somerset tradition. Once in Glastonbury they have sustained their own separate grouping, with modes of behaviour quite different from, and sometimes directly in opposition to, the adjacent mainstream cultural setting.

In this chapter we place the Alternative Community in Glastonbury in the context of its wider locality. The perspective is that of Cohen (1985), who views 'community' as a symbolic construct – as a body of idioms and representations which convey mutuality and togetherness, and also as a linguistic term which people invoke on particular occasions and in particular places. The Alternative 'Community' in Glastonbury, in this sense, is more something that the members conceptualise than a bounded group that an outsider could concretely observe. According to Cohen, a central aspect of community as something conceptualised relates to the community's boundaries – imaginary locations where, as one crosses over, key social idioms cease to be meaningful or else come to be given entirely different meanings. In this way, in terms of valorising certain idioms and being repelled by others, opposed social groupings – such as, in Glastonbury, New Agers and mainstream locals – respectively conceive of themselves as being distinct.

The symbolic construction of community life rests on the experiences of individuals. The reality of having come to Glastonbury is a central experience of most New Agers currently in the town and, in the form of biographies, we shall explore this element first.

Biographies

Sean

Sean was born in the Devon town of Honiton in 1956, where his parents were local tradespeople. He remembers being very musical at school, taking part in the school choir and the school orchestra. In his mid-teens he became involved in the school C.N.D. group, and amongst the peace literature he came across the life story and pacifist teachings of Gandhi who became one of the main influences in his life. Sean stayed on at school until he was eighteen, and became involved in a local rock band which afterwards led him to move to Bristol. There he lived in a large house of young people, where from time to time he would perform music. A couple of years passed and he decided to go to university to pursue his interest in philosophy. Later, somewhat dissatisfied with the analytical nature of Western philosophy, he travelled to India and

South America where he had a series of spiritual encounters in which he experienced himself to be in direct contact with God. Back in Britain, he felt his life had been changed and he went to live in an isolated cottage in the countryside where, supported financially by social security, he spent the time reading the works of many different gurus and composing music. When he married he and his wife moved nearer to Glastonbury and he increasingly became involved with the meditation and discussion groups there. After a few years, as he made more and more contacts, he began to compose short pieces of music for a New Age video company and to lead a meditation class himself.

Marion

Marion was born in 1943 in Holland. She left school at the age of sixteen and took a job as a secretary. At the age of twenty-one she married, and she stopped working shortly afterwards when she became pregnant with her first child. Her husband was a senior manager in a catering business, so they were financially comfortable. Over the next ten years Marion had four children and, although she did no paid work, she was a very active member of parent–teacher organisations as well as becoming elected to the council of the village in which they were living. Her husband's job transferred the family to England and Glastonbury in the late 1970s. Very soon Marion started attending workshops and courses in the town on such subjects as meditation and 'realising one's full potential'. Her growing feeling was that, though she had raised four children, no recognition had ever been given to her as a woman, and this in the long term had led to a lack of self-worth. Further, she came to believe that her family lifestyle was too materialist, and she wanted to live on a smallholding and become self-sufficient. However her husband and teenage children were unwilling to make this sacrifice and wished to return to Holland. Soon afterwards she left them to share a house in a rural area, and started attending the meetings of a regular spiritual group who came together on a weekly basis. The group itself had decided not to live communally although the members kept in close contact with one another nearly every day. Marion started a small jewellery-making business on the government's enterprise allowance scheme, and she became an active participant in the life of the Alternative Community, contributing regularly to a newsletter and organising holiday events in the Assembly Rooms.

Stephen

Stephen was born in 1945. He did well at school despite suffering throughout childhood from prolonged periods of asthmatic illness. His parents encouraged him to take up a profession, and so, leaving school at eighteen, he joined a legal firm as a clerk and worked his way up. He stayed with the same firm for twelve years. As time passed the asthma attacks increased in frequency, particularly when he was suffering from stress. He also began to suffer severe stomach complaints and, at the age of thirty, was diagnosed as having a stomach ulcer. At the same time he started to attend a local rebirthing group. Learning to re-enact the moment of birth as a positive, as opposed to negative, experience he came to understand that his asthma was related to his reluctance to breathe when he was first born. He had not been ready to emerge from his mother's womb, but was forced to – and consequently had spent a life being coerced by others to do things he did not really want to do. Through his contacts with the group he met a number of people living in Glastonbury and became more and more attracted to the place. Eventually he decided to give up his job and move there to find a more satisfying and less stressful way of living. He also felt it would be his way of 're-birthing' his life. Once in Glastonbury he supported himself financially by doing part-time bookkeeping for small businesses, and working some hours helping in a shop. He began to undertake regular day-long fasts and to eat only raw foods, and he also became an active helper with arts events in the town, as well as attending the rebirthers' support group every week. He felt he had found somewhere where he could be accepted for himself and for his own emotional and environmental needs. In 1990 he was buying a piece of land with a number of others which they hoped to use to grow food, and as an 'outdoor space'.

Rachel

Rachel was born in 1963 in Wales. Her parents were both doctors with high expectations for their children. Rachel was sent to a private school, which she did not particularly enjoy, and until her mid-teens was very quiet and introverted. At the age of around fifteen or sixteen she started to rebel against what she saw as the repressive atmosphere and rules of the school. With like-minded friends she began to visit the summer music festivals, and to spend time listening to music and experimenting with various drugs. Meanwhile her parents, horrified at their daughter's behaviour, tried to restrict her activities and get her to pay more attention to her schoolwork. As a result, Rachel found her situation at home intolerable, and began to look for ways to leave. She had met a Canadian Traveller, Rob, who was living in a bus with a convoy of other Travellers and their vehicles, and she began to have a relationship with him. His visa had expired and he was considering moving back to Canada. One day Rachel came home and announced to her parents that she had married this man and she was leaving home to live with him in the bus. After six months Rachel became pregnant and at the age of seventeen gave birth to her first child. Out of contact with her parents she spent the following six years as a Traveller, with Rob, and had another child. Towards the end of this period, her relationship with Rob was deteriorating; Rachel was fed up with looking after two children on the move with little or no help or support from him. She also suspected he was seeing other women. On the basis of a strong intuition, confirmed by a tarot card reading, she packed up her possessions and, taking the children, arrived on the doorstep of a friend's house in Glastonbury. She was rehoused in a council house in Glastonbury, and started working part-time in a café and re-establishing her relationship with her parents.

These biographies, relating events by which people can come to be engaged in the New Age lifestyle, offer a sense of the Alternative Community as a community. A perspective on this community and what it means to participate in it can be clarified by the following three points:

Firstly, there is a continuum of involvement and experience in the Alternative Community. Some, like Rachel, had never held jobs or even filled an adult role in mainstream British society, whilst others, such as Marion and Stephen, had held or continued to hold 'traditional' job or adult roles, such as housewife or lawyer's clerk.

Secondly, though people may have strong spiritual or emotional experiences, which catalyse their becoming involved in New Age beliefs in general and in Glastonbury in particular, one is encountering here a more complex process than sudden religious conversion. A number of more mundane factors are salient such as change in lifestyle, or crises in relationships and in the workplace.

Thirdly, Luhrmann, discussing involvement in witchcraft in present-day England, suggests that the acceptance of magical beliefs by people whose outlook has hitherto been secular and scientific is not so much a sudden acceptance of the irrational, but is rather a slow absorption of a new set of values, beliefs and, above all, meanings for the events of everyday life. 'A new definition of evidence, new assumptions, new common knowledge – these changes systematically alter the way yet-to-be interpreted events are noticed, organised and analysed' (Lurhrmann 1989: 176). This rings true with the Glastonbury biographies. As Stephen became more involved with the rebirthing group his friends' account of his 'negative birth experiences' became persuasive as an explanation for the asthma from which he suffered and his stomach ulcer; but this was a gradual process. Especially to the point, as he took on the values and explanations of the group he also found a reasonable justification for giving up his job and moving to Glastonbury.

Notions of Community

There is something distinctive about the New Age 'community' in Glastonbury. To draw this out, one may usefully contrast it with the utopian religious communities in North America in recent history, which, according to Rosabeth Moss Kantor (1972: 2), have emerged in successive (though overlapping) waves. Up to 1845 the North American communities had overwhelmingly religious agendas, such as the Aurora and Bethel communities with their emphasis on the purification of Christian organisation, and the Hutterites and Amish colonies whose presence stemmed from religious persecution in Europe. Then, from the early nineteenth century, the communities that sprung up had a more overtly political or economic rationale, probably associated with the sense of individual dislocation connected with the rapid growth of industrialisation. From this period one would include the Shakers and the Oneida community, whose peasant livelihoods were based around the production of 'local' goods such as furniture or steel traps. A third period started in the 1960s with the so-called 'commune', a social grouping said by Cantor to have a more psycho–social basis, connected with people's concern to 'find themselves'. Now, all these various communities, from different historical periods, are extremely diverse in terms of beliefs, values and social organisation; famous for their celibacy, the Shakers would assuredly be horrified to be mentioned in the same breath as the 1960s' Children of God who through extending sexual favours acquired new members with a technique known as 'flirty fishing' (Wallis 1979: 69). Nonetheless these communities do have something very significant in common, namely spatial, or residential, exclusiveness – they are physically enclaved vis-à-vis the outside world. This is the respect in which the Alternative Community in Glastonbury, also a utopian community, is different. Interspersed with the mainstream population over an area whose radius stretches ten miles out from the town, and internally highly diverse, both in terms of its members' practices and the particularities of their beliefs, this Community challenges us as to whether, and in what sense, it actually constitutes a community. This is especially valid in view of the fact that in Glastonbury the label 'alternative *community*' is widely used by New Agers and non-New Agers alike. To begin with, it is worth inspecting what the word community generally means in English-speaking cultures.

The principal meaning of community, we propose, is a sense of closure with respect to a heterogeneous body of people. Heterogeneity suggests variety and difference, and the idea of closure implies that the people concerned enjoy a common purpose. In short, the idea of community seems to be saying: 'in spite of differences we are one'. Community, in this manner, connotes a rather distinctive type of social grouping. This is because in human society, for most people most of the time, the salient social identities relate to social *categories*. The notion of social category connotes homogeneity – which is why, as is evident from the previous chapter, to talk of New Ager as a social category is so difficult. Social category implies an association of people in terms of specific qualities which they have in common (e.g. adults, children, men, women, workers, Catholics). One concludes from this that the term community has an ideological function. Community acknowledges diversity and cleavage within the social fabric, but then insists that they do not matter. This being so, it is important to examine the vested interests of the people who invoke the term.

'Community', then, is exactly appropriate as the self-appellation for Glastonbury New Agers. We have commented upon the heterogeneity and diversity in the New Age several times already, yet the New Agers in Glastonbury certainly enjoy a common purpose, which is to manage relations with mainstreamers, who are responsible for a good deal of unpleasant opprobrium. The vested interest here is that the Glastonbury New Agers, all of them, are concerned to represent themselves as the moral equals of, if not morally superior to, the mainstream. For Glastonbury New Agers, the word 'community' amounts to what Victor Turner (1974) calls a dominant symbol. With its double connotation of shared morality and physical togetherness, it provides the basis to mount further symbolic elaborations relating to the boundary between New Agers and the wider society.

Anthropological approaches to the study of community that focus on the conceptual (community as an idea in people's minds), as opposed to the concrete (community as an objectively observable body of people), are therefore highly pertinent. Such perspectives, especially those provided by Benedict Anderson and Anthony Cohen, may usefully be elaborated on.

For Anderson, the notion of community is important in order to help make sense of the perplexing idea of the nation-state. The nation-state is akin to a community, and it is, above all, something 'imagined':

> It is *imagined* because the members of even the smallest nation will never know most of their fellow-members, meet them, or even hear of them, yet in the mind of each lives the image of their communion . . .

> In fact, all communities larger than primordial villages of face-to-face contact (and perhaps even these) are imagined. Communities are to be distinguished, not by their falsity/genuineness, but by the style in which they are imagined. (1983: 19)

In Anderson's opinion, the historical availability of mass-printing technology was crucial in facilitating the spread of the myths and stories which, at the level of nation-state, provide the content for this shared imagination.

Cohen, addressing precisely the small-scale level of settlement or locality, argues, for his part, that it is through symbolic interpretation more generally that communities are imagined.

> The community itself and everything within it, conceptual as well as material, has a symbolic dimension, and, further, this dimension does not exist as some kind of consensus of sentiment. Rather it exists as something for people 'to think with'. The symbols of community are mental constructs: they provide people with the means to make meaning. (1985: 19)

We may return to the Alternative scene in Glastonbury with the notion of a conceptual, imagined and symbolic community, and briefly rejoin the New Agers whose biographies were told earlier.

These New Agers' motives for coming to Glastonbury were quite different, yet they felt the worth of being surrounded by like-minded people and of a sense of identity with the place (Cohen 1982). The predominant symbolic idiom by which Glastonbury is recognised – again, shared by all – is its spirituality, which imparts an animating and manipulable power. This power, concentrated at such places as the Tor and the Chalice Well, is, in turn, linked to symbolically propitious times of the year – the solstices. Both summer and winter solstices are times when very large numbers of people gather on the Tor or at the Chalice Well for individual or group meditation. Even New Agers who do not seek out these venues at these times would recognise them as focal symbols – as conveying what it is to be New Age. Such recognition denotes a belonging to the town's Alternative Community: in conversation discussion of these places is reverential. Thus Rachel would look to the Tor and see it as the 'Goddess' to be prayed to; Sean, at the end of a long journey, would observe its Tolkein-like figure on the horizon and feel a welcoming sense of home-coming. Later, both might attend the same ritual, holding hands around the ruined church tower at the top of the Tor, and feel moved.

Cohen maintains that the meaning a symbol conveys does not have to be exactly the same for all those who 'share' it. He exemplifies this with the C.N.D. symbol – the circle with its three distinctively-positioned radii. Prominently displayed at any peace march this symbol serves as a focus of association for all who sympathise with the campaign for nuclear disarmament. However within the peace movement there are many branches, from anarchists through to Christians, whose opinions often conflict – and whose understandings of the symbol are therefore likely to differ. Yet this is precisely the strength of the 'symbolic construction of community'. Cohen writes:

> They [the symbols] can thus provide media through which individuals can experience and express their attachment to a [community] without compromising their individuality. So versatile are symbols they can often be bent into these idiosyncratic shapes of meaning without such distortions becoming visible to other people who use the same symbol at the same time. (1985: 18)

There is more than a hint of this in Rachel's and Sean's feelings about Glastonbury's sacred place.

But the notion of symbolic community has some limitations, for community implies that people's togetherness includes a sense of continuity, which can be spurious. People's conceptualisation of their social world also includes what classical anthropology would call segmentary principles. As circumstances change so communities disappear and reappear, dissolving and reforming at different levels. A familiar fact is that people may hold an idea of (smaller) communities nesting within (larger) communities – indeed Cohen indicates as much. But it is more than this. By fission and fusion, boundaries between communities may, at the one moment, evaporate and, at the next, manifest themselves anew. Thus among Glastonbury New Agers, that apparently most important of symbolic boundaries – between the Alternative Community and the wider world – would sometimes be denied altogether. On such occasions the debate would typically revolve around 'what it means to be in Glastonbury', with people's personal situations and interests determining how they lined up in the argument and how, accordingly, they construed the Alternative–mainstream divide.

These Glastonbury discussions could be articulated in any number of ways. For example, someone might query the very notion of 'alternative community', by so doing refusing to accept that a boundary with the mainstream existed. Thus one person said:

> Glastonbury is like a meeting place, a gathering of people to discuss ideas, it has no productive centre. We have common agreements but we're not really working together. Community means relating to each other as people rather than roles, we are too fragmented for that. Glastonbury yearns for community.

But there is an opposite point of view:

> Well, since I've lived in Glastonbury I've felt an incredible sense of warmth and trust with other people here. It's like we're all trying out different ways of being and living together, sometimes it goes wrong and we feel bitter, but mostly I feel surrounded by more laughter and love than I have ever felt before. I suppose it comes from being in a community.

Evoking 'warmth', 'trust' and 'living together', the second speaker experiences community (the Alternative Community) very strongly. For his part, the first speaker, invoking segmentary terms such as 'fragmented', denies it. As between the two, circumstances explain the differences of attitude. The second speaker was a woman who was absorbed in organising a local (alternative) event and also closely involved with a bi-monthly New Age newspaper.

Her experience of Glastonbury was genuine, but the existence of an idea of community was also rather directly in her interests. The first person was a man who worked in the area as a therapist. From an academic background, he gave as part of the reason for living in Glastonbury the large number of people in the area interested in his kind of therapy. For him the idea of the Glastonbury Alternative scene constituting a community was unimportant. In the conversation between these two people, with the symbolic importance of community at issue, their respective positions had polarised.

Boundaries and Sub-Groups

Read through any New Age journal, attend any lecture or workshop, and the conclusion might be that, in New Age thinking, people's ideal is to live in a boundary-free world. However, take a closer look at what New Agers say and do, and it is obvious that matters are more complex. The ideology of a boundary-free world should be examined first, but we then move on to consider the boundaries that do prevail – first, those between the Alternative Community and 'the town', and secondly, those between the various groups within the Alternative Community. These boundaries are importantly articulated by symbolic idioms.

A Boundary-Free World

> We stand on a threshold where human consciousness can take a quantum leap out of self-consciousness into all-consciousness, God-consciousness. (Sir George Trevelyan, quoted in Slocombe 1986: 15)

Central to New Age doctrine, these phrases, authored by one of the New Age's most prominent thinkers, convey the concept of a common and divine consciousness shared not only among all human beings but by plants and animals as well. Adapted to such cosmology is the notion of Gaia (see Chapter 8), which names James Lovelock's scientific theory that all living things are interconnected as a single, immense and self-correcting system, and which upholds as its central emphasis the communality of nature, humans and the world. Sir George Trevelyan writes of 'our relationship to the wholeness of life and the fact that the universe is a vast living organism' (ibid.: 12). Ruth attended a meditation group where the leader drew participants' minds to imagine two 'dragon lines' of energy spanning the circumference of the earth, pulsating as they did so. As she relates in her dairy:

'We were to see the earth as one whole with points of concentration of energy called "global chakras". Glastonbury is the heart chakra and there are other chakras (monetary chakras) at London, Tokyo, New York and Darjeeling – though the meditation leader added that Darjeeling has not yet been fully "realised". We were asked to imagine that we were a blue disc travelling from chakra to chakra in "love, light and peace", and we were to visualise each place on a pure bed of crystal. The symbolism of a holistic vision is clear in such a meditation; linkages between the different parts of the world are importantly represented as being without boundaries or divisions. That said, such holistic thinking failed to quell the development of subtle forms of internal division within this meditation group. At the end of one session, involving six of us in a small room sitting cross-legged in a circle, a woman commented that she had felt a cold energy next to her, almost as if it were coming from the radiator but not quite. I turned my head to see where in the room the radiator was and with a start realised that it was right by my shoulder. The woman continued to say that during the meditation she had challenged this "energy" a number of times but that it had not gone away – in fact each time it had warmed up. I suspect that all this was probably directed at my being present, but kept quiet. This was more or less confirmed when the leader of the meditation group approached me a few days later, saying she hoped that my being identified as a cold spirit would not stop me returning. In a meditation about going "beyond" boundaries and barriers, this seemed an interesting form of boundary awareness'.

The membership of the Alternative Community in Glastonbury comes from several different nationalities and backgrounds; as well as British, there are, in particular, many Germans, Dutch and Americans. Among New Agers, however, emphasis is invariably put upon the individual, and on personal qualities, rather than upon background – whether this be nationality, culture, class or occupation. But as context to this, in Glastonbury and other New Age communities, importance is also placed on the environmentally correct notion of the global citizen. Thus, popular for both events and meditations was the theme, 'One Earth'. For example, in Glastonbury a banner proclaiming 'One World' week was displayed in bookshops in October 1990. There was also the week-long 'Earthwork' celebrations, in April 1990, which put on a series

79

of lectures, therapies, meditations, music events and a street market – all to promote an awareness of the earth as an interconnected holistic entity. Its publicity used the 'one earth' symbol – our planet photographed from space. The organisers, reputedly acting upon a message received during meditation from Gandhi, felt the event could specifically bridge the gap between the environmental 'Green' movement and the New Age, as well as between the town and the Alternative Community. In Glastonbury and elsewhere, then, global citizenry is typically associated with an emphasis upon an awareness of ourselves as humans obliged to the planet. The revolutions in Eastern Europe at the end of 1989 were welcomed with great fervour in Glastonbury, being seen as a sign of the breakdown of global boundaries and of people interacting across cultures. A local theatre company put on a play about a man who yearned to become free and fly across national boundaries, which they later took on tour to an Eastern European country. The idea of a common humanity is everywhere.

The Alternative Commuity in its Wider Setting

That people more generally present themselves as members of exclusive social groups (for example, as 'New Agers', 'Alternatives') belies any notion of a boundary-free world. Tied to ideas relating to holism, 'freedom from boundaries' may well function as an ideological notion. In the case of Glastonbury New Agers, the representation of the universe as an entity where everything connects *obliges* New Agers doctrinally to uphold a social world without social cleavage. In the run of human social life, however, social identities inform the reality of daily affairs, and these are normally secured by individuals grouping up against, and then distinguishing themselves from, 'another side', the names assigned to denote such identity often patently evoking difference. In Glastonbury it is no different – hence the name 'Alternative' Community. Accordingly, we may examine the attitudes and concepts pertaining to 'the other side' by which the Alternative Community and the town established themselves as contrasting social groups.

One recalls that in the 1980s the division, Alternative/town, was commonly referred to, by the Alternatives, as 'Glastafarians' (Alternative incomers) versus 'Glastonians' (mainstream locals). And that, for their part, townspeople, and their kith and kin from the surrounding area, normally referred to New Age incomers as the

Hippies. But the term Hippy is rather broad, and it can also be confusing, for in the national media it has become common to refer to the growing Travelling Community as the New Age Hippies. Particularly to the point, the townspeople in Glastonbury would distinguish between the two New Age groups: the settled Alternative Community was more usually seen as harmless 'wee weirdoes' (we borrow the term from a taxi-driver near Findhorn[1] in Northern Scotland), whereas the Travellers were viewed as a definite threat. When talking, locals would make it clear to which group they were referring.

In Glastonbury, observable symbols distinguishing the (settled) New Agers from the mainstream, and signalling people's belonging to one side or the other were clearly present. Even to the untrained eye, the New Agers' personal appearance was often fairly obvious. The members of the Alternative Community stood out, in the main, by their dress. For both men and women, relevant indicators here were such things as silver or beaded earrings, hand-knit jumpers of primary colour or muted 'earthy' shade, strong outdoor shoes or sandals, and, in general, clothes made from natural fibres. Common was a peace sign, yin-yang sign, or rainbow displayed on some part of the clothing. However such symbolic differentiation had to be put aside in some situations. For example, quite a few New Agers in Glastonbury held white-collar jobs in mainstream society and wore a suit each work day – as they put it, temporarily donning the 'uniform' of the 'straight' world.

Between the Alternative Community and the townspeople an interesting division relates to attitudes towards social and medicinal drugs. The accepted and commonly used stimulants in British mainstream society are tea, coffee, sugar, cigarettes and alcohol, and in Glastonbury such social and legal conventions become challenged. Among the New Agers in the town, tea and coffee were not universally acceptable, and quite a few people would drink only herbal tea. Also many New Agers were teetotal, and sugar was generally avoided. In addition, homeopathic cures were preferred to (for example) antibiotics. However, in contrast, cannabis was smoked socially by large numbers in the Alternative Community, and although many New Agers strongly objected to taking 'chemical drugs', quite a few claimed that their original insights into the spiritual nature of the world stemmed from their experiences of taking 'acid' or other hallucinogenics. In short, New Age stimulant use clearly served as a symbolic means for rejecting mainstream social values. In mainstream society, stimulant consumption in ritual contexts (for example, the tea break, pub gatherings, parties) functions to heighten social bonds and so enhance the social structure. In the Alternative Community, entirely different stimulants performed comparable functions, to uphold the worth of an 'alternative' social structure.

Finally, the New Age community is conspicuously a religious and philosophical community; so symbolic division also arises in respect of people's talk. In Glastonbury mainstreamers do not fail to notice New Agers, thanks to overhearing conversations about 'holism', 'spiritual healing', Gaia, and much else that evokes a non-Western body of cultural priorities. The Alternative Community might speak English, but to mainstreamers much of what they say is in a foreign language.

There is a history of difficulties in the relationship between the Alternative Community and the town that informs and influences present-day social interaction in Glastonbury. Growing up in the area of Glastonbury in the 1970s, Ruth remembers groups from the Alternative Community camped out on a piece of common ground, and local people reacting very defensively. Reports and rumours of nudity, and even witchcraft, were rife. Cafés in Glastonbury hung signs in their windows saying 'No Hippies here'. Any friction there was has been heightened by the Glastonbury Festival, a pop festival which most years is held in a nearby village. This has grown into an international event and continues to be a source of immense local controversy. In the 1970s it was smaller, but even then it attracted a large crowd of 'alternatively dressed' people to an area which, one should remember, remains politically part of a Conservative constituency.

During 1990, when Ruth was in Glastonbury for the whole year, the Alternative Community was more integrated into the local area than seemed to be the case in the past, such as during her visit in 1987. This may be partly due to the number of Alternative children attending local schools. In addition the Alternative Community was playing a more active economic role in the town. Up to then the New Agers' economic position in the town was largely as a pool of unskilled temporary labour, but in the previous few years there had developed a degree of New Age economic control, resulting from members of the Alternative Community starting small businesses and taking over increasing numbers of the High Street shops. Some of these shops were exclusive to an 'alternative' and possibly tourist clientele, but others, such as the photocopiers, the health food shop and some of the cafés, were patronised by a wide variety of people. From a formerly marginal position, the Alternative-run shops had captured a lot of the trade in the town.

As well as this, a self-conscious effort was being made by some members of the Alternative Community to narrow the cultural gap between the two sides. Part of an on-going process, such endeavours paradoxically often only served to highlight differences and divisions – at least, so the anthropologist saw it. An example occurred in the Earthweek event in spring 1990, with its series of workshops, concerts and lectures. Tents and tipis were put up in the Abbey playing fields to demonstrate ways of living 'closer to nature', talks were given about conservation, and there was a variety of activities for children including face-painting. The aim of the week-long event, as has been mentioned, was to bring together the New Age and ecological movements, but it was also to provide seven days of environmental awareness in the town that would be open and accessible to all, bringing together the different sectors of the population. However the event was only publicised – and publicised very little to Ruth's knowledge – in New Age and Alternative journals. When the High Street was closed for a day of celebration, one local newsagent angrily claimed he had received no advanced warning and had lost much of his custom. Afterwards the event was described by a local councillor as comprising 'the great unwashed and professional beggars'. In contrast, Elana, who organised the event, wrote in the Mid-Somerset Gazette:

> Local people came and thanked us for such a lovely time and how nice it was to have our street closed! No one complained to us, no one commented on begging or dirty people. (24 May 1990)

In sum, this attempt by the Alternative Community to break down boundaries and hold an event with the 'town' ended up alienating local people. But other events, such as the annual Dance Festival where the High Street is closed for a night of dancing, proved more successful in integrating the various social groups.

In general the two main groups in Glastonbury, the Alternative Community and the locals, largely view one other with mistrust. Ruth was in an interesting position because she was involved with the Alternative Community and yet had also been brought up in the mainstream community just outside Glastonbury. Thus she was a local *and* an Avalonian (and an anthropologist). Being in all positions she observed only too clearly how quickly the Alternative

Community would dismiss the opinions of people from outside, labelling these views as 'old order'. On the other hand, when local people saw her as part of the Alternative Community, particularly when she was researching articles for the New Age newspaper she helped with, she was often treated very rudely and dismissively. This newspaper, the Glastonbury Times, described itself as a newspaper for the whole town, presenting local news from an Alternative point of view. A few locals did read it, but members of the Alternative Community were overwhelmingly both the purchasers and the contributors. (Since 1990, other newspapers and magazines, fulfilling a similar function, have appeared on the Glastonbury scene, for example *Free State: the Journal of the Free State of Avalonia*.)

Groups within the Alternative Community

It has been emphasised that the Alternative Community in Glastonbury does not amount to a homogeneous body of people. Far from it: an appropriate analogy is the Starship Enterprise whose crew, from a neighbouring spaceship, is an apparently uniform crowd, but once inside one finds that Scottie and Spok and the others are, in rather significant respects, very 'individual' indeed. In Glastonbury, for example, differing mainstream backgrounds have obvious implications for the sorts of knowledge and skills each person brings to the Alternative scene, and this, to some degree influences the networks of social affiliation that form.

In Glastonbury, the various New Age sub-groups, preferring to represent the Alternative Community as unified, would normally not criticise one another publicly, for in New Age ideology great emphasis is put on acceptance and mutual respect. But Ruth found that, once integrated into one group or another, or when people just felt comfortable with her, the divisions would be only too evident, based around widespread knowledge of other people's affairs, and articulated by gossip, which was pervasive. As well as this, people's networks and affiliations were continually shifting and changing, even within the daily round. For example, someone earning their living as an acupuncturist might spend most of the day-time hours around the healing wing of the Glastonbury Experience, including eating lunch with other healers. However they reside in a caravan parked in the grounds of a large house in an outlying village alongside a group of Travellers. Thus their social identification alternates from a sub-group of healers to a sub-group of Travellers – quite a social distance, on the face of it.

With memberships of sub-groups within the Glastonbury Alternative Community being both flexible and unstable, the identification and classification of New Age social groupings in the town is more satisfactorily achieved in terms of doctrinal raison d'êtres. New Agers claimed that it is because of rather specific beliefs that people get attracted to one another – that, as they put it, people 'connect up'. And it was the case that many groups are formed on the basis of sharing a commitment to a particular method of therapy or spiritual practice. For example the people who attended a 'rebirthing group' would generally pass the time with others who had undergone rebirthing. Another group had met by all being 'premies', or devotees, of the international guru, Guru Maharaj-ji. Groups formed around centres where particular teachers were based. Notions of family were commonly invoked to enhance feelings of sub-group solidarity.

Along another dimension, sub-groups could also be identified in terms of the two social focal points in the town, the Assembly Rooms and the Glastonbury Experience. In 1990, the Assembly Rooms attracted a wide range of people, including Travellers, a theatre group (which was based there), and an older, more prosperous group who had a financial investment in the building and who were anxious to maintain it as a community centre. Since the café, which is part of the Assembly Rooms complex, is set back from the road, and Travellers' dogs were often tethered up outside it, it rarely drew in townspeople or the wandering tourist, so the building was very largely patronised by people from within the Alternative Community. But in terms of social practice the Assembly Rooms might be seen as being relatively closer to the mainstream; coffee was available, and people would smoke and were likely to pop out for a quick pint of beer at lunch-time. This contrasts with the Glastonbury Experience where the prevailing ethos was purity of life – where there was a vegan restaurant and a wholefood shop selling 'pure' and 'natural' foods. In the Glastonbury Experience aromatic smoke was more likely to come billowing from the incense shop than from a neighbour's joint.

The relationship between the New Age Travellers and the settled New Age community was interesting. The two are socially quite different, obviously chiefly in regard to the Travellers' nomadic lifestyle, yet they clearly hold sufficiently similar values to be part of the broader New Age movement. Both are devoted to a general ethos comprising (in differing degrees) individualism, the rejection of consumer materialism, a movement towards living on the land, a non-monetary economy, spiritual values and the experimentation with an alternative way of living, as well as clustering around places such as Glastonbury and other sacred sites. As has been mentioned before, the Travellers are notable for their individualism, to the point where they feel they cannot speak for any other Traveller or present themselves as a group at all. This is certainly how they struck Ruth in practice. They ranged from people who favoured living in vehicles or camping in quiet rural places, through to young people who are urban-based and nicknamed the Brew Crew on account of their liking for cans of Special Brew beer. On the other hand there are a lot of similarities among the Travellers, which distinguish them from the settled New Agers. Travellers often have dreadlocked hair, and they uniformly wear unkempt or ripped clothes. Yet it remains that every living thing is seen by them as a free and independent being. When challenged about their dog running wild in a village near Glastonbury, one man replied, 'it's a free dog'.

Notwithstanding a shared general ethos, the way the settled Alternative Community in Glastonbury interacts with the fluid Traveller population which clusters around the town mainly during summer, was not straightforward. Some members of the settled Alternative Community were very supportive of the Traveller population; indeed, quite a few had actually lived as Travellers before settling in Glastonbury. People with land would often let Travellers stay on it, and at the Glastonbury Festival a separate and free area was created for them. However the Travellers were very unpopular with 'locals' in Glastonbury and, as is well-known, have a bad media image nationally. When Travellers caused problems in the town, this would backfire upon the entire settled Alternative Community and the latter's attitudes would then become more mixed. When the police were called to move on a crowd of drunken Travellers in the High Street, one resident New Ager commented, 'sometimes I think the Travellers and the police deserve each other'. Thus there was a feeling of protectiveness towards the Travellers in their dealings with the institutions of British society, but also a feeling of separateness in respect of lifestyle and beliefs. The feelings, in short, were ambivalent.

Living by One's Principles

In the following chapters in this book we shall describe how, in Glastonbury, New Age social principles implicate the gamut of human values – the spiritual, the environmental, the communalistic, the intuitive, and so on. Moreover, New Agers would attempt to conduct daily life in accordance with such standards and ethics. They would, in short, attempt to live by their principles.

New Age relations with the mainstream community in Glastonbury explain these two facts. The context is that, for New Agers in Glastonbury, being in the town is an end in itself. The town is not merely a convenient place to live out a preferred lifestyle: Glastonbury, the place, evokes a vital mystical aura. This being so, New Agers there must continually submit themselves to the gaze of fellow (mainstream) residents, in circumstances where, since they are settled in the town, they have also to engage in normal life, that is to say, make a living, bring up children, keep healthy, and so on. Such a situation meant that the Alternative Community was both sensitive about its lifestyle and values, which, in turn, had implications for the way it conducted this lifestyle and observed these values.

In the first place, New Agers in Glastonbury, subject to stigmatism from mainstreamers, in what they said or did had to address the mainstream world in a comprehensive way. Lest, by being New Age in only selected areas of life, they be accused of hypocrisy, members of the Alternative Community would ideally try to be New Age in all respects – i.e. in making a living, bringing up children etc. Here the relevant contrast is with New Age communities in Britain that socially insulate themselves from the mainstream, in spatial enclavement in communes, or through secrecy. For example, the English witches, magicians and Neo-Pagans studied by Luhrmann (1989), who mainly meet behind closed doors during evenings and weekends, may concentrate on just the mystical in New Age philosophy, devoting enormous energies to developing spectacular rituals, and to inventing rich and aesthetically elaborate mythologies to accompany them. For them, other aspects relating to the New Age need not feature.

Luhrmann has something else interesting to say about the New Agers she studied. She maintains that for the most part the witches and magicians do not intellectualise what they do: their beliefs (principles) do not especially dominate how, in the rituals, they proceed. This is despite the fact that these beliefs are spectacularly unorthodox from the point of view of both mainstream religion and Western science. This brings us to the second point about New Agers in Glastonbury, where in another sense they were vulnerable to accusations of hypocrisy. New Agers in Glastonbury, being conscious of mainstream scepticism, could only counter it by demonstrating New Age values in practice – as the cliché goes, by practising what they preached. Thus, for Luhrmann's Wiccans, principles function, in the situation of secrecy, mainly as rationalisations, or justifications of the rites their ilk engage in and which adepts pass down to novices. Meanwhile, for Glastonbury New Agers, subject to outsider scrutiny, principles had to govern what they did, lest their behaviour undermined the veracity of the New Age from within. By living by one's principles, one confirmed that the principles are good. However, this is not to say that in Glastonbury this is something New Agers always managed to achieve . . .

Notes

1. Findhorn is a large, closed 'alternative' commune, which has pioneered New Age and Deep Ecology living in practice. Ruth visited it in 1989 (see also Hendershott 1989). See Chapter 12.

5

Health: the Holistic Person

Attitudes towards health and disease in Western mainstream society are in the process of change, and have been so for the last couple of decades and more. This change is essentially the recognition of an intimate and mutual connection between body and mind. Back in the 1960s, Robin Horton, in a now-classic paper contrasting 'Western science' and 'African traditional thinking', commented that Western biomedicine had hailed germ theory with such open arms that in the industrial countries the social/mental causes of disease were almost entirely pushed aside:

> Modern Western medical scientists have long been distracted from noting the causal connection between social disturbance and disease by the success of the germ theory. It would seem, indeed, that a conjunction of the germ theory, of the discovery of potent antibiotics and immunisation techniques, and of conditions militating against the build-up of natural resistance to many killer infections, for long made it very difficult for scientists to see the importance of this connection. (Horton 1967: 59)

By contrast, in Africa, in the absence of germ theory, immunisation techniques, and so on, social and mental causes of disease assume enormous prominence especially in relation to the link between disease and social conflict.

The recent changes in Western thinking mean that Horton's comparison, between the industrial countries and Africa, can no longer be drawn so clearly. In Britain herbal medicines are now routinely displayed on the chemist's shelf for minor ailments, and a broad range of people use them. From natural childbirth techniques, concern over 'E' numbers and preservatives, yoga classes, herbal throat pastilles, and not to forget meditation and massage, so-called natural methods of healing are becoming increasingly accepted. According to Rosalind Coward (1989: 42), between 1984 and 1987, 34 percent of the population tried a therapy 'alternative' to standard biomedicine, with homeopathy undoubtedly being biomedicine's chief rival in this regard (Sharma 1992). Integral to the thinking of all such 'alternative therapy' are notions upholding the inseparability of mind and body. Alternative therapy, in short, endorses an holistic philosophy of the human person.

Yet biomedicine continues to dominate in the Western mainstream. Therefore when one considers the difference between the mainstream and the New Age regarding health practice, matters of mind–body philosophy continue at the centre of discussion. Whilst the mainstream remains in general equivocal about alternative approaches and therapies, among New Agers such practices have always been the norm. Thus the New Age enthusiastically celebrates what it calls the holistic vision of self, by which is meant the holistic constitution of the human person. Indeed, if many mainstreamers today are experimenting with alternative therapies it may well be that the influence of New Age ideas is partly responsible – which is something about which we shall offer some theoretical observations in Chapter 12.

The paradoxical juxtaposition in the New Age movement between holism and individualism is at its starkest with respect to matters of health; therefore it provides the organising framework for this chapter. On the one hand, the 'New Age person', whose well-being is at issue, is construed holistically. But on the other hand, practical action, directed towards sustaining that well-being or dealing with misfortune, is highly individualistic. Such individualism is reviewed by Rosalind Coward:

> Alternative therapies talk of a 'new age', an age where the individual is no longer part of a system or bureaucracy but is recognised in her or his full individuality. And frequently this new attention to the individual is represented as an attention to things 'spiritual'. (ibid.:11)

In New Age health practice, individualism is most usually discussed in terms of notions of responsibility and empowerment. Thus Burrows (1993: 19–20) indicates that wellness is considered by New Agers to be a matter of individual self-awareness, together with the recognition that the human organism has a capacity for self-healing. And Danforth, in his study of the New Age firewalking movement in the United States, describes how healing is seen by participants to be to do with personal development and spiritual growth; overcoming fear, individuals who submit themselves to the firewalking ritual consider that they have transformed themselves into 'new' persons (Danforth 1989: 263). Mainstreamers who to some degree or other involve themselves in alternative therapies merit comment in similar terms.

Individualistic practice is a second domain relating to health and healing where Western biomedicine and the New Age differ markedly. Relations between healers and patients exemplify this especially clearly. In biomedicine one submits oneself to the authority of the doctor, but in alternative therapy it is the opposite. Alternative therapy – homeopathy, aromatherapy, gestalt therapy, acupuncture, and so on – emphasises a patient-centred approach, stressing the importance that the client be fully engaged in every aspect of the healing process, and it upholds the value that knowledge be shared between specialist healer and client (Sharma 1992; Burrows 1993). New Age health practice, since it embraces such alternative procedures, definitely incorporates this perspective.

Why individualism in New Age health practice manifests itself in terms of personal responsibility is something that this chapter addresses. A further matter is whether, in African traditional thought, patient-empowerment is also present. This chapter offers some suggestions on these questions. In the final section we shall attend to some crucial differences between the New Age and tribal society; these importantly help with the explication.

The New Age holistic human person is described in some detail in Chapter 8, where we discuss New Age cosmology. A brief exposition is required now, so that we may introduce two concepts, 'spirituality' and 'energy', that constitute the contextual language by which very much New Age discourse on health, the body and healing is conveyed. The New Age 'person' includes four inseparable and mutually affecting elements: the physical, the emotional, the mental and the spiritual. (A social element is discussed in the next chapter.) The spiritual element is interesting since in New Age thinking 'spirituality' commands many meanings, and this makes the 'spiritual in the human' a demanding notion. A metaphor drawn from New Age ethics, spirituality specifies two key ideas in daily thought and practice. It evokes the idea of a personalised, non-institutionalised religion, and it refers to the non-material aspect of any thought or activity. Through spirituality the New Age constitutes two key domains: firstly the cosmos, the broadest possible domain of existence, in respect of which every human being is merged; secondly the holistic person. In relation to the human person, spirituality signals not just the presence of something on top of the purely physical, but that this something is equally, if not more, fundamental; spirituality expresses the individual's awareness that well-being relates holistically to the correct integration of all the human person's necessary aspects. For its part, 'energy' functions to express these ideas. A metaphor drawn from the notion of interconnectedness, particularly with respect to the cosmos as an holistic domain, 'energy' in its most elementary sense refers to any enhanced level of 'activity'. Energy may be used to describe an atmosphere in a room, or the appeal of a painting, or the quality of interaction between two people. With regard to a particular entity the discourse of energy therefore conveys the idea that this is something which is animated. In the case of the human person, energy combined with the idea of spirituality delineates a *being* with sacred properties.

Health in Glastonbury

In the New Age movement and Christian church alike, Glastonbury is considered as a place of pilgrimage and healing; very many people are attracted to the town and the surrounding area for precisely this reason. 'Healing', an ambiguous term in any context, refers essentially, in New Age thought, to establishing balance between the mind, the body and the spirit. In New Age parlance the practitioners of the many forms of healing are called healers.

The basis of Glastonbury's power as a healing centre is threefold. It is the heart chakra of the planet, it enjoys a situation on the intersection of powerful ley lines, and as its focal points it boasts the Tor and the Chalice Well and spring. Chakras (expounded in Indian vedic philosophy) and ley lines (in Chinese geomancy) basically connote the special concentrations of energy relating to Glastonbury, which, according to many people who have been drawn to the town, can be tapped into for purposes of healing. Strictly speaking, chakras are points on the human body where cosmic energy may be absorbed, but by metaphorical extension New Agers use the concept to refer to energy-auspicious places as well; ley lines are energy channels in the earth, linked to cosmic energies and joining up places of sacred significance. In Glastonbury all this is commonly spoken of in terms of the town having positive vibrations. Among local mainstreamers, as they discuss the Alternative

Community in the town, one of the more light-hearted banters is, 'I've lived here all my life, why haven't I felt the vibes?'

In Glastonbury over the last twenty years there has been a considerable growth in healers and healing, especially marked, in Ruth's reckoning, between 1985 and 1990. But the link between healing and Glastonbury has a long historical tradition. We have already described the Chalice Well, fed by a spring coming out of the hillside, with which many myths and legends are associated, which the dramatic red colouring of the water no doubt heightens. In connection with healing, its reputation can be traced back as far as 1582 when Dr John Dee, the astrologer and mathematician, declared himself possessed of the 'elixir vitae' he had found in Glastonbury. When the Pump Room in Bath reached the height of its popularity in the middle of the eighteenth century, Glastonbury was a further attraction nearby.[1] As mentioned before, the Well's surrounding garden is a place for meditation and contemplation

By the end of the 1980s, then, Glastonbury had become a centre for alternative healing, along with Totnes, another small town in the southwest of England. There is a spiralling situation here. The more that healers are attracted to the area and its reputation grows, so the more people visit and/or move to the area to take advantage of their services – so even more healers arrive. In addition people who have undergone healing sometimes train to become healers themselves. It is, after all, a way of earning a living in a 'spiritually attuned' manner. A resident of Glastonbury, in an ironic and comically intended article in the Glastonbury Times, the 'alternative' newspaper Ruth Prince helped produce, commented upon the almost overwhelming number of healers around:

> Following scenes involving over-committed healers chasing Glastonbury's last remaining sick person down the High Street, the Equal Opportunities Board has come to an agreement with the many Health Professionals. In future half the town must be sick between January 1st and June 30th. A mass healing will occur on July 1st. Then the other half will become sick. [Self-healing is abolished as an employment measure][2]

Thus in the town in 1990 there was the Natural Health Clinic which had been set up to support the more 'traditional' alternative methods such as acupuncture, herbalism, massage, reflexology and homeopathy. And there was also G.A.I.A., Glastonbury Advice and Information Agency, an information centre in the Healing Wing of the Glastonbury Experience, which aimed to put people in contact with the different healers and therapists. The specialists connected with G.A.I.A. offered a wide range of healing techniques, including therapeutic counselling, Shiatsu, Reiki healing, yoga, rebirthing, regression therapy, meditation, astrology and astrological counselling (to name but a few). They also arranged events, concerts and workshops. (This institution subsequently became 'The Isle of Avalon Foundation', which started a magazine *Avalon: Journal of Transformation from Glastonbury*.)

The physical aspect of health, healing and well-being is not excluded as a component in the Alternative Community's holistic vision of the self and to the process of personal transformation that membership in the community implies. In Glastonbury, a person's daily diet was seen as very important, especially in relation to inner spirituality; a 'you are what you eat' ethos prevailed. For reasons of both health and environmental ethics, many New Agers in the town were vegetarians and, indeed, in 1990 Glastonbury boasted one of Britain's few vegan restaurants. The wholefood shop even included a section for macrobiotic vegetarians trying to balance the yin-yang elements of their diet. The large house where Ruth lived was also vegan, and when retreats and catering days were organised there, vegan food would be provided. One person, who was a vegan and ate a diet largely consisting of raw foods, said she was bringing up her two children as vegans because in order to become pure it was spiritually beneficial to eat only of the earth. However, in line with the diversity of thought within the Glastonbury Alternative Community, others ate a wide variety of food including animal meat. Ruth got involved in a conversation with a rather defensive group of meat-eaters who were complaining about born-again vegetarians, where it was agreed that it was not so much what you ate, but that you appreciated and gave thanks for the life-force that had been sacrificed. The uniting factor behind the seemingly disparate views about diet in the town was concern over the way in which food is produced, for example the importance of using organically grown produce wherever possible, and a recognition of food as having a strong influence upon the individual at all levels.

As may be expected, the New Agers in Glastonbury saw food as being integrally important with respect to cleansing, purifying and/or to heightening spiritual experience. Thus some participants in the Harmonic Convergence in 1987 went on a fruit and nut diet beforehand to prepare their bodies. Then again, there was a man who fasted for two days before his wedding. Fasts and diets were common leading up to significant dates in the year, for example astrological dates or festivals such as the Solstices, Beltane or the Equinox. The association of food with spirituality is evident in the Rainbow Diet, which is famously associated with enhancing the spiritual experience. Sprouted beans, nuts and fresh foods are the basic constituents of this diet, for they contain the most 'chi', or life-force. Some people in Glastonbury would incorporate diets as part of their normal nutritional regime. Ruth met a woman who for liquid sustenance would only take water from the spring at the Chalice Well. Weighed down by gallon containers she carried it around in the back of her estate car. Another person, who had a history of gastric problems connected, he said, with stress and emotional difficulties, would fast for two days each week and spend another day eating only raw fruit and fruit juices. Food, for him, was a particularly sensitive concern. One day, after a heated discussion had gone on around him, he claimed that he had terrible indigestion resulting from his whole body being in a state of shock from all the aggressive energy. Holistic notions relating to the close connection between body and state of mind are plainly in evidence here.

Healing Practice

The distinctive character of New Age practice directed towards the restoration of health derives from a special combination of three arresting features. Firstly, there is the importance attached to patient empowerment, such that the individual is deemed to be largely responsible for his or her well-being and recovery, which means, in turn, that the specialist healer is regarded more as a facilitator for such process than as someone to whose authority an afflicted person must surrender his or her agency. Secondly, New Age healers are invariably inspirational figures. Indeed their charismatic impact may rest uneasily alongside the notion of patient empowerment, such that some New Agers in Glastonbury were ambivalent about the very idea of specialist healers. Thirdly, New Age healers advocate a wide range of manipulative techniques on behalf of the recovery of good health. In the subsections to follow, with Glastonbury in mind, the respective emphases are on each of these aspects in turn. In addition, these subsections also reveal that, for New Agers, knowledge about healing comes from a combination of several different sources – from practical participation in healing activity, from abstract instruction from gurus and teachers at first hand, and from pamphlets and other literature. The latter cover all manner of different therapies, are authored by teachers and gurus and copiously available from bookshops, healing centres and by mail order, and, once in the New Age community, get readily passed from hand to hand. We shall select examples relating to each such source of knowledge.

Practical Participation: Spiritual Healing

Spiritual healing is extremely important in the Alternative Community in Glastonbury. Along with many of the healing practices described as New Age, such as herbalism and acupuncture, it is associated with earlier centuries and other cultures. It is also familiar in mainstream Western society, where it meets with greater or lesser acceptance, and its roots can be traced back to the New Testament. But the New Age movement imposes its own meanings on elements that it shares with (and which it may have appropriated from) other traditions. Therefore to discuss spiritual healing in Glastonbury one may deal with it simply as it is practised in the present-day as part of a broader commitment to New Age beliefs.

The large spiritual healing centre established in the town in 1990 is evidence of the importance of healing in Glastonbury; it consisted of a meditation and healing workshop led by two healers belonging to the National Federation of Spiritual Healers. For the three years prior to 1990 the group involved with the centre had been meeting one evening each week with a steadily growing and supportive attendance. When Ruth arrived in Glastonbury in October 1989 she started to go to the meetings and on each occasion there were about thirty to fifty people, all crowded into a relatively small room, many of whom had travelled from up to twenty miles around. The leaders opened the Glastonbury Healing Centre during Easter 1990. It occupied a permanent site at the bottom of the High Street, and a prominent event with many speakers and special workshops was held to celebrate the occasion. The Centre was one of the few alternative shops/centres on the far side of the road, and people commented on how wonderful it was to spread the 'healing energy' to the end of the town.

Thanks to her education at the Centre, Ruth learned that spiritual healing consisted of the transference of healing energy from the healer to the patient. One person, who was receiving spiritual healing for a physical complaint, said it made her feel very deeply relaxed, like a meditation, even to the point that she found it quite difficult afterwards to walk or talk. The most technical description of spiritual healing that Ruth ever heard was that when the brain rests the nerve cells vibrate in different ways and different directions; however when one concentrates upon one thing they all start to vibrate in the same direction so that flares of energy build up around the area needing healing. This results in a harmonious exchange of energy between the healer and the person being healed such that the latter assumes the responsibility for his or her recovery whilst the former catalyses the process by providing technical knowledge and general encouragement. Ruth attended a workshop on 'self-healing', led by Audrey Muir-Copland, which revolved around the suggestion that personal crises are often linked to an old misery which one finds difficult to let go. If there is a resistance in the mind to going forward in life there will probably also be a resistance in the body, which she referred to as 'biofeedback'. Often healers find a concurrence between the two; for example, problems with feet or walking could suggest a problem with moving forward mentally or emotionally; problems with the shoulders or back could be linked to taking on too much responsibility. She explained that one has to find a way of releasing this negative energy.

An important forerunner of certain ideas and practices in the New Age movement, and cited by several commentators on New Age history, is nineteenth-century spiritualism, and it is indeed the case that what New Agers call channelling (Chapter 9) is substantively similar to spiritualist ideas such as those upheld in North America around one hundred years ago. However the spiritual healing being discussed here is altogether rather different. Spiritualism refers to the agency of a disembodied (human) spirit working through a (passive?) intermediary for the sake of the psychological betterment of the living, whereas New Age spiritual healing, corresponding with the rather broad notion of spirituality, implies living agents in joint sacred work. Yet, despite the important difference, spiritualism and spiritual healing both isolate the specific needs of specific individuals and, as individualistic practices, may in their contrasting ways reflect personal dilemmas heightened by, respectively, the beginning and the close of the industrial era. Such dilemmas may relate to a loss of confidence in traditional institutions and structures (including orthodox medicine), leading to mystical/healing practices designed to bypass them altogether. In late nineteenth-century North America, the context was the general upheaval in the urban environment connected with waves of immigration, whilst spiritual ideas in the post 1970s' New Age movement have arisen in the context of a deliberate rejection of traditional ideas associated with family and established church. Returning to the matter of historical connection, perhaps one might say that the knowledge that spiritualism was once very popular in the West as a non-mainstream practice is found reassuring by present-day New Agers, while through quite independent initiatives they sustain vaguely comparable practices relating to present-day problems and anxieties.

The Charismatic Presence

In the Alternative Community in Glastonbury, specialist healers were conceptualised as falling into one of several categories, namely healers proper, shamans, teachers, and gurus. These categories embrace a charismatic approach to healing, and differ in accordance with the particular charismatic techniques applied. Such specialists' exclusive skills in facilitating ordinary people's personal and spiritual quests were generally rooted in their own profound spiritual awakenings, and these people will normally have spent long periods studying spiritual matters. By their inspirational example they demonstrate to others the possibility that they, too, can experience the same.

Healers are people who manipulate available spiritual power in order to relieve people's (internal) physical, mental or spiritual problems and sufferings; such spiritual power may be present either externally, within the 'cosmos', or internally within people themselves. The techniques by which this is done are very many and varied and have been described elsewhere many times. Rosalind Burrows' PhD thesis (1993) does this extraordinarily well (see also Hanegraaff 1996). In Chapter 9, we shall mention such techniques as channelling and crystal healing, which were popular in Glastonbury.

The *shaman* is a particularly compelling type of specialist. When Ruth was in Glastonbury in 1990 no one publicly practised shamanism as such (this has since changed), but everyone in the Alternative Community was familiar with the notion. Taking explicit inspiration from Amerindian shamanistic practice, New Age shamanism, in both ideas and practical accoutrement, is similar to the Inuit (Eskimo) shamanism described in Chapter 10. The key New Age metaphor, in the case of shamanic practice, is the 'journey', which implies a far more active, even aggressive, intervention with spiritual forces than occurs with channelling; such a journey implies the person's direct contact with a 'non-ordinary reality' (Jakobsen 1999). Again, this can be an external (to the cosmos) journey, or a journey within (the self). Harvey (1997: 118) comments that the latter is more typically New Age, notwithstanding the inspiration drawn from Amerindian shamanism where the journey is always to a spirit's domain. Gabrielle Roth's shamanism, for example, refers to a journey uncovering successive, and higher, levels of the self; for Roth such a journey is facilitated by dance (Roth 1990; also Albanese 1992: 81). Van Hove comments, about New Age shamanism, that it is not surprising that it is so fashionable on the New Age circuit, for it allows the possibility of touching deeper reality without having to surrender individual autonomy (1996: 192). As Jakobsen emphasises, curing, of oneself or another, is always the aim (ibid.).

Teachers are people who, rather than intervening directly in people's well-being, have at their disposal supremely insightful knowledge that ordinary people can take note of, and so be better equipped to accomplish their well-being through their own efforts. Spirituality is an important component of such insight. Some New Age teachers' fame extends well beyond the confines of the New Age, and their knowledge is relevant to the conduct of all aspects of life's affairs. Those such as the Caddys (Peter and Eileen) and David Spangler at Findhorn, having founded communes in the name of their particular spiritual insights, have come to propound complex cosmological systems, drawing on extraordinarily wide ranges of philosophical and religious knowledge (Hendershott 1989). Other teachers are associated with more limited areas of spiritual practice. For example, Leonard Orr (below) is well-known for his expertise on rebirthing.

Finally, *gurus* are inspirational persons of great power. These are controversial figures in the New Age movement, for 'guru' implies a person 'of the spirit', or of divinity, and this seems to contradict New Age egalitarianism, whereby *all* are held to be divine. But several members of the Alternative Community in Glastonbury were absorbed by the insights and interpretative powers of particular gurus, some of whom enjoyed worldwide reputations, mostly established in the context of teaching and healing communes (or ashrams). For example the Indian guru, Maharaj-ji, of the Divine

Light Mission, commanded a number of devotees in the town, one of whom travelled two or three times a week to Bristol, thirty miles away, to be with a larger group of followers who would show videos of his most recent talks and hear of the experiences of people who had been converted into recognising his powers. Maharaj-ji was considered to be deeply spiritually imbued, enabling him to teach secret techniques of meditation that would be learned in stages as a process of initiation; for followers this meant two hours of meditation each day. Maharaj-ji's techniques were considered to heighten spiritual experience and to help people realise their full potential in day-to-day living in the material world. Some devotees had made pilgrimages to Greece and Rome to hear him speak in person.[3]

We may also mention again that charismatic *texts* abound in Glastonbury. Ranging from brief pamphlets to substantial books, such written literature in many and various ways expounds on the different types of healing, details the spiritually inspired insights of teachers, and reveals the divinity of gurus; many are authored by the healers, teachers and gurus themselves. Other literature provides historical and philosophical depth to New Age culture, for example by demonstrating how eastern religions have inspired its deep reflection about the person and the universe, or by showing that its practical conduct bears witness to the order of things among the North American Indians (and so on). New Age culture is a highly literate culture and in Glastonbury there is a vast array of such literature readily available from all manner of different outlets.

With regard to the charismatic texts, one important matter is the criteria by which a given piece of literature qualifies as New Age. Containing systematic, although often rival, descriptions of how things are in the world, New Age literature, generally expressed in sophisticated language, is commonly similar, in terms of topic or mode of presentation, to mainstream philosophical texts. Indeed academic treatises upholding the anthropic principle, or the philosophy of Teilhard de Chardin, find themselves being warmly embraced by New Agers as well.[4] Qualification as a piece of New Age literature is, in our view, an empirical and contextual matter: a text is a New Age text when it is elaborated within the New Age agenda. This can often be difficult to demonstrate, not least because some 'New Age authors', who quite clearly espouse very many key New Age ethical standards from within an unequivocally non-mainstream context, protest that they are anti-New Age. But once it *has* been demonstrated, the text's contents may be counted as an aspect of New Age cosmology, which anthropologists then have it as their task to explain (and not judge). In this regard consideration of the circumstances of ordinary New Agers will be a vital matter, for ordinary people are crucially important in legitimating the creative efforts of the texts' authors by giving them credence.

Glastonbury and its surrounds, we have mentioned before, has attracted many important New Age figures. Sir George Trevelyan, who died in 1996, was a frequent visitor to the town, Robert Coon lives there, and William Bloom, a key interpreter of the New Age, resides nearby. Very many significant teachers on the New Age scene have visited at one time or another. Yet other charismatic figures are well known in the town by their writings and by their repute, rather than for any physical connection with the place. But not everyone in the Alternative Community in Glastonbury, Ruth observed, was enamoured of gurus and their ilk. In the town were many people who were there directly as a result of having turned their backs on cults and teachers, including people who had once associated themselves with New Age ashrams, in America and elsewhere, for example those focused around Bhagwan Shree Rajneesh (Osho) or Maharaj-ji (Maharaji). New Agers sceptical of gurus declared that the quest should be for something less constricting than the doctrine of one person. In any event, not a few people in Glastonbury took the view that for a single person to be regarded as the unique focus of enlightenment or spiritual elevation is in fact contrary to egalitarian social ethics, and as running against the notion that everyone is a spiritual being. For them, to quote Gabrielle Roth (1990: 123), to be your own sacred teacher is the trip. In fact many New Age teachers acknowledge the validity of this position, and accordingly represent themselves, as has been noted, as 'facilitating' or 'coordinating' other people's spiritual development rather than as directing or instructing it. But perhaps this is not entirely the point. Here one returns to the charismatic texts that importantly inform New Age practice. The fact of the matter is that New Agers who reject direct contact with teachers are not bereft of guidance, as the titles on their bookshelves, both academic and New Age, indicate: *The Tao of Physics, Small is Beautiful, The Mayan Factor, The Spiral Dance* (respectively the products of Capra's physics, Schumacher's economics, Argüelles' techno-mysticism, and Starhawk's witchcraft). For everyone in the Alternative Community, a charismatic presence vitally informs the New Age experience. In this book, 'teacher' is used as a suitable generic label for this presence.

Teacher's Wisdom: Physical Immortality

Physical immortality is the belief in being able to avoid death, whereby a person may decide consciously to remain in his or her own physical body, which implies slowing the external ageing process. Notions of individual empowerment are obviously intrinsic to this process, and such ideas have gained considerable popularity among elements in the New Age movement:

> We are at the end of the old Aeon and at the dawn of the New. At every such major planetary change, all ideas undergo revaluation. Many conventions are overthrown, certain old ideas become useless, and new ideas suddenly become useful.
>
> Physical immortality is the most useful new – yet extremely ancient – idea now available as we enter the New Aquarian Aeon.[5]

In the field of health and disease, physical immortality represents *in extremis* the relation between mind/body holism and notions of individual responsibility. As an example of teacher's wisdom it is well worth expounding, and not least because of the way that it relates to other, less controversial, New Age ideas.

For physical immortalists the crucial notion is that people themselves should truly accept responsibility for their own life in the world and affirm that they truly love this life; then they will be able to indefinitely sustain their individual physical bodies. People who die are those who have 'deathist' urges – negative attitudes towards life, which in turn, lead eventually to physical decay:

> There are no dualisms in Immortal Thought. There is always a movement towards synthesis and alchemical Union. As William Blake once said: *The body and the Spirit are One, not two. They are literally the same thing.* All conceptions of separate bodies – physical, etheric, astral, spiritual – are harmonised and united as One Purified and uplifted incorruptible Body in Service to the Divine and in support of Life on this Earth and throughout the Universe.[6]

Although physical immortalism is one spike on the umbrella of New Age doctrine, it cannot be pointed to as an universally accepted belief in Glastonbury; many people in the town greeted its ideas with scepticism. Indeed, some people were striving towards the opposite goal: to develop a loving acceptance of death within themselves. Reincarnation, with its opportunities for past and future lives, was a common subject of conversation in the town. Ruth had a long talk with a person who ran retreats on death and bereavement, who felt that people who became physical immortalists were probably those who were very over-concerned with – perhaps afraid of – death itself. This was shown by the way in which they placed so much emphasis upon death and had built up a whole philosophy around avoiding it. But he thought it was a very interesting philosophy, because it challenged people's preconceptions about death.

The elements of New Age thinking that embrace physical immortalism can be traced, on an international basis, to the Rebirthing Movement, led by Leonard Orr and Sondra Ray. Originating in America, this practice/therapy/philosophy of life, to which we return in Chapter 9, has become very popular, and by contextualising physical immortality the latter has been legitimated and lent a greater degree of acceptability, when otherwise, certainly in Glastonbury, it would have remained a marginal, fringe idea. Rebirthing consists of confronting the trauma of birth and stimulating the remembering of past lives. Its significance for physical immortality is that it explores in great depth the ideas of self-responsibility – of making affirmations in one's life and then realising them – upon which physical immortalists rely. When Leonard Orr visited Glastonbury, Ruth attended a question and answer evening with him where the subject of physical immortality inevitably arose. He said to become physically immortal was to reach a certain level of spiritual awareness and consciousness – to stay alive is to be one with God. The death urge, he believed, is what keeps people from being fully alive, and senility is a childish way of gaining attention. He mentioned that when he was 'back-pedalling spiritually' he had suffered from senility for two years. When someone asked him if death was not part of the natural cycle, he answered, quoting the Bible, that death is the wages of sin and that people reincarnate to pay for their sins. He concluded, with a mischievous grin and twinkling eyes, 'Staying immortal is the trip'.

Robert Coon, one of the major teachers of physical immortality, lives in Glastonbury and Ruth and he discussed his ideas over many conversations. His wife is also a physical immortalist, and for a period of time a group caught up by their ideas would meet with them every week. Robert Coon has written booklets (from which the quotations, below, on the subject were excerpted), and our understanding of his thinking comes from a mixture of literature, personal conversations and workshops. Many of his readers and much of his popularity actually come from outside Glastonbury. Citing the Bible, just as does Leonard Orr, he discerns physical immortality in the doctrines of most major world religions – not only in Christianity, but also in Judaism, Islam, Taoism, Hinduism, Shinto Religion, and not to mention Arthurian myth. He explains the process of developing physical immortality in technical terms,

> It is possible to make a transformational shift of bodily structure and energy to both higher and lower frequencies. As wavelength patterns throughout the living form shorten and increase vibratory frequencies, the individual reaches a level above entropy and decay. At this point, an observer may think that the Immortal has dematerialised because he or she is no longer visible. This is not accurate. 'Bodily Translation' is a more descriptive term. The immortal body maintains its essential structure as it subtly shifts in and out of the visible spectrum.[7]

According to Robert Coon, immortals are currently in existence around the planet, but they desist from making themselves manifest because they wish first of all to be accepted by all of humanity; at the moment they are in retreat from public consciousness because in the past they were rejected or not understood. It is this acceptance that is the 'task' of the Aquarian Age: not only have we mortals reached a point in the development of our consciousness where we are able to choose not to decay on a physical level, but it is also time for the 'reintegration of ALL Immortals back into the global culture'.[8] In order to work toward physical immortality Robert Coon recommends self-examination of negative preconceptions, and particularly training the body through diet, fasting and prayer.

Birth and death are the two elements of an individual's life over which they are deemed to have little or no control. Most world religions have developed doctrines which reveal this and which help people to accept it. For a doctrine to declare that a person can choose to remain indefinitely within one physical body that does not decay is very striking, for it implies, in stark contrast, the appropriation by the human individual of an ultimate control. As we said, this is linkage between mind/body holism and practical individualism at an extreme.

Techniques

A very wide range of healing techniques, which clearly reflect New Age ideas about the human person, are available in Glastonbury and tried out by New Agers in the town, and large numbers of different types of healers travel to Glastonbury from all over the world. We should like briefly to capture this range of techniques and, covering three very different types, will draw on reports from magazine publications that are widely read in the town. The Alternative Community is highly literate, the written word is an integral part of their world, and so magazine articles on healing are very much part of their way of life.

The first example concerns the power of massage as an agent for relaxing the body so that healing can occur. Discussion of this is given prominence in the Spring 1990 edition of *Kindred Spirit*. The writer tells us that massage is, indeed, a catalyst for much more:

> it is often through receiving a massage that people first begin their journey of self-discovery and exploration of the integral link of the body, mind and spirit – the holistic principle. The body has a precious innocence to it and seems less devious than the mind.[9]

Through touch, the article continues, it is possible to get in contact with the body, and with the emotions and memories of our past which are locked up in our physical self,

> For the body is never separate from the thoughts and feelings, the childhood influences and attitudes, the personality that builds up around one's emotional experiences, or the posture and physical structure one forms to create an image in which to function. The body reveals one's personal life history, and stored within the muscles and tissues are memories of all that has happened to make us happy and sad, fearful and hopeful, and a whole human being.[10]

The second example comes from the magazine, *Global Link-Up*. In Spring 1990, in a section called *The Power of Sound*, two healers write on the role of sound in both healing and personal transformation on which they run classes and workshops. The first, Jill Purse, believes that in the West we have lost our voice and become 'sound-polluters'. She sees sound as powerful on two levels; firstly as a means to keep the body healthy, and secondly as a means of keeping in tune with others:

> When traditional societies chant together, first and foremost it is like sonorous yoga, to resonate the body so that it is healthy and to resonate with yourself and with those closest to you. In church for example you might sit in the family pew and literally come into resonance with your

family and all the people that are in the church. Many churches are situated on very ancient sacred places where there is a kind of mediation
between heaven and earth.[11]

The third example is 'colour therapy'. In this the patient is healed
by being exposed to and then absorbing different colour rays, and
different colours are appropriate for different conditions. For example, pink rays are good for people with addiction problems, and for
relaxation and letting go of stress. Orange is good for hyperactive
children, and blue is known as the colour for more general healing.
Marie Louise Lacy, in *Kindred Spirit*, writes,

> It's not by chance that blue jeans were introduced and are worn round
> the world for any occasion. Everything that happens is trying to link us
> to a deeper purpose for being here and for us to look at that. The
> colour blue is linked to faith and trust, integrity and loyalty, all the
> attributes we need today, and helps us find the purpose for incarnating
> at this time.[12]

Mind/Body and Personal Responsibility

In keeping with the idea of the holistic person, wellness, in New
Age thinking, implies a proper balance among the various elements (physical, emotional, mental and spiritual) that constitute
the human being, and illness that such a balance is lacking. Indeed
people in Glastonbury would criticise different social groups in
these terms. Thus academics were deemed to place too much
emphasis on the mental and not enough on the emotional or intuitive, and people who became wrapped up in the spiritual and paid
little attention to the physical and the mental were accused of
being 'ungrounded'. It follows that healing, and the maintenance of
well-being, consists of restoring or sustaining the correct balance.
This contrasts with Western biomedicine which, focusing solely on
the physical, must speak of health and illness (employing
metaphors of violence) in terms of the invasion of the physical
body from the outside and of the concern that such contaminating
elements be expelled.

New Age interpretations in these terms were summoned in relation to Ruth's own experience towards the end of summer 1990
when she developed a virus which came and went over a period of
a month and left her feeling faint and nauseous. As she reports in
her dairy:

'I went to my own [National Health Service] doctor, but she said there was very little she or I could do except that I should look after myself and wait until it left my system. At the same time I was helping with the "alternative" newspaper in the town. My relations with the woman running it were deteriorating, the newspaper seemed to be going through a period of unpopularity and there were few helpers to put together the autumn issue. When I became sick I phoned up and said I would have to stay at home for the day. But aware of the pressures of getting the newspaper ready to go to print, I returned the following day, not feeling completely better. After a few hours I began to feel physically very drained and decided to go home again. The woman I was helping said to me,

> I'm rarely ill, perhaps the odd cold but that's all. It's because I let my emotions in and out freely, when I'm angry I scream and so I don't get any blockages. The reason why you are ill is because you suppress things. This is your chance now you are here in Glastonbury to let go. You are trying to hold down a job and career, have a monogamous relationship, trying to please others. Now you are in Glastonbury you have a chance to throw it all off and to really experience yourself. All the resentment and frustration you have is manifesting itself on a physical level.

Thus I came to feel that my condition was entirely my own fault. It was evidently something inextricably linked with my personality, and so I was now fully responsible for regaining my health'.

We have cited in this chapter several examples illustrating New Age attitudes to health where the idea of balance within the total human person is very clearly on display. Thus New Age diet reflects the notion that physical ingestion has direct spiritual implications; spiritual healing plays on the concept that resistance in mind and resistance in body are linked; and ideas about massage see the physical body as a repository for things mental and emotional. The question remains, however, as to whether there is a relationship between, on the one hand, the holistic person, and, on the other hand, the fact that, in New Age health practice, both health and illness are deemed to be basically a matter of personal responsibility. Does the latter in some way directly result from the former? In fact it seems that it may not, and therefore, in relation to matters of healing, we should seek another explanation for New Age 'personal responsibility'. As much is suggested by differences between tribal society and the New Age, which also clarify what the notion of personal responsibility in the context of health practice means. Like the New Age, tribal society generally upholds the concept of the holistic person, but it differs in that it normally declines the idea of a direct, unmediated impact of a person's demeanour on their overall well-being. In Western alternative therapies it is specifically this latter notion that personal responsibility describes.

Rosalind Coward, in her critique of the alternative health movement, inspires this line of thinking, thanks to the contrast she draws between New Age health concepts and the ideas about illness and misfortune which prevail in ancient, or 'early' society. This contrast is valuable since we can assume (for the time being) that, in terms of social organisation and beliefs, early society and current tribal society are much the same (this is something we shall refine and discuss in Chapters 10 and 11). In both New Age and early society, Coward comments,

> It is the state of the whole person, the spirit or personality which predisposes an individual towards illness. But the difference between earlier 'spiritual' accounts of illness [exemplified today in tribal society] and contemporary accounts based on the idea of personality [for example, in New Age thinking] is that *the individual is much more directly and personally responsible for illness.* (1989: 77, our emphasis)

Coward explores this one step further by examining the link, in the alternative therapies in the West today, between an emphasis on spiritual (mis)behaviour being influential in illness and an underlying stress upon personality, or emotion. For example, in the New Age,

> there is an extremely hazy area between spirit and personality in reference to the whole person . . . for although in the past [tribal society], connections were made between illness and the spiritual state of an individual, there has never before been a theory which connects illness with the state of the personality. The connection between illness and personality *gives an individual an even greater responsibility* for his or her illness than previous 'religious' explanations of illness as expressions of God's displeasure. (ibid., our emphasis)

Many African societies, including those that Horton had in mind when he contrasted African traditional thinking and Western science, qualify as 'tribes' in terms of their types of social structure. Accordingly, these quotations introduce the similarities and differences between New Age and African conceptualisations of misfortune rather well. Both New Age and African thinking, in contrast to Western science, attend to the circumstances as well as to the mechanics of accident and illness. Thus, in biomedicine, germ theory explicates very well the mechanics of illness, but it evades questions about time and place, explaining away via such concepts as bad luck or coincidence why, for example, one person gets struck down whilst another seems to live a charmed life. Meanwhile, New Age/African thinking is able to explain that misfortune falls to that particular person, at that particular moment because the person's demeanour is somehow not currently in balance (cf Evans–Pritchard 1937). Levi–Strauss (1966: 11) labels such New Age/tribal thinking 'magical' and aptly characterises it as incorporating an all-embracing and uncompromising determinism, where, in place of notions of coincidence and luck, people invoke something quite specific. Yet for all this, according to most African understandings, illness and misfortune are not caused directly by the afflicted person, but are rather mediated by an external agent; it is witches, spirits, ancestors etc., offended by human misdemeanour, who inflict the illness (or whatever) and so decide that the misfortune should occur. This contrasts with New Age thinking where (as has been seen) such an external mediator is more normally absent, and where illness and distress arise, above all, directly from within the victim, from internal disturbance triggered from following the 'incorrect path'. A substantive illustration of such a difference is provided by Danforth when he compares firewalking rituals as events of healing among American New Agers and among Greek peasants (for present purposes, standing in for African society). In the case of the Americans healing comes about because, thanks to submitting themselves to the ordeal, people are able to harness internal powers; whilst for the peasants, shackled by orthodox religion, the ritual's function is to summon external supernatural powers relating to God and the saints (Danforth 1989: 270). An explanation for direct personal responsibility in relation to New Age health practice should clearly incorporate an account of why, in African thinking about health and misfortune, such a notion is broadly absent.

We suggest that one should look first at the fact that, between African health systems and Western biomedicine, there is something in common. This is that they are both mainstream in the sense that within their respective societies they comprise the dominant orthodoxies. Thus the relevant difference between African and New Age health practice may be that between mainstream doctrine and non-mainstream doctrine. We suggest that in the African realm, the society's official gods, spirits and other central religious forces are available so that, with regard to the flow of human affairs, the burden of immediate responsibility for how things turn out may be relieved from the shoulders of the ordinary human being; thus in African thinking about health practice, where illness is held to be inflicted by the ancestors etc., direct blame for the misfortune which has occurred is shifted away from the afflicted person – to their considerable psychological benefit. But this cannot be the case in the New Age. New Agers, since they have decided that the (Western) mainstream is not for them, are constrained to fall back on their own resources regarding the conduct of daily life, and this, in the realm of health and illness, disposes them to consider both well-being and its restoration (in times of misfortune) as primarily a personal concern; with respect to the interpretation of illness this translates into the notion of personal responsibility. Finally this leaves Western biomedicine as the residual system, with its dualistic thinking about the nature of the person, and its mechanistic causes of illness as affecting the human being in solely his or her physical dimension. Such a system is plainly caused by highly exotic social organisational and cultural circumstances!

The Final Question

In Chapter 9, on New Age cosmology, we shall deal further with matters of New Age spirituality, but already it is clear that dimensions of this notion force one to raise difficult questions. We air such questions immediately since, in our view, they refer to issues of enormous significance regarding the 'construction' of New Age cosmology (Chapter 11). The nub of the problem refers to matters of cosmological holism. When New Agers uphold holism in this context they mean it either as 'the entity in its complete form', or else as 'the entity as it locks into a wider system'. What is the relationship between these two perspectives on holism?

With regard to health, this question reduces to whether a person's well-being is in the hands of internal spiritual forces or whether powers relating to some sort of transcendent spirituality have a bearing on personal well-being. For the most part, New Age health may be understood in terms of the former, such that it is the individual's spiritual constitution, as this balances with other

aspects of the holistic person, that is the cause of their bodily fortune; the 'human entity in its complete form' is the basis of well-
being. Yet we have also encountered spiritual ideas relating to a
universe, to a global ecology, or to an 'other reality' domain, commonly labelled cosmos, whose powers (or energies) some New
Age healers harness for human good; such powers make themselves available for human well-being because the 'human entity
locks into, or is subsumed by, this wider system' (Pomroy 1998).
For New Agers, the notion of cosmos largely functions as part of
how New Agers construe the world beyond, yet sometimes it is
clearly believed to be relevant for human well-being as well.

The question is whether such internal and external spirituality
should be understood as all of apiece, or whether these are quite
separate (though superficially similar and often brought together)
elements of a constructed cosmology. For New Agers themselves
internal and external spirituality are generally thought of as two
logical dimensions of essentially the one thing:

> Holistic worldview . . . sees . . . health as the dynamic, creative process
> of living in harmony with nature . . . In holistic health the emphasis is
> on the functional relationship among the various aspects of the whole
> person. (Rick Ingrasci, quoted in Satin [1978: 125–6])

In Chapter 11, we argue that, in terms of the construction of
New Age cosmology, it is vitally important that these two notions
be separated out.

Notes

1. Information sheet, Chalice Well, Chilkwell St., Glastonbury.
2. 'Column 23', Dominic. *The Glastonbury Times*, Autumn 1990, p. 23.
3. Another extremely well-known guru is Bhagwan Shree Rajneesh, whose psy-
   cho-religious healing therapies are informed by Sufism, yogic breathing,
   Tibetan practices, Taoism, Buddhism, Jainism, Hinduism, Hassidism, Jung,
   Reich and humanism. Bhagwan was formerly a professor of philosophy at the
   University of Jabalpur. Communes in his name have been established in many
   countries around the world. Bhagwan translates as 'God self-realised' (Thompson and Heelas 1986: 51, 16, 17).
4. Teilhard de Jardin, the Jesuit priest and inspirer of the New Age in its Christian
   dimension, coined the term 'omega point' to capture his view that a consciousness is imminent in the universe, to which human consciousness is
   attuned, and in respect of which evolution is occuring to an eventual point of
   convergence (Teilhard de Chardin 1959). The anthropic principle insists that
   the universe (or the planet), to have the properties it does, especially those

which permit the existence of life forms and human consciousness, is extremely improbable. The principle invites the conclusion that chance and coincidence could not have given rise to what it sees as such extraordinary circumstances, and that some sort of guiding hand may therefore be present. Teilhard's work offers one sort of suggestion as to what this guiding hand might be.

5. *Physical immortality: history, theory and techniques*. Robert Coon. The Omega Point Foundation, Glastonbury.
6. ibid., p. 14–15.
7. ibid., p. 26.
8. ibid., p. 43
9. 'A language of love', Nitya Lacroix. *Kindred Spirit*, Spring 1990, Totnes, p. 7.
10. ibid., p. 8.
11. 'The power of sound', Jill Purse. *Global Link-Up*, April/May 1991, Gloucester, p.12.
12. 'Colour for Healing and Harmony'. Mary-Louise Lacy. *Kindred Spirit*, Summer 1990, Totnes, p.26.

6

Relationships: Communitas or Counter-Culture?

An extreme lack of social differentiation – contrasting markedly with almost all human societies – is the notable feature of New Age social relationships in Glastonbury. People do engage socially with one another, for all manner of purposes, yet what an anthropologist would call 'social structure' is hard to discern. Turner (1969) identified these characteristics – lack of social differentiation, absence of social structure – when he depicted communitas, the primordial, anti-structural state that, according to him, underpins the possibility of real human society. As Turner saw it, during periods or circumstances of liminality in ongoing social life, when structure is stripped away, communitas is exposed as the sole human social experience. The question that frames this chapter is whether the Glastonbury New Age community should be appreciated as a liminal community.

In this chapter, we shall describe the social organisation of the Alternative Community in Glastonbury, and show both how it is different from social organisation in the Western mainstream, and how the New Age individual, as inherently a *social person*, is qualitatively distinct compared with the mainstream person. The question of communitas aside, New Agers in Glastonbury, like people in any social community, come to occupy certain basic social positions – 'men' or 'women', 'parents' or 'children' – that imply particular types of social relationships, for example gender relationships, family relationships, and so on. These will be our particular topics for consideration.

The difference between the New Age and the mainstream here relates to the fact that, in the New Age social world, holistic and individualistic principles interpenetrate in a way that a highly

113

distinctive moral quality is imparted to New Age social relationships and to the New Age 'persons' who participate in them. With
respect to human interaction this interpenetration is evident in the
value that New Agers put on the social provision of 'space'. The
position here is an intriguing and paradoxical one. On the holistic
side, a sense of (imagined) community and interdependence permeates New Age social affairs, providing an inherent backdrop for
everyday social life. On the individualistic side such everyday
social interaction is strongly marked by an emphasis on personal
autonomy. A case may be made for saying that the former permits,
even if it does not directly cause, the latter. As New Agers in Glastonbury see it, an inherent mutuality provides the support (and
therefore the 'space') which allows people to develop their own
individual connections in the manner that they see fit. This is different from thinking in the Western mainstream where people see
communal life more as the product than the condition of individual social action and the particular roles individuals occupy. Reminiscent of communitas, three notable features of New Age social
organisation result from the individualism that consequently
shines through in the conduct of everyday affairs in the Alternative
Community. First, in the Alternative Community people play down
the value of – they 'de-signify' – specific social roles; this, it will be
seen, has an intrinsic bearing on how New Agers in the town think
about the social nature of the human person. Second, among New
Agers gender roles are less marked than in most human communities, in the West or elsewhere – though this is sustained in the context of a strong cultural emphasis on the difference between the
masculine and the feminine as intellectual principles. Finally, the
value of personal autonomy is very much in evidence in procedures for the resolution of conflict. We shall devote a section to
each of these topics.

In Glastonbury, relations between people are about the
exchange of energy. 'She's got good energy', 'just feel the aggressive energy at the meeting', 'your energy is so forceful': these were
the common ways by which members of the Alternative Community would mark the distinctive, and highly variable, quality of
human social interaction. In New Age culture, the importance of
'energy' is that it provides a common denominator in terms of
which different types of relationships can be discussed and compared, and the contrasts with the mainstream made clear. 'Energy',
in the human social situation, is, for New Agers, akin to an
electrical current: along with the semantically similar concept of

'vibration' it expresses the idea of a 'charged' social atmosphere. Thus social events in Glastonbury would be described in terms of the amount and type of energy that they contained, and people were believed to be able both to generate and to manipulate energy, thereby having an affect on others in the various social arenas (see the example of the meditation groups, described in Chapter 9). As one may expect, from the discussion of energy in the context of human health, there are spiritual connotations in all this, to which the following extract, from a letter in the summer 1990 edition of the magazine *Kindred Spirit* bears witness. The authors of the letter, Ann and Paul Adams, describe being caught up in the famous Poll Tax demonstration in London, March 1990,

> It soon became obvious from the banners that it was the Poll Tax demonstration, which we had completely forgotten about. The atmosphere was very tense and excited . . . We went back to the Café and went and sat down. About five minutes later the vibration level went up and all hell appeared to have broken loose outside. We looked out of the window and it appeared to be raining – then we realised it was rocks, pieces of scaffolding and glass flying through the air . . . We went to the back and sat down in a corner, deciding there was work to be done. We went into meditation straight away using the Charing Cross as our focus as this is a very powerful energy point. We started to say the Great Invocation together, silently. As we reached the word 'love' the whole place started to buzz, as we said the word 'Christ' the whole thing went wouf, like a fountain of energy, for a moment I couldn't remember the next words to say. We continued this way for what seemed a very long time but it was actually only a few moments . . . As soon as we'd gone into meditation and sent up the call we felt an enormous group of people with us, some we recognised as being part of our local Fountain group but thousands and thousands more, like points of light . . . We could feel the energy pulsing down through us and into the Earth, and how it spread out gradually from around us and around the Charing Cross. At first it felt difficult for the energy to push through the enormous cloud of negativity and then, gradually, the Love spread and the atmosphere became calmer.

De-Signifying Formal Roles

In Glastonbury, upon meeting someone from the Alternative Community for the first time, one would give them a hug. Walking down Glastonbury High Street, it would not be uncommon to pass one or two couples of either the same or the opposite sex, engaged in a long and presumably meaningful embrace. It was also not uncommon, once one had become a part of the Alternative Community, to find oneself as a participant. As Ruth Prince describes it, when one is more at home with the ubiquitous British handshake it is somewhat disarming, at first, to have a stranger tightly squeezing one's whole body. When she read about 'Rajneeshpuram', the Bhagwan Shree Rajneesh community in Oregon, it could as easily have been Glastonbury:

> On the streets people called out gaily to one another and walked with their arms about one another's shoulders. In an office you might find one staff member teasing another and the whole group howling with laughter. Also a good deal of hugging went on. Tourists looking out of the smoky windows of their buses would see people embracing in the tea tents, in the vegetable garden, and behind the trash mashers and wonder what was going on. (Fitzgerald 1968: 274)

The handshake and the hug, both of them expressing mutual recognition, differ objectively only in the proportion of the body coming into contact, yet the hug reflects the general propensity for physical contact in the Alternative Community, which contrasts sharply with mainstream British society. The symbolic meanings in this regard are worth exploring.

In Glastonbury, New Agers would so far as possible interact with one another as complete persons, and not, in the more restricted way characteristic of the mainstream, as incumbents of particular social roles (for example, relating to family hierarchy or workplace duties). Social interaction in the Alternative Community was based on a desire that social barriers between individuals be lowered at the earliest moment. The New Age friendship relationship indicates this very well: this is a distinctive type of friendship. In Glastonbury friends were, in a manner of speaking, 'instant friends'. Upon first meeting, people would presume immediately that the crucial values of trust and affect held between them. This is unlike mainstream society where, because people normally relate to one another in terms of significant formal roles (not forgetting the formal role of 'stranger'), friendships are generally built up cautiously: the individuals concerned must deconstruct the respective formal roles while the values of trust and affect are substituted in their place. In Glastonbury, with such formal roles barely in evidence, caution might be cast to the wind. The 'hug versus handshake' contrast epitomises this nicely. The hug expresses very well the unreserved acceptance of another person in

116

the New Age community, whilst the handshake expresses the more conditional acceptance evident in the mainstream, in both friendship and other social roles.

A developed complex of roles, which reflects the existence of social differentiation, implies social restrictions upon people that, to be sustained, require the exercise of power or authority within the community at hand. In contrast, where formal roles are 'de-signified', individual autonomy will flourish as a value. The latter occurs in Glastonbury. Indeed, in New Age thinking even the human individual's personality is considered, analogously to a social role, as in some sense external, or imposed, and therefore as constraining. As New Agers see it, true individuality accordingly rests with the physical self and the soul. New Age attitudes to occupational roles, and to the traditional nuclear family, exemplify such social patterns very well.

With regard to occupational roles, Ruth noticed immediately that in Glastonbury one was rarely asked 'what do you do?' She reflected on this in her dairy towards the end of her stay in the town:

'Since I was an anthropologist, I would discreetly try to volunteer as much, feeling that people ought to be aware of the fact when talking to me. However as I hung around cafés and houses engaging in long conversations and doing nothing very obvious with my time, I always seemed to be surrounded by others who appeared to be doing much the same. For example, no one really discussed how they supported themselves financially, which, for me, was a source of frustration: I knew how I was supporting myself doing "nothing" all day, but what about everyone else? To a certain extent this remained an enigma; a person's source of money was not considered important as a topic of conversation except among those engaged in small businesses. At length, by the time I finally came to leave Glastonbury it had become fairly clear that many people were either collecting social security cheques or living from private incomes; others did a variety of part-time jobs, combining different work'.

Why was the discussion of job roles so infrequent in Glastonbury? It was not the absence of work that made people attach little standing to, and devote less time discussing, work roles. In fact, as we shall mention in the next chapter, in the Alternative Community people did regard work occupations as something important – at the very least in the sense that they should be satisfying. The point is, people's jobs were not regarded as a focal point in their lives. The individual's spiritual well-being mattered far more, which is something highly personal, and moreover equally valid whatever work one does. Indeed, in a work situation, emphasis was less on the work being done than on the development of harmonious relationships. Thus when Ruth was helping with the preparations for the Harmonic Convergence in 1987, a group attunement would be held every afternoon, where, sitting in a circle and holding hands, those involved would meditate for a few minutes. Likewise there was the situation in the house where Ruth lived, where people would come on short-term courses on New Age themes; there was vegan catering and she would frequently do the cooking. Each morning Ruth would be greeted by the leader of the course with a long hug, and it was the same when he left in the evening. Once she worked part-time helping organise a course, and the man repeatedly became very emotional about their working together. Ruth commented to him that placing so much emphasis upon the emotional in a work situation was unusual for her, to which he replied,

> How can you separate work and the 'personal' [as Ruth had called it]? Everything is personal. We are working together and sharing energy together, and so we are bound to go through an emotional process together.

Turning to New Age domestic organisation, the general downplaying of formal roles means a comparative lessening in the value attached to the traditional nuclear family and a correspondingly widened area of reference for intensive social relationships. In Glastonbury 'family' was a word with many meanings. It certainly did not imply an adult male and an adult female living in the same residential unit with varying numbers of children parented by both. 'Family' could equally be applied to a group of adults living together with no blood ties; or to a single parent; or to a spiritual group which meets regularly; or, clearly in a metaphoric sense, to describe the feeling of communality in the whole Glastonbury area. The leader of one spiritual group, whose members did not live together but had all moved to the Glastonbury area and bought houses there, described the group as 'like the family you would wish for'.

Many New Agers in Glastonbury, however, did live in nuclear families – though this is not to suppose legal marriage between the respective male and female adults. Yet because, among New Agers, formal roles are generally played down, the whole character of such families was qualitatively different from the mainstream. Thus in the Alternative Community people would commonly teach their children from the beginning to call them by their Christian names rather than Mum or Dad. (It is interesting that when the children began attending a mainstream school, they would often start using Mum or Dad.) Within a nuclear family unit there was evident dislike of the categorical positions of husband, wife, or parent (versus child). Often parents would resist being authoritarian, believing that the words of the child should be listened to with sensitivity (see Chapter 8). Likewise effort was made not to segregate the work of the female and male parents. It was most uncommon that one partner would have a full-time job whilst the other stayed at home to look after the children, so attempts were made to share the workload. (We discuss this in detail later in the chapter.) That said, a gendered division of labour similar to the mainstream normally did develop to some extent. Thus Ruth only ever observed one 'partnership' where the majority of the domestic duties fell to the man.

But in the Alternative Community domestic organisation based around a recognisably nuclear family was only one option. There were many single parents in Glastonbury, and a lot of the older people had come to the town as divorcees. When people talked about ideal living situations, the notion of the two-parent family beloved of the mainstream commonly brought looks of horror to many people's faces; for them it was clearly not a desirable option. People would cite memories of the 'restricted energies', or 'claustrophobia', of their own natal family to explain why they would have no part in one now; according to some members of the Alternative Community, the nuclear family was 'old age'. However, people would often talk about the isolation of single living, and about the heavy work load of bringing up a child alone. Against this, while some people did live in large communal households, the commune was frequently viewed with acrimony and distaste, recalling the high rate of failure of this form of social living in the 1960s and 1970s. People commonly said that communes did not allow enough space for the individual. For them, kibbutz-like arrangements, where domestic management and childrearing are organised communally, would be out of the question. In contrast, the 'green village' was often cited as the ideal – as striking the correct balance between the needs for community and individuality. One person said,

I've lived by myself, with others, with my wife, tried out all sorts of situations. And now I'm convinced that the idea of people living together with communal land is the best idea yet. The idea is that people live with their own living space and a small piece of land around them. But at the same time there is communal land where vegetables, etc., can be grown communally, people share the work for that, and a common building where people can meet together when they want company. In that way you get your own individual space and also community.

Another said,

Ideally I would like about four other benders or mobile homes on the field, working together on the land, yet each of us also having our own space and autonomy. I don't even want to be part of a monogamous couple anymore, I feel I can live independently and have one or two 'sweet friends', I think others are also reaching that point.

In Marge Piercy's novel, W*omen on the Edge of Time*, people lived close by one another, had sexual relationships with a number of others, and there was no notion of ownership of others; children were conceived separately in test tubes (Piercy 1976). A person with whom one had such a sexual relationship was called a sweet friend. The conception of children apart, this, in the name of autonomy, was very much many New Agers' ideal.

New Agers, then, experience a sense of togetherness the while that they pursued their affairs largely autonomously. By such togetherness the Alternative Community in Glastonbury would imagine the dissolution of the boundaries between human individuals such that people mesh into one another. Such togetherness is not restrictive and implies a generalised support, which is as much psychological as it is material (see Chapter 7 on the material elements in New Age life). Its manifestation in Glastonbury indicates that it goes to the heart of how New Agers conceptualise the human individual. Its vital symbolic idea is love.

Truly a dominant symbol, love, in the New Age, has various meanings, and, in Glastonbury, was summoned on many different types of occasion. In the first instance, as an ideal to which people aspire, love evokes a perfect way of being, in which aggression finds no place. For New Agers 'unconditional love' therefore implies deep affection, positiveness and altruism; from the object of love nothing is expected in return, nor is there any desire for it (or he, or she) to be anything other than it is. As well as this, in Glastonbury love was considered to be unlimited. Thus it was thought possible to love many others at the same time, and this meant, on a practical level, that even within the context of the nuclear family, its traditional confines might be played down, with people becoming involved in one another's families, taking additional lovers, and so on.

There are further meanings. Love refers to oneself, underlining the fresh awareness and the raising of consciousness that are necessary for participating in the New Age movement. Love may also be applied to a task, as will be noted in Chapter 7. Altogether on another level, love applies to the world: accepting the world as it is is seen as a true expression of love. (Critics of the New Age movement cite this as evidence of its political passivity.) Lastly, it was said in Glastonbury, the 'world beyond' (e.g. the mainstream world) is devoid of love, from the point of view of both relations among people and one's veneration of oneself as a divine being. Significantly, for New Agers in Glastonbury the opposite of love is fear.

A social world, expressed by love, where formal roles are played down and togetherness and autonomy mesh together, is manifest, in Glastonbury, in three main domains of living. First, love is reflected in communality. In Glastonbury this was especially so in the context of spiritual retreats and group meetings. As we shall see in other chapters, people attended these for their own purposes, yet beforehand there would be an expression of collective strength as, getting in a circle and perhaps joining hands, people 'attuned'. Everyone would tell the group their name and why they 'felt moved to come', and there would then be much sharing of feelings and experiences. And it was usually not until much later that people would get round to telling each other where they came from, whether they had a job, and other such role-related details. Second, love is evident, in interpersonal relationships, as friendship. As Paine has described it, friendship implies a mutual sense of worth between two people, yet at the same time it is a relationship that people will have established voluntarily. Friendship is also a private relationship in that what they choose to disclose to one another is a matter solely for the people concerned (Paine 1969). We have mentioned that in Glastonbury, friendship is instant, so people often rapidly disclosed to others matters of considerable intimacy. Thus it was common to tell people whom one knew only slightly all the personal details of one's life. Ruth remembers standing for an hour in the High Street on a busy market day hearing about a dream a woman had had the day before. Prior to this she had only casually said hello to her once when she met her in the nearby café where she worked. Finally, love is evident in a generalised mutuality, such that people's lives blend into one another. In Glastonbury, it was overwhelmingly one's own business how one conducted one's affairs, yet each person's identity participated in the affairs of everyone else. According to the New Age teacher, Sir George Trevelyan, who frequently visited Glastonbury, this is because of the common spark of divinity which exists between living beings, which makes up an 'holistic common thread' (Trevelyan 1986: 15).

These values condense in the New Age conceptualisation of what it is to be a human being: the fundamental social values in a society will centrally be reflected in the way human beings in that society think about the very nature of the human person. Upon the New Age human being, communality and autonomy converge, such that the 'person' is conceived of as an entity suspended in relations with others. Thus, for New Agers, along with their physical, spiritual, emotional and mental components, human persons are also constituted by inherent interdependence. Through the idea of love such mutuality in the human person is provided with an ideal moral and emotional substance. Love, it is evident, expresses an inherent capacity in the human being, as well as the intensity of sharing existing between any two people by virtue of their common humanity. Ann and Paul Adams' invocation, during the poll tax riots, of universal Love as the key energy in social healing, confirms this perfectly. In Glastonbury, love connoted an awareness of *being* a New Ager and an unqualified acceptance of *others who are* New Age.

Gender

Among New Agers, many important ethical and intellectual qualities are modelled in terms of putative differences between man and woman: some such qualities are described as masculine, other (opposite) qualities as feminine. But that said, as New Agers reflect on daily life they are generally rather resistant to the notion that men might assume particular roles and women other, quite different ones. In short, in New Age gender *thinking*, the ethical (masculine versus feminine) and the practical (male roles versus female roles) seem to point in opposite directions. When it comes to real *social activity*, it will be seen, the relation between these two aspects of New Age gender thinking underscores pervasive ambiguities, which in turn leads to frustration and conflict.

A perspective should be put on this, however. On the matter of New Age activity, divisions relating to men and women remain secondary to the emphasis on the individual and to the 'de-signifying' of social categorisation and formal roles. For example, the Alternative Community in Glastonbury was generally very aware of feminist issues; some women in the Community had lived in the women's peace camp at Greenham Common, and in the case of many other women their decision to become involved with the New Age movement had meant leaving former roles as housewives. Yet gender roles were largely muted, which is one of the reasons why, in Glastonbury, feminism was often criticised as being 'divisive'. And the muting of gender roles, rather than gender politics as such, was why men were encouraged to find the feminine within themselves.

Gender Thinking: Essence and Roles

The dance is One: a movement of energy through time and space according to a casually determined design. The two 'partners' are as its dual poles – the one an impulsion, the other a response. Yet how to distinguish these two within the dance; for each is fused with the other, connected in such a way as to be the entity of relationship. Indeed, without one or the other there would be no dance, no movement, no energy in manifestation.[1]

The New Age invokes a model of the social person based upon the balance of male and female elements. In Glastonbury this was explained in terms of masculine and feminine essences existing within both men and women, which need to find a harmonious relation. In this context the above quotation plays upon the energy of interaction between the genders: mutually dependent, the masculine and the feminine are seen as dual poles of the same entity, different but inseparable. The person as a whole constitutes this primary entity. New Agers in Glastonbury would say that within a woman there would obviously be more of the feminine essence and within a man there would be more of the masculine essence. However it was felt important for each sex to recognise the presence of the other essence within themselves.

As to the content of the respective masculine and feminine essences, insight was provided by a woman healer with whom

123

Ruth came into contact, who specialised in putting women in touch with (the female in) themselves and supporting them in following their spiritual paths – which sometimes meant leaving their families and partners behind. According to this healer, therapy lies in ritual, notably drawing upon the female archetypes of the mother, crone, warrior and virgin. Much Christian religious ritual, she would assert, is male-based, praying to God our father. In contrast, feminine spirituality is about cycles, such as the link between the woman's menstrual cycle and the moon and the tides.

The healer described the 'male' and the 'female' by evoking the relationship between a priestess and a priest, in a series of oppositions. These clearly resonate with the way commentators on the New Age in general have described New Age gender ethics: the feminine as nurturing and intuitional (etc.), in contrast to the masculine as rational and aggressive (etc.):

female/priestess	male/priest
chalice	spear/sword
void into which the seed can be dropped	
dark receptive vessel	light and form
chaos	order
clear channel	
nurturing	
prophetic	

In addition, there is female and male in combination:

An electro-magnetic partnership whereby the magnetism of the priestess draws things into her, and the priest draws things from her.

In the New Age movement, the ethical implications of the contrast between the masculine and the feminine are famously manifest in the veneration of the feminine. People in Glastonbury would talk of the restoration of the Goddess. This was seen as part of the redressing of the balance from a formerly male-dominated spiritual hierarchy and society, which may be seen, continuing to exist, in the Western mainstream. According to many people in Glastonbury, as well as a number of feminist theologians, the establishment of the patriarchal Christian church suppressed an earlier and more Goddess-centred faith. Indeed 'The Mists of Avalon', Marion Bradley's novel about the Arthurian myths, which describes the suppression of Goddess-worship, is based around Glastonbury (or 'Avalon') (Bradley 1984). Glastonbury itself is often described in terms of a feminine identity:

> Glastonbury is one of those places where the very shape of the landscape speaks to the people who visit or live upon Her slopes. For it is here that the Body of the Goddess can be seen outlined in the contours of the small group of hills which rise out of the flat Summerland meadows.

> The Goddess appears in different forms to different people and as Her nature changes with the seasons, She presents Her many faces to those with eyes to see. For some people the whole Island is Her spread and Birth giving body.[2]

New Age thinking here may be clarified with respect to controversial theory that holds that, virtually as a universal, human societies link the male principle with culture and the female principle with nature (Ortner 1974). According to anthropologists who uphold this theory, this linkage obtains because males in society are associated with that which is humanly constructed, for example public political life, whilst women are associated with what is biologically given, for example childrearing within the domestic domain. New Age thinking seems, at first glance, to offer a permutation on this equation. Among New Agers the feminine is indeed linked to what are seen as biopsychological tendencies – the emotional, the intuitional and, as intimated in the above quotations, the earth. But by New Agers such tendencies are elevated to express key public ethics. Thus in Glastonbury nature was seen as something to be revered, as something which we are part of rather than control, and towards which there should be minimum intervention. Social values, rules and conventions, it was believed, should respect, even imitate, nature. Correspondingly, the masculine in the human person should make way for, even submit to, the feminine. However it is in fact wrong to line up the New Age with Ortner's theory. This is because it is clear that New Age gender essences do not correspond at all with the nature/culture opposition. The point is, for New Agers the woman/female is much more than merely natural (biological). The feminine is especially suffused with spirituality, most strikingly in the Neo-pagan element in

New Age cosmology: the Earth/Goddess. Here the feminine is decidedly cultural. Moreover, the Earth is considered to be a distinctively creative force (Sjoo 1992: 170). But one may not leave it here, for one should note that anthropologists who have detracted from Ortner's theory have concluded that, far from being universally applicable, the link of male to culture and female to nature is peculiarly part of Western ideology (McCormack 1980). Supposing this is correct, New Age gender thinking actually fits perfectly into the pattern of rejecting the mainstream (i.e. orthodox Western values). If Western values celebrate such linkages, the New Age, in common with very many non-Western societies, it seems, declines the linkage altogether.

When one turns to roles in life, New Age thinking starts to become intriguing because here gender is played down. New Age historiography might describe the veneration of the feminine replacing male domination, but with regard to the present time, gender-specific roles are something not to be emphasised – as the following quotations, drawn from conversations in Glastonbury, indicate (note, however, that they all come from male respondents):

> The gender issue is all a personal thing, and it would all become irrelevant if and when the system is changed. What we have to do is to recognise our male and female energies and then people would not treat each other differently. It's not about a battle between the sexes, not about division, but about joining together.

> We now have a person rather than man or woman. Feminism was a necessary first stage, but I don't believe there is much difference beyond the physical, just cultural beliefs, values and processes. The witch used to be the leader of the village, and there was a strong female witchcraft movement. Men killed off herbalists as a sort of professional colonialism.

> In the age of Aquarius the man and the woman will not be differentiated between, although we have yet to find a way to transcend the biological and reproductive differences. Still I see each sex as having the capacity to do things equally and not even to do them in a different way.

We slip in one additional quotation:

> . . . by experiencing a new synthesis between the masculine and feminine aspects of our nature we can begin to heal the wounds of our psyche thus becoming more fully integrated individuals. (Freeing the feminine. Advertisement for the Wrekin Trust conference, 27–28 October 1990)

Reflecting this thinking, children in the Alternative Community were encouraged not to emphasise sex differences and gender roles. When a young boy started to wear girl's clothes his mother remained unperturbed and was happy to walk around with him dressed as a girl. 'He needs to explore that side to himself', she said. It was also common for young boys to have long hair, or at least to maintain one long lock of hair down the centre of their back, which they would either plait and put beads in, or wear loose. As the fathers of many of the children also had long or shoulder length hair, this would only get registered as unusual when the young boys went to state schools. The parents and teachers Ruth spoke to said they tried to help their children recognise the 'sex difference', but not to place a great deal of importance upon it.

Concerning the relation between the two aspects of New Age gender thinking, this is not hard to discern. Since masculine and feminine essences co-exist within each human person, one can conceive of them being balanced out, and this underscores the relative equivalence of men and women when one contemplates social roles. But there seems to be ambiguity here. The notion of the two essences being 'balanced out' clearly justifies the idea that men and women should be much the same in the roles they perform. But whether it instructs New Agers to think about roles in these terms is another matter. Among New Agers in Glastonbury this ambiguity clearly feeds through into real daily activity. When in daily life men and women are doing similar things, people can legitimise this in terms of the essences balancing out; but, equally, when they are doing different things, people can legitimise this in terms of the essences being different. Thus in the Alternative Community the battle of the sexes was by no means fully assuaged. The pervasive impression was that, at an ideological level, women's standing, compared with the mainstream, was enhanced, but at the level of daily activity it was 'business as usual'.

Gender in Everyone Life

When the woman healer in Glastonbury spelled out the differences between female and male principles, Ruth's initial reaction was that the categorisation of the female in such terms as 'dark receptive vessel', and 'void into which the seed can be dropped', implied passivity, particularly in comparison to the male notions of 'light and form' and 'spear'. The healer replied that she did indeed feel that women have a passive role as the receiver. Some of the female notions that she elucidated are obviously direct references to biological differences, but they are also very revealing about the underlying conceptions of the 'new feminine' in New Age thought: the *idea* of the feminine is honoured, but the characteristics for which women are respected are not necessarily ones which render them any more equal in political or economic terms. As Rosalind Coward writes,

> The issue is not really whether women's genitals are revered or reviled, but the fact that women by virtue of their bodies are rendered symbols. Far from being a new ethic, this is a time-honoured way in which women have always been treated. When any group (whether it be sexual or ethnic) becomes a symbol, the individuals in that group will be defined from the outside and suffer from that identity. (1979: 185)

Fieldwork in Glastonbury confirms this rather pessimistic view of women's position in everyday life. Either women submitted to subordinate social positions, or else they voiced frustration that New Age ideals (of gender equality) did not seem to hold in practice. Albeit that two of the main property owners in the Alternative Community were women, and that women ran a number of businesses in town and so had a substantial degree of power in the public domain (Chapter 7), it is equally the case that for many New Age women that Ruth encountered there was dissatisfaction both with their personal positions and with women's treatment within New Age society in general. This they expressed trenchantly:

> These green hairy types [i.e. typical New Ager women], they've got the knowledge and the language to express themselves, yet they're no more emancipated.

> At least you knew where you stood with straightforward chauvinists.

> They [the men] worship the Goddess, they keep talking about the Goddess, and yet they can't talk to women.

> The New Age doesn't actually do a thing about changing the structures of hierarchy.

It is certainly true that New Age men would treat women as either a 'breed apart' or else as having different competencies, which invited much discussion in terms of the idea of male versus female essence. For example, the New Age movement is very popular with women (Puttick 1997), which must partially be due to its veneration of the feminine, in contrast to the Christian church. In Glastonbury one leader of retreats disclosed that he received many more woman clients than men. Mentioning that within the woman there will be greater feminine essence, he suggested that women's greater presence at retreats must be because women tended more to discuss their feelings in a group, and because they placed more importance upon their emotional selves. Men, he said, 'were more likely to choose the lone path'. In general, women were often described, in Glastonbury, as being more 'in touch' with nature, more involved with their emotions and thus more 'wild'. In contrast, men, in male therapy groups, were trying to 'get in touch with the feminine inside themselves', in order to learn to experience and to express their emotions more effectively.

New Age marriage and partnership clearly illustrates the idea that women have different competencies, and hence should fulfil different tasks. Marriage as a monogamous relationship was not afforded a high status in the Alternative Community in Glastonbury, and people more often had a succession of partners in their lives. So partnership arrangements were especially interesting. Particularly notable is that in four recorded cases of people simultaneously having a sexual relationship with more than one person, and all or most parties knowing about it, the person having the multiple sexual relationship was a man; the women 'sharing' him remained monogamous. In two of these cases the man had explicitly stated that he did not want the women to have other relationships. In one of these the women agreed because they felt the man was a special spiritual being. There was also the matter of primary responsibility for children. Thus, although Ruth did meet male single parents, in the majority of cases when partnerships broke up the women kept the children and were resultingly tied to the domestic domain; formal childcare facilities in the Glastonbury area in 1990 were almost non-existent, although there was a strong informal network. Ruth's partner, Anthony, once commented, casually:

> Why is it that when I drive up Glastonbury High Street I see lots of women walking arm in arm, or with a pushchair and a couple of children? And then I see the men separately. They have this way of walking with a determined expression, looking straight ahead beyond the crowds and into some far vision. The strange thing is, I never see the women and men together.

Women's frustration was evident in an incident that arose over electing new members to the board of trustees for the Assembly Rooms. One woman felt strongly that the gender ratio among the trustees should be equal, and so proposed to fellow members of the board a form of positive discrimination to get more women elected. Her request met with a negative response (from both women and men), so she resigned her own position. Later, she wrote in the *Glastonbury Times*,

> The latest 'intellectual' justification for considering actual equality of numbers unimportant is that we are all a combination of male and female, striving for inner balance (roll on Nirvana!). The arguments put forward in these situations, in Glastonbury as elsewhere, are classic and very familiar. For example: 'It doesn't matter what sex a person is, it's who they are that counts.' 'If it's more men that come forward, what are we supposed to do?' 'I can't see what all the fuss is about. There are other priorities more pressing than this'.[3]

The opinions that so frustrated this woman reflect the increasingly prevalent view, in the New Age generally, that feminism is old hat, political, and divisive.

One might, finally, balance this discussion in favour of men. We mentioned earlier the female healer who helped women find their spiritual paths and true selves, and in passing noted that following such a quest often led to the women abandoning families and partners. What one husband, left behind in this way, had to say offers another dimension to the dynamics of gender relations in Glastonbury:

> Well I think men get a really bad deal in this sub-culture of ours. What do we do? We try really hard to work on equal relationships. But if a woman wants to leave the relationship in order to 'find herself', we are expected to stand out of her path and feel good for her. And if we say anything we are immediately accused of being oppressive and patriarchal. There is nothing we can do, we are just powerless.

The Resolution of Conflict

The notion of harmony continually comes to mind when one ponders the New Age ideal: harmony with nature, and harmony with others. People in Glastonbury would talk about acceptance, and about their aim to 'work through their anger at life'; and they had a vision of a peaceful future society, the 'new age'. All this is in line with love as the pre-eminent New Age value. In the Alternative Community, aggressive behaviour was certainly very largely, and often successfully, avoided. For example, Ruth recalls witnessing a person getting angry at another, who in turn became frustrated and upset – whereupon a third person stepped in, saying 'I think it's time for a group hug'. Yet, inevitably, situations of more intractable conflict would arise. However, there were processes available for both explaining and reacting to such conflict that are distinctively New Age, and which chime in very well with the ethic of individual autonomy. These processes especially drew upon Freud's notion of projection.

In Glastonbury Ruth both observed such processes and was sometimes caught up in them herself, so we may describe them in terms of her direct and immediate experience. As she wrote in her diary:

> 'Because my engagement with the alternative community has been active, and because I have felt my values and "New Age" values clash on some issues, it is an aspect of my fieldwork where I have very much felt myself to be a tool. As a tool I can feel my subjectivity. I have been working alongside someone [a New Ager] with a very confrontational personality, a very strong and forceful personality, so have experienced quite a lot of conflict at close quarters'.

The central notion in New Age thinking about conflict is that expressions of anger and displeasure can be understood in terms of key elements in the personality or mental state of one or other of the conflicting parties, rather than in terms of objective rights and wrongs in the situation at hand. In Glastonbury, 'projection', which paperback psychologists use to describe the transference of feelings from one person onto another, was the means by which conflict, deemed as the individual's responsibility, could be both conceptualised and resolved. In New Age thinking, projection is essentially a pejorative notion, for it generally appeals to basic shortcomings in a person's personality. But there is normally no specific implication that such shortcomings, and the negative feelings which surround them, should be rectified immediately, and by providing a body of ideas through which 'being angry' commands a measure of understanding, the notion resonates closely with the New Age values of 'acceptance'. Moreover, appropriately to the value of non-aggression, there is the means for the conflict itself to become rapidly dampened down. Two complementary perspectives are available here: projection either explains someone's anger in terms of their own shortcomings, thus *diffusing* the import of such anger; or else it explains someone's anger as having been invited because of shortcomings in the recipient, thus *justifying* the anger. These sorts of social sanctions, by focusing on people's internal states, appear to operate on two, interrelated levels. Firstly, a specific meaning is attributed to the idea of conflict such that the objective issue of dispute is deemed to be not worth persisting with. And secondly, the possibility is held out that people whose behaviour is unacceptable will eventually be able to bring their deepest personal attitudes to social living into harmony with New Age ideals relating to love. Two case studies, which Ruth experienced in different ways, may illustrate; Ruth will describe them in her own words.

Diffusion

Projection, in the form of diffusion, is exemplified through people's attitudes to the experience of a young man called Tommy.

The incident began when Tommy came over the road from the café and sat down in the room with Jim and myself, saying how upset he was feeling. He was distressed because Sarah, who worked in the café, had accused him of playing in a very sexual manner with a three-year-old girl who was running around. Sarah said she had seen Tommy pull up the little girl's skirt. In return Tommy said that he had not been playing with the little girl sexually, although he did have a very strong monthly sexual cycle which he sometimes needed to express. However he was adamant that his sexual expression did not extend to three-year-old girls, and felt completely insulted that he had been accused of being a child-molester. At this bitter complaining, Jim intervened, saying that there was no point in being annoyed at Sarah because she was just 'going through her stuff' and should not be made to feel in the wrong for being overly sensitive. Jim said that 'her stuff' was at the moment obviously manifesting itself as an ultra-sensitivity to sexuality. He said that however misplaced was her antipathy towards Tommy she should not be put in the wrong for it.

Linking Sarah's sexuality to the allegations she makes about Tommy's sexual behaviour, Jim explains to Tommy that Sarah is just projecting her feelings about her own life on to him. She tries to make him feel bad about his sexuality because she feels sensitive about her own. Jim's interpretation is intended to cool the conflict by reducing the impact of what are potentially explosive accusations. Not only does it take the responsibility for the situation away from Tommy, it also explains Sarah's apparently anti-social behaviour as not entirely her fault. In this way Sarah's displeasure is diffused, and Tommy's annoyance abates.

Justification

The other side of projection is where someone voices annoyance, but this is held to be understandable because shortcomings in the person who had caused such displeasure had in fact invited it. In the following example I was the person, it appeared, with the shortcomings.

I had started to help run a small business with a woman who had just taken it over after her partner left Glastonbury. The business involved producing an 'Alternative Community' newspaper, and the woman was very anxious about her ability on the technical side, which her partner had mostly looked after. As a result, a lot of the working tensions in the office revolved round the word-processor. Contrary to many others in Glastonbury, Jill welcomed confrontation. She had spent a period of time at a Bhagwan Shree Rajneesh community, which sees conflict as a means of freeing people from social conditioning, and waking them up (Thompson and Heelas 1986). Such influences were evident in her social interactions, which alienated a lot of people in Glastonbury.

One day, towards the end of my stay in Glastonbury, Jill started to get irritated because I did not know how to use the printer. A deadline was approaching and the atmosphere was becoming increasingly strained. My lack of knowledge was effectively the straw that broke the camel's back, and Jill became very angry with me,

> I'm amazed at you, you've spent all these years at a university and yet you don't know how to use a printer. Can't you learn? Honestly, you don't seem to have any sense of personal direction, you always seem to have to be taken through something as if I am teaching you, as if this is a 'tutorial'.

This was a familiar jibe at my position in the academic world, which was Jill's usual line of attack whenever any conflict between us arose. She continued,

> All you need to do is put the printer on; how are we going to reach this deadline? I can't cope – all these years you've spent at a university have repressed you, and this should be your chance to let go and find your true self.

On to my mental state, then, Jill projects her frustration and annoyance. She justifies her anger, not through me being technically incompetent with a computer programme, but as being warranted because of my maladjusted internal condition.

While in Glastonbury I realised that the way I thought about the idea of projection was influenced very strongly by my own personal involvement in conflict. Therefore it was important to check my understanding of the notion, and I did so with a knowledgeable third party. I asked him to elaborate on projection in his terms and to explain its role in social dynamics in Glastonbury. He took my understanding a step further,

> In projection you take something which is objective and you place a subjective value onto it. But in Glastonbury people act on a meta-level with projection. They are conscious of what projection is. So, while most people just project, in Glastonbury 'projection' is part of the language and people start manipulating and projecting their projections.

By this reasoning Jill is engaging in a double projection. When she associates my incompetence with the printer with my lack of personal direction, this, on her part, is conscious projection. A manipulation of the idea of projection is taking place here (thus Jill justifies her anger). But projection is occurring at another level as well, and in Jill's case we may reveal this as being similar to Sarah's projection in the previous example. At this level Jill's anger will be understood as stemming from her own fears about technology. Jill may be barely aware of it, but she projects these fears onto me, and so it is that I come to be on the receiving end of her displeasure.

Our comment is that, just as New Age ideas about health link the well-being of one's physical body to spiritual and mental well-being, so, by the idea of projection, conflict situations are explained in terms of the personality states of the people concerned. This means that potentially acrimonious debates on the facts of such situations (for example, as to whether my lacking certain technical skills made me poorly suited for working in a newspaper office) are set to one side. But this is not all, for ideas relating to projection also capitalise on, and so reinforce, important ideas (mentioned earlier in this chapter) about the malleability of personality. As Jill's comments to Ruth indicate, especially when one throws off mainstream shackles one's personality – certainly in the long term – is eminently changeable.

Conclusion

The principle of individual autonomy dominates New Age social interactions, yet New Agers construe the human individual as an inherently social being. Western mainstream conceptions, by contrast, are very different. As Marilyn Strathern puts it, thanks to the experience of the industrial process, mainstreamers conceptualise the human person as individuated – sealed off, even – in relation to fellow humans (Strathern 1987b: 281–2). Only outside the West do societies incorporate mutuality, or relatedness, as an essential component of what it is to be human. New Age thinking on the matter situates it clearly in the non-Western camp.

The contrast with the mainstream invites the question, again, of how to explain New Age social organisation in Glastonbury. Such social organisation is unlikely to have been determined by the needs of cooperation since, as people go about their lives in the town, not much cooperation occurs (Chapter 7). Egalitarianism, autonomy and the downplaying of formal roles together smack strongly of communitas. Yet the contrast with the mainstream suggests an alternative. New Age social organisation may take the form it does largely for contemporaneous political reasons, namely to express social principles counter-cultural to the mainstream. This is something Chapter 11 adjudicates on.

Notes

1. *The Way of the Goddess*. Authoress unknown. Earthsong Press, California.
2. Kathy Jones, *The Goddess in Glastonbury*. Ariadne Publications, Glastonbury, 1990, p. 5.
3. Comment, Ann Morgan, *The Glastonbury Times*, Summer 1990, p. 4.

7

Work: the Spiritual Task

Non-mainstream principles inform the organisation of work in the Alternative Community in Glastonbury. This is important to note, since it makes the point that New Age individualism with regard to matters of economic life is very different from the individualism that informs Western industrial capitalism. In the context of work New Agers enjoy remarkable autonomy regarding conduct, and this autonomy is different in kind from that which colours 'Western economic man'. With the focus on the Western mainstream, Macpherson captured this difference very well some time ago, when he observed that 'individuals defined as choice makers in the (Western) market are managed and manipulated – the choices they make are those that producers wish them to make' (1964: 496). Thus in the mainstream, the individualism evident in choosing to abandon work in favour of a meditation session, or in electing to pursue a lifestyle based totally around subsistence preferences, is definitely not a valued option. By contrast, New Agers, unconstrained by market priorities, positively entertain a far wider range of economic goals, precisely including meditation and subsistence.

But there is something else distinctive about New Age participation in work, which refers to the quality of participation itself. A recurrent theme in this chapter concerns the New Age emphasis on spiritual appropriateness regarding how one makes a living. Merely to state that New Age work patterns embrace a broader range of economic goals than the mainstream is clearly inadequate to grasp the significance of such a value. The salience of spiritual values regarding work clearly awaits explanation.

'Hands to work and hearts to God', runs an old Shaker proverb. The Shakers, whose utopian communities peaked in number in the late nineteenth century, mainly in North America, famously extolled hard work as a way by which the individual became closer to God – a doctrine to which the Shakers' finely crafted furniture and buildings, produced at the zenith of the movement, pays tribute. No such maxim exists in the Alternative Community in present-day Glastonbury, also essentially a utopian community, though there are many artists and craftspeople living in the town. Thus New Agers rail against what they see as an overemphasis upon work as such, coupled with losing the ability to play, which they insist is one of the chief problems of larger British society. When Ruth Prince was in Glastonbury, a major concern expressed by people in the Alternative Community was the problem of earning a living within the larger capitalist framework in a way that was consistent with such beliefs. For some New Agers, moreover, the context for this, which had long been causing them some considerable distress, was the fact that, while they desired in this way to live 'apart' from mainstream society, they nevertheless remained economically dependent on it in the shape of the fortnightly dole (i.e. government social security) cheque. Hence the importance, to which most New Agers in the town were becoming greatly attached, of the development of an independent New Age economic infrastructure. Thanks to the endeavours of certain individuals and groups, this, in 1990, was slowly beginning to evolve.

In this chapter, we begin by offering some respondents' views about work which emerged during conversations in Glastonbury. Then we introduce the idea of 'economic infrastructure'. This concept, enunciated in the Alternative Community itself, has distinct theoretical underpinnings and meanings, informed particularly by the writings of the economist, E.F. Schumacher, which have been very influential among New Agers since the 1970s (Schumacher 1973). With a series of case studies we exemplify how, as it has emerged in the Alternative Community, such an infrastructure has taken on a highly individualistic character. This, it will be seen, includes the development, in Glastonbury, of a vibrant 'informal economy'. Finally we discuss the notions of 'manifestation' and 'prosperity consciousness', twin doctrines which, for New Agers, serve as a justification of, and legitimacy for, the material accumulation which, as a distinctive New Age economy starts to flourish, inexorably seems to occur; manifestation and prosperity consciousness is an ideology of accumulation without exploitation.

Attitudes to Work

The individualistic ethos is readily apparent in people's attitudes to work within Glastonbury. Corresponding with this, the jobs people hold in the Alternative Community, and the manner in which they hold them, varies enormously. However, the need to earn a living and at the same time practise a spiritually attuned lifestyle, is replete with contradictions, and, when Ruth was in the town, this was a growing subject of discussion.

Among the New Agers in Glastonbury, there was a continuum of involvement in the mainstream economy. At the one extreme, some people in the Alternative Community managed to hold full-time mainstream jobs, for example as teachers, office-workers or social workers. This may be seen as a reflection of the permeable boundary in Glastonbury between the Alternative Community and the larger British society (Chapter 4). But better it reflects the existence of situational ethnicity. Judging by the circumstances of these people, the cultural boundary between the New Agers and the mainstream continued to persist the while that, day in and day out, a stream of individuals moved across it, as if by osmosis, from one side to the other, and back (Barth 1969).

On the whole, however, the more that people were involved in the Alternative movement the keener they were to explore means of earning a living independently of the organisations and institutions of larger British society. Thus one person had worked as a computer programmer for a large mechanical parts firm. But she had often felt a strong disparity between her obligations at work and her spiritual life at home, saying she was uncomfortable in the work environment. Then she got a new job with an environmentally-oriented organisation, and she said she felt more positive and able to integrate the two. However within six months she had given in her notice and bought a ticket to Asia in order to follow the spiritual quest more fully. Another woman had trained as a teacher, and worked in a comprehensive school in the Midlands. After going through a course of healing, she said she wanted to give up teaching and become a healer herself with the National Federation of Spiritual Healers. A further example of this was a man who worked as a chemist but was at the same time training part-time to become an acupuncturist, intending, once trained, to give up the chemist's job completely. These people, representative of those in Glastonbury who sought a job lifestyle consistent with New Age values, would often invoke the term 'spiritually attuned'.

By this they meant that they were looking for the sort of employment which expresses and 'nurtures' their spiritual self, or their 'deep self'. This deep self reflects the New Age holistic person. In the context of the holistic person the individualistic ethos which pervades New Age practices generally takes on, in the domain of work, a specific character. As we explain shortly, nurturing the spiritual self invites, in the context of work, a profound emphasis on the value of self-reliance.

Albeit that working in the mainstream was not widely desired and was ideally to be avoided, there remains the question of how people in Glastonbury conceptualised a mainstream job as a daily experience. It is clear that for many people such experience had little or no intrinsic value. It was important, if at all, merely as a means to make some money, and as such it was felt that one could be happy washing dishes or working in a factory because that was not the focal point of one's life. Others claimed, however, that though apparently meaningless, a mainstream job could have something to teach them, even if only in a negative sense. One person, who was employed in a factory and took this view, told Ruth,

> Spiritual happiness doesn't depend on your occupation, people place far too much emphasis in life on success. I feel the dependence in life upon one thing, directing your energies towards just one thing, is out of accordance with nature. In fact I think that the emphasis upon goal and success are actually responsible for many of the atrocities in the world such as running roughshod over civilisations, destroying natural resources and being out of harmony with ourselves and other people. For the people of Northern Tibet they don't have this ethos and yet they lead their lives fully.

There was a further category of people in Glastonbury, who, in the field of jobs and employment, took a highly uncompromising view about the larger society. With respect to people in this category, the boundary between the mainstream and the New Age on the matter of work was very strong: for them, the dole amounted to their sole economic engagement with the mainstream. These people's complete dislike and distrust of conventional job roles throws into relief the difference between mainstream economic life and New Age beliefs regarding the emphasis of the latter upon the spiritual. Their image of the mainstream was that of a nine-to-five workday, an inflexible job structure, and a high income which traps one with material possessions and a grossly inflated standard of living. In the mainstream, they would point out, the employment situation is generally one where the person is working for a hierarchically structured capitalist organisation, which treats people as human fodder rather than as individuals. Such an opinion resonates with Marx's theory of alienation, though, consistently with the non-political worldview the New Age movement has adopted, none of the people in Glastonbury heard speaking like this ever mentioned Marx. A better observation is that this sort of talk explains very well why, among New Agers more generally, the individualistic ethos, in the domain of work, connotes the value of self-reliance. For the New Ager the point about capitalist organisation is that, because it neglects the individual's spiritual integrity, it stands as the enemy of the idea of the holistic person. Capitalism, treating the worker as barely human, thus denies the importance of both human agency and self-direction; therefore the New Age, by way of opposition, must celebrate them. Hence the New Age doctrine that the individual's economic fortunes and strategy should rest in his or her own hands, and, correspondingly, that long-term relationships of economic dependency should be shunned. We have seen already this value of self-reliance to be manifest in the scope New Agers enjoy to engage economically with the mainstream as much or as little as suits the individual concerned. And in the discussion, to come, on both the New Age economic infrastructure and the informal economy, it is clearly evident with regard to New Agers' relationships with mainstreamers and among themselves.

New Age thinking about work as an idea underscores all these various conceptualisations. The notion of work, by definition as something compartmentalised from the rest of one's life, was something which many respondents distrusted greatly, associating it firmly with the larger British society. Ruth had a conversation with one man about different types of occupation, and he commented that he would like her job because she seemed able to wander round and be able to do what she liked when she liked [projection of an aimless anthropologist!]. He said,

> My problem with making a living is that I can't tie myself down, I can't take someone else dictating to me a specific two days to work [he had recently lost a casual job]. I see the work trap as illegal, it's a commitment which ties you down to all sorts of things you weren't aware of before, like getting a mortgage. If I were to set up a block of gold in the street surrounded by a fence, and once you entered that fence you were trapped there with the door closing behind you for the rest of your life, would that be legal?

The boundary between the Alternative Community and the mainstream society is both exemplified and reproduced by this sort of attitude. New Agers, negatively stereotyping the mainstream 'other', are able to establish an image of all that they do not want, and thus develop a positive picture of their own distinctive values. The rejection of 'work' as a separate category of activity is a consequence of this. Ann Morgan, in an article in *The Glastonbury Times*, continues with this theme, and develops it further in the direction of a positive alternative,

> The need to earn a 'living' has become paramount in our consumerist society, to the extent that we have become stressed. We are out of touch with our bodies and our emotions, and have become focused on the mental task of keeping up with the 'rat race'. We work like stink and are often too tired to play, except slumped in front of the telly or getting 'out of it' in the pub.
>
> Green consciousness means honouring ourselves as part of the physical and spiritual world. It's not just the earth that needs healing but us too.
>
> We need to relax and play as much as we need to work, even though it does seem as if we are in the middle of the third world war, fighting to protect the very planet we live on.[1]

Certainly there was a great emphasis, in the newspaper office where Ruth helped, upon what was considered to be the 'false' distinction between work and play that was seen to exist in the wider society. In this office the prevailing ethos emphasised the rejection of strict boundaries between 'work life' and 'life outside', and it also stressed, among other things, that with one's work colleagues one should enjoy positive relationships. The development of friendships was considered to be part of a proper work process, as was giving oneself time to stop and have conversations, or being permitted the spontaneity of leaving the office and climbing the Tor on a sunny afternoon, even if it meant delaying the particular task at hand. This repeats itself in other New Age settings, such as the Findhorn commune where, while people generally work long hours, when someone declares that they 'need space' and so takes time off, everyone else must accept this with equanimity whatever they really think (Pepper 1991: 142). However in the newspaper office in Glastonbury, it was noticeable that as deadlines approached such an ethos was not quite so prevalent. This reminds Ruth of Glastonbury in summer 1987 when local celebrations for the Harmonic Convergence were being organised, and there was the suggestion that an ex-army officer be brought in to make sure the preparations were completed on time. (This ensured the resignation of at least one key helper.)

It is interesting that, overall, New Age attitudes to work closely resemble those that have been reported from many non-Western societies. Thus in their famous study of the economy of the Tiv of central Nigeria, the Bohannans report:

> *Tom* means work. But there is no Tiv word for the . . . meanings of the English word 'labour': 'an instance of bodily or mental toil, especially when painful or compulsory.' . . . The opposite of *tom* is not 'play' among the Tiv, but rather 'laziness' . . . (Bohannan and Bohannan 1968: 65)

Albeit that many of those Ruth spoke to in Glastonbury said they would prefer to live independently of the larger state structure, it was common, as has been noted, for people to be supported by social security payments. In the Travelling Community, in particular, where people uphold a particularly strong individualist and independent ethos, there is a clear contradiction between the determined aim as far as possible to live 'outside of society' and a person's economic dependence upon the state. In general, members of the Alternative Community in Glastonbury recognised such a disparity between ideals and reality. It was a continual topic of discussion, debate and controversy. Both the settled New Agers and the Travellers were trying to find ways of earning their living and 'getting off the dole' but, as they would often complain, the leap between the two is hard to cross, and it is not helped by the fact that the legal penalties for 'cash in hand' work are severe. Accordingly, the search has been to develop a distinctively New Age economic infrastructure.

Economic Infrastructure

From summer 1987, when Ruth first went to Glastonbury to do research, through to 1989 and 1990, when she was there for a much longer period, the physical outlook of the town changed considerably. Walking down the main street in 1990 it soon became obvious that the number of shops selling what are awkwardly termed New Age, or alternative, products, had doubled over the past three years. Mostly sited towards the bottom of the High

Street, leading to a top/bottom division of 'straight' versus 'alternative' enterprises, such shops enjoyed a wide range of business, variously purveying organic and whole foods, recycled products, clothes, jewellery, decorative furnishings, statuettes of earth goddesses, perfume oils, Celtic shields, crystals, ritual swords, and books; some shops doubled as therapy centres and cafés. One member, who had himself opened a shop front on the High Street, commented on this trend,

> The Alternative Community needs to find a way to support itself; to survive we have to develop an economic infrastructure. There's a growing alternative tourist trade in Glastonbury – people visiting the town as a sacred site and for its reputation as being part of the alternative movement. This is replacing the traditional tourist trade of coachloads of visitors to the abbey and we need to tap into that.

'Tapping in' on the 'alternative' tourist trade, and 'developing an economic infrastructure': these were the Alternative Community's key concepts relating to its struggle to earn a living consistent with its beliefs. Economic infrastructure essentially refers to an economic process rather than to a body of institutions – though the presence of 'alternative' shops and businesses is clearly a physical indication of this process. It connotes an independently self-sustaining economic system, existing alongside the mainstream economy and operating in accordance with New Age values. Directing and justifying such a system are powerful intellectual ideas, upon which New Agers call, which impart a distinctiveness to the particular economic activity which the system implies. There are two key bodies of thought here. The first is Schumacher's text, 'Buddhist Economics', which has been highly influential in green politics, Deep Ecology and 'alternative economics' since the mid-1970s (Schumacher 1973: 44–51). The second is the notion of the 'informal economy', first developed by Keith Hart to describe key dimensions of economic activity in urban West Africa (Hart 1973). In the next section, these ideas will be illustrated with some Glastonbury case studies; but first the ideas themselves.

Schumacher's articles and lectures over twenty years and more have inspired and influenced the environmental movement to the degree that a college devoted to the pursuit of 'environmental' thinking has been opened in his name, and 'small is beautiful' – Schumacher's aphorism, conveying his advocacy of small-scale technology in economic development – has entered common parlance. Familiar to virtually everyone in Glastonbury, Schumacher's economic ideas have entered the standing of holy grail among members of the Alternative Community in the town. 'Buddhist Economics' outlines Schumacher's attitude towards work and earning a living; the author begins by explaining the title,

> Right Livelihood is one of the requirements of the Buddha's Noble Eightfold Path. It is clear, therefore, that there must be such a thing Buddhist Economics. (1973: 44)

For Schumacher the logic of the modern mainstream economy is the minimisation of labour, the maximisation of short-term production, and the use of people as tools; in this economy, moreover, consumption is the sole end purpose of economic activity. Right Livelihood, Schumacher argues, should in contrast be based on small-scale enterprises, where 'the aim should be to obtain the maximum of well-being with the minimum of consumption'. (ibid.: 48). An intrinsic element of Right Livelihood is what Schumacher calls the Buddhist approach to work,

> The Buddhist point of view takes the function of work to be at least threefold; to give a man a chance to use and develop his faculties; to enable him to overcome his ego-centeredness by joining with other people in a common task; and to bring forward the goods and services needed for a becoming existence...To organise work in such a manner that it becomes meaningless, boring, stultifying, or nerve-wracking for the worker would be little short of criminal; it would indicate a greater concern with goods than with people, an evil lack of comparison and a soul destroying degree of attachment to the most primitive side of this-worldly existence. (ibid.: 45)

This three-pronged position on work is replicated in many of the attitudes heard expressed in Glastonbury. Firstly, people in the town were looking for work which was creatively satisfying – for the individual. Thus 'conventional job roles' were often distrusted because they suppressed the individually innate and creative spirit. For this reason, a flexible attitude to work – an attitude careful not to inhibit the human spirit – was favoured, and prevailed. Ruth's own experiences in working with New Age enterprises and events in Glastonbury, mentioned already, confirm this. Perhaps epitomising them was the advice she received when helping in an office to prepare for the Harmonic Convergence of 1987, where she was told to come in 'when you feel moved to' or 'with the flow'. Schumacher's second observation – about overcoming 'ego-centeredness' – is particularly

interesting in relation to Glastonbury, for it highlights the complementary relationship between individualism and community in the
ideology of the New Age movement. Thus in the Alternative Community in the town the notion of community and working together
was very strong, and yet work was a highly individualistic matter,
with, for example, most New Age enterprises being owned and
managed by just one or two people, though sometimes casually
employing one or two others. The salient point here was that
the Alternative Community considered itself to be a caring community, and this demanded that New Age enterprises be considerate
in respect of their impact on other members of the Community.
The third prong of Buddhist economics – bringing forward the goods
for a 'becoming existence' – is highly pertinent in respect of the
Alternative Community, for it underpins the stance against materialism and consumerism that was strongly emphasised in Glastonbury, and also the recognition, which many New Agers in the town
clearly expressed, of the need to develop an economic infrastructure
which is 'sound', and not based upon ecological or human exploitation.

In the context of an 'alternative' infrastructure in Glastonbury,
'informal economy' refers to a body of economic practices which
have gradually evolved as burgeoning immigration has swelled
the Alternative Community's numbers. As occurs in many areas of
Britain where low-income populations are concentrated, people in
the Alternative Community would stretch out their incomes by
taking on and combining, concealed from the surveillance of
mainstream fiscal institutions, different forms of work and economic support. Ullrich Kockel, writing about New Agers who
have emigrated to the West Coast of Ireland, maintains that the
idea of informal economy in such a context should be understood
as encompassing more than matters of tax evasion, to include the
following positive features: non-monetarized exchange [barter],
occupational pluralism, lack of commercialisation and market orientation, and primary goals other than utility or profit.[2] These features ring true for the basic economy of the Alternative
Community in Glastonbury, although, that said, in relation to certain luxury goods shops, such as those selling items like 'alternative' ornaments and handmade shoes at high prices, some
mainstream ideas, not excluding the profit motive, were becoming
increasingly accepted. Thus barter – the swapping of goods and
services in a strategic way according to need – occurred frequently. For example, in one office the main tenant allocated half

the space to a man running a word processing and accountancy service, and in return received two days per week free word processing. Occupational pluralism, where individuals work part-time in a variety of occupations requiring different skills, was certainly common. Thus a person might work in a bar (or a café, or a shop) and perhaps also make a small income as a musician, gardener or healer. This was something many people applauded, for the reason that it gives a person the chance to explore, and take full advantage of, different aspects of his or her personality. The further dimensions of informal economy were more evident in the recently established High Street shops and other, properly constituted, businesses. These enterprises' goals were invariably a little less than solely commercial, as the case studies below illustrate.

The various types of New Age business enterprise in Glastonbury, each one developed through shared discussion and the exchange of ideas as well as on the strength of individual initiatives, constituted the growth point in the New Age economic infrastructure in the town in 1990. The ideological context of these enterprises was submitting oneself to work which nurtured the inner self, which implied a commitment to throw oneself as far as possible to the mercy of one's own personal resources. However an interesting fact here is that to set up their businesses, not a few people had taken advantage of the Enterprise Allowance scheme set up by Margaret Thatcher's government in the 1980s. With the consequence of small businesses, free market basic wages and the ethos of individualism one might be forgiven for seeing the bottom of Glastonbury High Street as a perfect exemplification of the Thatcherite dream! Yet the case studies which follow do not tell this story, for, as hinted already, these were not standard capitalist enterprises. Their rationale would appear to revolve more around making a living than making a profit, for they commonly incorporate strongly informal and even overtly spiritual dimensions which seem to nullify capitalistic ideology and logic. Above all, flexibility informs the organisation of these enterprises: there is overgenerosity, and there is apparent stinginess; there is ingenious self-reliance, and there is concern for providing opportunities for others; there is interest in accumulating money and material resources, and there is ideology which states that the means by which money and material resources accumulates should avoid the need directly to exploit others.

Case Studies

Ruth Prince studied a number of Glastonbury enterprises in greater or lesser depth. But as regards people's financial situation it was often difficult to get even basic information, largely because the sorts of questions one needed to ask were inappropriate by the standards of New Age culture. People were in general far more interested in talking about the delights of organic tomatoes or the dreams they had the previous night, than how they managed to pay the rent. However, the following case studies amount to a representative sample, and display quite well both the types of enterprise that were emerging and how people were structuring them as the enterprises developed. Virtually all these enterprises, as has been intimated already, are businesses operated by one or two people on ostensibly market principles with a strong entrepreneurial flavour, though with rather varying emphases on profit.[3] At a superficial glance, as we shall see, 'enterprise allowance culture' might indeed be an apt description of such activities. Yet at the same time such enterprises clearly incorporate distinctively New Age meanings. The cases are all slightly fictionalised.

A Newsletter and Information Publication

This enterprise was devoted to 'networking', the making of contacts with spiritually-attuned folk in other places, which in the New Age movement is considered to be a vitally important part of 'spreading the light'. A combined newsletter and information publication, the enterprise used to be based in Totnes in Devon, another focal point of New Age activity in England, but in February 1990 the two owners moved to Glastonbury; in Glastonbury it was run from the owners' home, so this cut down on expenses. The publication consisted of a magazine, which came out three times a year and was free. It had a very short editorial section, and space was mostly taken up by the advertising which supported it. The newsletter's function was principally to disseminate information about the 'human potential movement' through southwest England. The owners also published a mailshot which came out once a month advertising local events. In addition, they would do the layout for similar small scale publications, varying their fees according to the nature of the venture concerned and what it could afford. Thus they did the layout for Glastonbury's 'alternative' newspaper with a basic fee of £100, whereas another printer had previously been charging £185. The jobs they took on, the owners said, depended very much on whether they 'warmed to them', and they were prepared to work through weekends and in the evening to get something done.

A High Street Café

This was a vegan café and bakery in the High Street whose owner was also a caterer and supplier of vegan food; those employed by the enterprise sometimes referred to themselves as 'food evangelists'. Over the years the enterprise had changed from being a restaurant to a take-away, and the owner altered the image quite regularly. Around five women were involved in the café's daily operations, and they lived together as well, pooling their incomes to feed and look after their children. They made their own tofu and cakes/pastries which they supplied to the local wholefood shop, and they also distributed their goods as far afield as London.

The café took on frequent casual labour, paying £2 an hour (much the same as the lowest wage levels being paid in the mainstream at that time), and Ruth took a job there for a while. Others worked there washing dishes in exchange for food. The five women regarded themselves as a family, and one of them explained that they were basically a group of single mothers who had clubbed together to beat the poverty trap so that they could run a crèche, share in bringing up children, etc. Also, thanks to their involvement in the business they were able to run vehicles and give their children things like fruit juice to drink.

A Spiritual Community and a Guest House

The Ramala Centre was run by an airline pilot and his wife who had received a message that they were 'to take the light to Glastonbury'. So they came, and found a huge ramshackle old house, which they managed to buy for almost half the asking price. Their finances, they claim, were largely secured through the grace of external intervention: through 'manifestation', money had 'come into their lives'. The concept of manifestation, a distinctly New Age notion, connotes a spiritual process whereby needed resources are deemed to materialise expeditiously as free gifts. It is mentioned in the literature on the Ramala Centre, entitled the 'Story of Ramala',

In the first year alone over 700 visitors came to the Ramala Centre and David and Ann were introduced to the Law of manifestation. As work needed to be done in the house, and that need was expressed, so people appeared at the front door to fulfil that need.

The people who came to the centre would live and work as part of the community in return for a small salary. The guest house and bed and breakfast side of the enterprise was where the more 'prestigious' members of the New Age movement would stay when they came to Glastonbury. The charge per person per night was set at a normal commercial rate.

An Example of a Mixed Income

This instance is of a man in Glastonbury, very keen on holistic ideas, who believed it possible to combine widely varying economic ventures. In his case such ventures ranged from the provision of computer services, through to badge-making and small-scale farming – all to form a mutually supporting and coherent enterprise. He also believed very strongly that work and play should not be segregated, and that we should simultaneously be involved in both. We should feel free to 'play in our work', and equally we should strongly resist the 'nine-to-five mentality', for this means closing ourselves off from work after hours.

The man owned a field on which he lived in a trailer. In 1990 he was taking a course on permaculture which he hoped to implement on the field. Also, he eventually intended to run weekend workshops on the field on 'new man' topics. It is believed that he bought the land with money he inherited from his parents. As to the computer services side of the enterprise, he rented an office in Glastonbury for which he paid around £30 per week. He would design and print New Age newsletters and other small publications. But he said that this side of things did not support itself and so he was moving to share office space with a friend for nothing, who in return would get free access to his computer.

A Spiritual Healing Centre

This enterprise, mentioned in the previous chapter, was set up mainly by two healers who originally had operated from their home, or else had attended clients in their homes, and who had then rented a room in Glastonbury to hold weekly meditation and healing workshops for which there was a voluntary charge of £1. In late winter, 1990, the two healers announced that they needed £3,000 to set up new premises. To finance the move they were appealing for money to add to their own fund-raising. This was to come from straightforward donations and also from 'manifestations'. By Easter 1990 the healers were able to move to the new premises, and they held a raffle and a weekend of concerts and workshops to further raise money. By mid-1990 this healing centre had been running for three years with a regular attendance, though it had moved venues more than once. People in the town had evidently come to assume a long-term commitment towards sustaining and maintaining it.

A High Street Shop

Now a High Street shop-front business, this enterprise started life in a tent in the nearby village of Molesworth, and then expanded considerably. In 1990, it consisted of a recycled photocopying, printing and stationery store, in which a variety of publications authored by the owner and others on the subject of Travellers, festivals and sacred sites were sold. The man who owned the business employed people to work in the shop at a flat rate of £10 a day. This works out at less than £2 an hour, and well below mainstream wages for comparable jobs at this time.

Manifestation and Prosperity Consciousness

Sheltered by a rowan tree in the courtyard of the Glastonbury Experience, and ensconced on a carved and ornate wooden seat, New Agers in the town would often pass many long hours, especially during the summer, occasionally buying cold drinks or a salad from the nearby café but mostly playing the guitar, chatting and watching people pass by. Travellers rested with their dogs, and the scent of incense would flood the air as tourists from outside the town strayed in cautiously. The Glastonbury Experience is an open space. Above the courtyard and behind the balcony are a maze of rooms, many of which are used for workshops, yoga, meditation meetings and individual therapy sessions.

As to the economy of these services, some of them would be free, or those leading them would ask for donations. For many others, however, there would be a minimum fee. And this being so, down in the courtyard people there would be complaining about people charging money for spiritual teachings. In short, within the Alternative Community there existed an uneasy marriage between spirituality and materialism. Many healers had to charge in order to support themselves and continue healing; however, particularly among those who could not afford to pay, there was a feeling of bitterness, along with complaints about the exploitation of spiritual energy for personal gain.

Money, materialism and spirituality; it is evidently a difficult matter for many involved in the New Age movement to combine the three, and especially so for people providing specialist services. There is a distinct echo in other New Age scenes regarding the controversy surrounding the healers in the Glastonbury Experience. For example, in America, New Age firewalking leaders, who make quite substantial sums of money from weekend instructional retreats, agonise over how this squares with the 'countercultural', and therefore anti-capitalist, ideology (Danforth 1989: 282–3). And in Findhorn, resident members of the commune reflect on the high charges imposed on guests who have come to share the Findhorn experience, reasoning that since manifestation should ensure the commune's material well-being, such charges ought to be unnecessary (Clark 1992: 102).

In Glastonbury people approached the problem in a variety of ways. Thus some healers would simply ask for donations, whilst others (including the retreat centres) had a sliding scale of charges. But yet others charged quite large fees, seemingly without any scruple. Charging for this sort of work was sometimes explicitly justified on the grounds that having to raise money to attend healing is intrinsic to the challenge and thus part of the preparation for treatment. Thus advertising literature for one course read, 'Manifesting the fee of £45 is part of the learning – affirm that God is your supply – ask Divine Mind to support your intention'.

There has accordingly developed a New Age philosophy which, in distinctively New Age terms, wittingly or unwittingly legitimises the accumulation of money; this is 'prosperity consciousness'. Much as physical immortality lies at the extremes of New Agers' attitudes to health, prosperity consciousness arouses very great controversy in the Alternative Community in Glastonbury. It rests on the idea that one can have a positive attitude towards attaining, and living with, material wealth. Contrary to the prevalent anti-accumulation ethos that hangs over much of the New Age movement, prosperity consciousness effectively disposes of the guilt many people feel at their own consumerist lifestyle. One respondent felt it represented the Californian rather than the European element of the New Age, and whilst Ruth was in Glastonbury the idea aroused only very modest interest.

New Age ideas relating to the cosmos (Chapter 5) underwrite the concept of manifestation and permit one to elaborate on the meaning of prosperity consciousness. According to New Agers, transcendent energies are benignly at work when those who need resources find, thanks to manifestation, that they have become blessed with them. Prosperity consciousness is the explicit ethical counterpart of this. It expresses the idea that, by virtue of one's personal spiritual attunement one can attract money to oneself. Thus Stuart Wilde, known as a 'teacher of financial assertiveness and practical mysticism', has authored a book entitled *The Trick About Money is Having Some.* In an important interview in the magazine *Kindred Spirit*, he argues that money is a necessary factor 'to drive the motor of your spirituality',

> Some people say 'How can you be so commercial Stuart?', but it is nothing to do with being commercial, it is all to do with emotion. It is like how do you feel powerful and resonant and at one and at peace with yourself if some guy's trying to cut the electricity off?[4]

He goes on to say:

> In other words, if this spirituality and the balance and the kindness and the softness work then in theory the universe has got to open up to you and give you what you want . . . financially, because if it does not then you are doing something terribly wrong.[5]

There is clearly a highly individualistic ethic behind prosperity consciousness in that it essentially describes how acquiring money fits in with the well-being of the self. The goal of Stuart Wilde's teachings is to make people into 'latter day metaphysical warriors', to raise their personal power, create their own 'battle plan', and take on the material world and make it work for them.

But in taking on the material world Wilde is recommending a distinctively non-mainstream entrepreneurship. His broader 'therapy', which contextualises prosperity consciousness, recommends an extended period of time during which individuals withdraw themselves from concern with the affairs – economic, political and material – of the rest of the world, and instead concentrate upon the self.

The number one lynchpin of what I teach is detachment. So you dry clean your emotion as much as possible, given that you cannot detach from everything because you are still here. But you detach from the emotion, so you are not really into who wins the F.A. Cup, you are not really into whether or not they bring in the Poll Tax, you detach. If you percentile that over a period of years you can watch the whole of the world go past and it does not make you callous, because in a way I see detachment as infinite love, because you allow everything to be without disturbing it.[6]

Wilde does not comment upon the possible consequences of a large number of people following such a philosophy of detachment, indeed he does not address the question of collective action at all. This is consistent with what is said by another proponent of prosperity consciousness, Leonard Orr, the physical immortalist. Responding to the question, put to him when he visited Glastonbury, as to whether prosperity consciousness was not just greed, Orr declared,

At the moment when one needs shelter you stop picking food off the trees, one enters the game of economics. One person having money doesn't necessarily take it away from the other. Every individual chooses whether or not to be greedy, this is not conditioned by how much money they actually have.

One supposes that the logical conclusion of such a philosophy is that when everybody attracts money, there will be a kind of universal abundance. One cannot escape the feeling that there are remarkable similarities here with the ideology of free market capitalism.

End Comment

New Age attitudes to work consist of a package of functionally related ideas, specifically a rejection of mainstream practice, the notion of the spiritually imbued person, and the value of self-reliance. There remain, however, important questions regarding the 'construction' of these activities. These particularly refer to the manner in which the mainstream is conceived: it is stereotyped by New Agers in terms of capitalism and consumerism. With regard to the construction of such a stereotype, the question arises as to the salience of ideas relating to spirituality. Chapter 11 identifies this as a relationship between New Age stereotypes of the mainstream and New Age notions of the holistic person.

Notes

1. 'Comment'. Ann Morgan. *The Glastonbury Times*. November/December 1989.
2. U.Kockel, 'The West is learning, the North is war: reflections on Irish identity between New Age and postmodernity'. Unpublished paper, 1989, p. 4.
3. In the Glastonbury area in 1990 Ruth Prince discovered just two economic enterprises being owned or managed by more than just a couple of people and yet which might be said to be at least peripheral to the Alternative Community: a small food distribution cooperative and the Somerset county-wide organic farmers' cooperative.
4. Interview with Stuart Wilde. *Kindred Spirit*, Autumn, 1990, Totnes, p. 11.
5. ibid., p. 9.
6. ibid., p. 13.

8

Education: the Reincarnated Child

And a woman who held a babe against her
bosom said, Speak to us of Children.
And he said:
Your children are not your children.
They are the sons and daughters of Life's longing for itself.
They come through you but not from you,
And though they are with you yet they belong not to you.
You may give them your love but not your thoughts,
For they have their own thoughts.
(*The Prophet*, Kahlil Gibran)[1]

Education, understood as introducing people, especially children, to a particular mode of social living, and inculcating them with its distinctive priorities and practices, has a paradoxical quality in the New Age context. The emphasis, in the New Age, on personal autonomy stands uneasily beside the desire of the New Age adult to lead the child to appreciate the New Age ideal. New Agers, as will be seen, resolve this by stressing a certain quality in the relation between socialiser and socialised. The New Age situation may be explicated by looking first at the process of education more generally.

Education, in all societies, consists of developing sequences of negotiations between two parties, typically parents and offspring. This suggests that the child, in the educational process, may objectively be specified as an independent agent. But, running counter to this, adults normally exact compliance from the child, thanks to the fact that power and resources lie overwhelmingly on their side. It follows that, at the heart of the educational process, there is a fundamental contradiction with respect to the relationship between socialiser and socialised, which all societies, through their representations of this relationship, must somehow address; their respective social organisations seem very much to control the form such representations take. Thus societies with authoritarian social organisations tend, in their depiction of education, to deny the child's agency altogether: the child, with regard to how he or she thinks and behaves, is conceptualised merely as the adult's (parent's) appendage. In contrast, societies which uphold the value of personal autonomy proclaim exactly the opposite, and go so far as to declare that, in some vital sense, all genuine insights in life lie with the child. In these latter societies, such a complex of understandings means that the child's education may be seen very much as a process of (the child's) self-determination. As might be predicted, such is the situation which obtains in Glastonbury, as the following brief discussion indicates.

In the Alternative Community in Glastonbury, children – even the 'childlike' – enjoyed a high status and positive value. Consistently with New Age spiritual beliefs, which emphasise individual expression and individual creativity, children, as full individuals, were in some crucial sense seen as inherently wise – much as is suggested in the quotation from Kahlil Gibran which heads this chapter. In Glastonbury, in a way that strikingly parallels the respect that New Agers afford non-Western societies, children were often pointed to with a sense of reverence: they had something that the adults have lost. One parent told Ruth Prince,

> We have to let our children develop in such a way that they don't lose this way of being in childhood. Children have a spiritual awareness which we adults ourselves need to rediscover before we can tackle the problems of the world.

In therapy, people often talked about 'rediscovering the child within'.

As to the substance of the childlike characteristics that, in Glastonbury, people sought to sustain in their children or else rediscover in their adult selves, two features stand out. Firstly children were thought of as being more in touch with their emotional selves: children, New Agers would observe admiringly, are quick to express emotion – they let their emotions flow freely. Secondly, and most importantly, children were considered to be more intuitive, and so more open to, and accepting of, the spiritual realm.

Children were seen as being without the doubts, fears and cynicism that trammel most adults; for children, tree spirits are not only possible, they are plausible. It follows that children were considered to be highly appreciative of learning about new, and particularly spiritual, elements in life. Accordingly, when adults talked about 'getting in touch with the child inside', they were referring to expressing emotion freely, living life in its full profusion of dimensions, and being more open to the spiritual world.

Finally, with regard to the context for the development of such ideas, therapeutic goals, not surprisingly, are most important. An example, where the inner child is regarded as crucial, is 'Voice Dialogue', a therapeutic method intended to reveal the 'sub-personalities' present within the one individual. In a magazine article where this was discussed, one of the two therapists who advocated this method described her first experience:

> It was amazing! I was a one-year-old! I had dropped into being this tiny little child who was sort of all curled up inside this cave and never talked to me, had never communicated, had always kept herself to herself, for all those years, 35 years! She had never allowed herself to be with another human being! Very, very little, very tentative, I didn't want to look at him. I just wanted him there, wanted him not to intrude on me, but wanted his warmth there, not to hold me, not to intrude on me, not to talk to me. I just wanted him to be there with me. I was 35, and I hadn't a clue that I had a child like that in me.[2]

We suggest that the New Age idea of child self-determination constitutes a very valuable resource for the movement as a whole. This relates to the New Age's distinctive conception of the nature of the human person. The emphasis, in the New Age, of the inseparability of mind and body stands starkly in opposition to mainstream dualism, and this means that matters to do with the mental or the emotional serve a crucial symbolic function in relation to the New Age movement's anti-mainstream advocacy. It follows, in this context, that ideas specifically to do with children are critically important. This is because these, in at least some respects, are shared as between the New Age and the mainstream, and so serve as potential vehicles of communication between the two sides. Thus in both the New Age and the mainstream the child is considered to be especially emotional and accepting. But by coupling these qualities in the child with other values, such as wisdom and intuition, the New Age upholds an overall conception of the child that the mainstream is going to recognise immediately as extraordinary, and very different. Accordingly, the mainstream stands opposed. There are clear parallels here with the way that the New Age manipulates gender values (Chapter 6).

In this chapter we report on observations in Glastonbury in respect of both the practical and intellectual dimensions of child education. We shall consider how in the socialisation of children the values of a community are self-consciously articulated, and also the complementary fact that in the contact New Age children have with the formal educational institutions of the wider society, the boundaries and conflicts between that society and the Alternative Community are thrown into stark relief.

The household Ruth lived in in Glastonbury consisted only of adults, yet in the Alternative Community generally the presence of children was never far away. Whether sitting in a courtyard café, watching a play or listening to a band in a smoke-filled room, at almost any hour of the day one would look around and see a clutch of children running about absorbed in their own social adventures. The only time children were absent was during meditation meetings or spiritual discussions, yet even this was a point of dispute and contention for some people. With respect to New Agers, to observe the process of socialisation is to witness the inculcation of individualistic values central to involvement in the Alternative Community.

We start by discussing informal education, which refers to the crucial socialising relationship between parents and children. Then, turning to formal education, we begin by presenting a case study of a specialist school run according to New Age ideals. After this we consider the circumstances of New Age children attending the local state school, where relations between the Alternative Community and the mainstream becomes the central issue.

Informal Education – 'Free Beings'

Individualism captures very well the capacities attributed to the younger generation in the Alternative Community in Glastonbury. The essence of the child, in New Age thinking, is as an autonomous being, with an existing personality that only needs nourishment to develop. In Glastonbury such autonomy and individuality was recognised as existing even from before birth. As part of the 'birthing process', it was common, in the town, to hold a small ritual during labour to welcome the person entering the world. This ranged from the simple saying of prayers, to the lighting of incense and to chanting and playing drums. Correspondingly, the Alternative Community was quick to criticise the 'seen and not heard' philosophy of the larger British society – the ethos that children's opinions are unimportant, and not sufficiently worthy of 'adult airspace' to be expressed publicly. As one mother said,

> I had a child five years ago when I was forty so I've had plenty of experience of being an adult and not having a child, but I find British people in general seem to hate children. They send them off to bed as early as possible and seem to avoid contact with them, not like other countries where the children are running around the cafés at 11 pm at night. We don't have to be strict disciplinarians as parents, there are ways of getting our point across creatively without being dogmatic. Some of my friends always let their child interrupt them when they are having a conversation because they believe everything that the child has to say is important and needs to be recognised.

Interestingly, in response to this statement, a man who was not a parent observed,

> I understand what you mean, don't get me wrong, I love having children around, it's just that if a child keeps interrupting I find the energy channels around adults get blocked.

Children in Glastonbury, then, were generally treated as independent agents who, no differently from adults, are capable of making choices to suit themselves, from bed-time to matters of schooling. The child's rights in this regard were clearly expressed. One person commented,

> I think children should be able to choose whether they want to go to school or not. If they don't, why should they be forced into doing it? They can learn as much from a tutor, or even listening to other people and spending time in nature. Not that they even teach them the really important things at school anyway, like how to make a fire with only wet wood.

Likewise, an adolescent in Glastonbury, in an interview published in *The Glastonbury Times* (the town's alternative newspaper), confirmed the fact that the desire for autonomy, and the power to determine one's choices, was well articulated by the young people themselves,

I think that everyone should get a year off from school when they get to about fourteen. It's just a break in the conditioning and it's just when you start finding out about life, and it's good to give the system a break.[3]

The relationship between New Age parents and children in Glastonbury was normally marked by amicability, consistently with the quality of the social relations which obtain more generally in the Alternative Community. Parental discipline was understated and adults would explain to their children that it 'would be a good thing' if they did or did not do a certain thing, rather than directly commanding them ('do this' or 'do that'). Only when a parent was severely fraught would they ever consider hitting a child. In the home, a child's education mostly took the form of negotiation. For example, a request to the child that he or she play outside might be presented as, 'Adam, how would you feel about being outside while I meditate. I really need the space in the creativity room'.

There are quite remarkable parallels here between the New Age and many societies in the non-Western world, especially so with regard to the so-called peaceful societies, including familiar peoples such as the Pygmies of central Africa, the Bushman of southern Africa and the Inuit Eskimo of northern Canada. These societies, disdaining inter-personal conflict and aggression virtually at all costs, take indirect socialisation virtually to its limit. Draper, speaking of the Bushman, comments that in that society adults do not punish or lecture – they soothe and distract, and get the child interested in something else. She adds: no aggression from the parent means that no aggression gets learned by the child (1978: 36–7). Among the South Fore of New Guinea, another peaceful society, there is similar childrearing practice, where the chief strategy when infants appear to be becoming aggressive, is distraction through the gambit of heaping affection upon them (Sorenson 1978: 17). Of interest is that individualism is pervasive in South Fore society, which is something that Sorenson links to parental permissiveness, such that young children, as they explore the world, go virtually unrestricted, pursuing whatever it is that attracts their interest (1978: 19–24). Finally, with regard to Inuit socialisation, Guemple refers to adult–child 'negotiation': as the child investigates the environment, the adult, rather than interfere, should outmanoeuvre and exhort. This, in Guemple's opinion, connects in with Inuit philosophy about the nature of children which holds that the child may be presumed to be socially whole from shortly after birth and therefore requires not so much to be taught as to be guided and directed – thus, in education, adults are considered to be drawing out what the child is deemed to know already (1988: 134, 137). From the Glastonbury evidence presented in this chapter it is evident that, on the matter of child education, New Age philosophy and practice chime in closely with all three of these societies.

As to what underlies 'amicable' child-rearing practices, academic research on the Israeli kibbutz proposes a psychodynamic motive. Thus Elizabeth Irvine (quoted by Spiro [1972: 13–14]) suggests that kibbutz adults are likely to have been rebels in their younger years and so in parenthood find it difficult to take on authoritarian duties since this involves identification with the parents they have rejected. In the kibbutz, as is well-known, responsibility for bringing up children is commonly assumed by the 'community' as a whole. By the kibbutz placing child-rearing in the hands of community specialists, adult kibbutzniks are relieved of the necessity of having to exercise authority themselves, as well as of the fear of alienating their children as they themselves were alienated. In the case of the Alternative Community in Glastonbury, though child-rearing is neither rigidly institutionalised nor indeed a matter of collective responsibility, a similar argument would hold. Much like Israeli kibbutzniks, the New Agers in the town, having committed themselves to a crucially new design for living, are in effect rebels – against their natal families or, more broadly, against the norms prescribed in mainstream society. Moreover, in Glastonbury, children are encouraged to join together into independent peer groups, and this may at least partially be explained by their parents' reluctance to take on the sorts of roles they themselves had previously been alienated by. With the kibbutz in mind, Melford Spiro sums up these sorts of ideas,

> a dominant theme is the maintenance of amicable parent-child relationships. 'We want our children to be our pals', is the way in which this desire may be summed up, and to destroy the barrier that conventionally exists between parents and children. We don't want our children to duplicate our own experiences. We had little in common with our parents and, indeed, we rebelled against them. 'We don't want our children to rebel against us'. (1972: 13–14)

In Glastonbury, formal collective upbringing like that in the kibbutz was, as we have indicated, rare, and the closest that was encountered was the instance of the group of mothers running the café, mentioned in the previous chapter, who lived together and brought up their children collectively in order to 'beat the poverty trap of single parenthood'. However a more diffuse shared responsibility for childrearing was in some measure evident even among people who lived as 'traditional' nuclear families, where it was not uncommon for the children to spend a lot of time away at friends' houses from a very early age.

We noted, at the beginning of this chapter, that education (in its broadest sense) is a most revealing dimension of community life, for in the socialisation of children key social values are clearly exposed. Parents, as they interact with their children, consciously or unconsciously inculcate something of their own experiences and priorities, and perhaps their rebelliousness as well. Correspondingly, children's social attitudes and means of expression reveal what their parents have taught (the school system, the media and age peers are obviously other important influences). Testimony to this is a story a friend recounted of walking down from the Tor behind a woman strolling with her toddler son. The little boy kept stopping, picking up stones, and saying, 'Mummy, what kind of energy is in this stone?'

A similar experience happened to Ruth when flat-hunting. She and her partner, Anthony, arrived at a big old house and rang on the door bell. It was answered by a five-year-old boy who proceeded to show them around the flat, which took up one floor. As Ruth's diary recalls:

'As we climbed the stairs we caught sight of some adults, yet they did nothing more than raise their heads and smile. We felt that how we got on with the child and generally dealt with the situation was being treated as a test of the kind of people we were. At the end of the tour we were brought downstairs to meet the parents who were the owners of the house. The little boy proceeded to sit on my lap and ask several quite personal questions while the parents half-listened and half-talked with Anthony. The boy pressed my stomach and said "do you have a baby in there?" I replied that I didn't, and then he asked "would you like to have a baby in there?" "Someday perhaps", I answered. Then came the next question, "are you going to have a baby with that man there?" He pointed at Anthony. It seemed safest again to reply, "someday perhaps". Without appearing to change his line of inquiry, the boy then moved to the next and final question, "so, do you have any caffeine in you?"'

The image people from his natal home and immediate social circle have of the wider mainstream society accounts for this last question; for many in the Alternative Community, caffeine, seen as the mainstreamers' preferred stimulant, represents mainstream values.

Another example connects in with the ethos of environmental awareness. In the Alternative Community in Glastonbury, Green issues were impressed upon children very strongly. The adolescent boy interviewed in *The Glastonbury Times* (see above) commented, rather amusingly,

> What we're all interested in is the environment. Pretty much everyone's aware of the greenhouse effect. I've stopped using spray cans now for graffiti, unless they're ozone friendly.[4]

In the same interview certain 'alternative' attitudes about mainstream society are again clearly revealed,

> There's a lot of weird people in Glastonbury but there's a hell of a lot of nice people who became Hippies and drop outs. They are not just run of the mill, average housewives, secretaries or business people but they have escaped from that reality.[5]

In Glastonbury, the New Age children's community play was a particularly interesting example of a collective vehicle for inculcating in children the values of parents. The story was set in a town called Vegansville, and was based upon some rulers who ate too much food and nightly gorged themselves in a 'chocolate frenzy'. The players had costumes with big hoops inside to make them look really fat and bloated. Then there were the people who just ate vegetables, who were kind and good. Their lives revolved round notions of love; they were gentle people. But they were dominated by their chocolate loving rulers. Eventually the vegetable eaters won the day and were liberated from the rulers, and everyone lived happily ever after . . .

Formal Education

The laws of the British state, that dictate that children should receive some formal level of education at school or at home, and also a genuine concern that their offspring need professional instruction, mean that the Alternative Community in Glastonbury has to give some thought to the educational institutions of the wider British society. This has often led to both anguish and confrontation

– as will be seen. Thus one woman, to whom Ruth talked about motherhood, said she was torn between bringing up children in a protected environment free from the values of violence and aggression of the outside world, and running the risk of over-protecting them, which in turn might lead them to rebel. Therefore, among the New Agers in the town, alternatives to mainstream schooling have, not surprisingly, been sought. Some people, who could afford it, have sent their children to Rudolf Steiner schools, whose understanding of the role of the educator strikes a sympathetic chord with New Agers, and others have joined together and set up small, independent schools, usually run by parents. But yet others have elected to go with the larger state system, and to have their children educated in mainstream primary or secondary schools.

During the remainder of this chapter we shall first look at a specialist 'alternative' school. Then we shall examine the problems encountered by parents who submitted their children to the state system.

A Specialist School

In Glastonbury, Ruth spoke to many parents with very young children who hoped that a small parent-run primary school might be set up in the town; but in 1990 the only such school in the area was in a nearby village. She came into contact with this school at the end of its first year of operation, which for the school was a period marked by instability since it was still evolving a basic structure. Her involvement with the school was quite limited as she was never present while classes were in progress; there had been a large turnover of teachers during the academic year and the parents felt that to introduce another stranger into the classroom would be to disrupt the children still further. Ruth's information about the school comes from extensive conversations with the adults involved. However what she did learn concurred with accounts about similar projects elsewhere.

> We want to look at the whole and everyone's needs within that whole. In my vision living itself would be an education. It should be about who we are and how we live, a natural and integrated part of what we do. It was industrialism which put up these boundaries between work, education and life.

This was the ethos behind the school and the vision of education voiced by one of the parents, who was also a teacher. One should look at the steps that were taken towards fulfilling such a vision, and how they were reflected in the teaching style in the school.

The administration and organisation of the school was originally in the hands of a group of founder-trustees, some of whom came from an educational background, who desired that education be a more fulfilling process. These people had spent three years considering various ideas before getting together with a group of parents to look for some way to put their ideas into practice. A building was found, which the parents converted into a space suitable for a school, which thereby came into being. There were no mandatory fees, although a donation of £400 per term was asked for, and the remaining monies were raised through fund-raising activities, which the parents organised. In its first year the school was beset by problems of getting, or keeping, professionally trained teachers. In the interim between such teachers as many as seven or eight lay people stepped in, none of whom plugged a gap for very long. One of the teachers gave as the reason for resigning that she felt the Trust was not allowing her enough autonomy. She complained that Trust members were continually interfering and questioning her teaching methods. Then, following a series of similar incidents, the relationship between the Trust and the parents deteriorated, to a point where the Trust withdrew and the school was run solely by parents. Basically the parents had rejected being subordinated to the Trust, and took on the running of the school in order to determine its direction satisfactorily.

The children in this school came from a variety of backgrounds, and from an area up to ten miles around. Some had been unhappy in state schools, and their parents had worried about them and looked for an alternative. At the beginning of the school year there had been eighteen pupils in the school but the numbers had dropped. Ruth was told by a man who was both a teacher in the school and a parent that children were encouraged to share toys, and other resources, and that many of the teaching sessions were held with both children and teachers sitting cross-legged in a circle. When asked about gender roles he said that they endeavoured to reduce them; inevitably the 'usual differences' emerged, but they tried not to encourage them. He also said they aimed to make teaching an interactive task, with the distinction between the teachers and pupils played down. The children were to be viewed with respect, particularly out of regard for their sensitive spiritual awareness. As for recreation, they played no competitive games.

A mode of teaching long out of fashion in mainstream education informed the methods to bring about these sorts of ideals and practices: small classes, teaching by topic rather than by subject discipline, and an emphasis on extensive contact with nature. The school was one big classroom, with only the infants separated from the rest, and the teacher/pupil ratio was high; it was felt easiest, by such organisation, to respond to individual needs, and also to ensure that the children were not restricted to interacting with one age group. Teaching by topic meant that a single theme was looked at from a number of different angles. The Native Americans were a favourite theme: by looking at the structure of the tipi the children were taught geometry, by finding out where the people lived they learned geography, and they learned music by singing Native American chants – sitting in a circle. Another exercise initiated by the school was looking at things from other people's perspectives. A teapot was placed in the centre of a circle, and everybody was told to draw it. Two teachers sitting in different positions in the circle got up and looked at each other's pictures. Then they enacted a small drama in which they asked one another why they had not drawn the same picture. This was intended to show that different people look at things in different ways. As to the importance of having a close relationship with nature this was borne out in weekly visits to a plot of ground where a group of people were living without water or electricity; there the children were given the opportunity to learn that people can and do live without modern conveniences. These occasions also provide children with the chance of running wild in the woods, and for leadership roles to emerge different from those of the classroom.

When Ruth was in Glastonbury the long-term future of the school was uncertain. The parents had decided not to apply for it to be granted official status, nor to follow the demands of the National Curriculum. One problem was that the school only catered for pupils up to the age of eleven, and so most children would have to be streamed off into the state school system. However the parents, when Ruth knew them, were more preoccupied simply with how to keep the present school going.

The following extract from a poem, entitled 'Teacher', was found on the notice board at Park School, Dartington, and printed in *The Glastonbury Times* as representative of how the teacher/pupil relationship ought to be. It represents New Age ideals in Glastonbury very well.

'Teacher'

I will know you.
I will touch you and hold you
and smell and taste and listen
To the noises that you make – and the words, if any.

I will know you.
Every atom of your small, lonely
Aching, raging, hurting Being
Will be known to me
Before I try to teach you
I must first reach you.

And then, when I have come to know you, intimately,
I will insist, gently, gradually, but insist
That you know me.
And later that you trust me
And then yourself.

The State School System

Sarah, aged eight years:

I don't like going to school, everyone's so straight.

Rowan, mother:

When my children go to school I try to dress them so they look as trendy as possible. If they were dressed and looked like a couple of Hippy kids, that just wouldn't be fair on them. Besides, they refuse to wear anything that's a bit Hippy-like, they want to fit in and be like all the other kids.

In Glastonbury and the surrounding area, children whose parents were involved with the Alternative Community stood out to a lesser or greater degree. Children are sensitive to differences among peers, and whether it was a long lock of hair at the back of the neck, the battered old car, the father's pink trousers or long hair, or the tofu in their lunch box, Alternative children in the state schools were not difficult to spot. Also, the local state primary school had been the focus of a particular problem. In recent years a car park situated next to the school became host to several Travellers' vans and buses. The local mainstream newspaper gave vent to accusations of hepatitis and aggressive dogs, and set off a tidal wave of resentment in the town. One of the 'local' mothers with children at the school told Ruth,

> I hate those Travellers and all the Hippies, I do. They just let their dogs run around right next door to where my kids come out of school. And they're all filthy, the kids even. I say live and let live I do, but not with them around, they don't let me just live.

Children from the Alternative Community could not help but absorb such remarks and attitudes, particularly since Glastonbury is situated in a rural area with an otherwise fairly homogeneous mainstream population. However while they were indeed often conspicuously 'different', they seemed to be present in sufficient numbers to withstand much by way of bullying or aggression from other children. Most Alternative children and adolescents passed through the state system happily, and many of those Ruth met were doing well and forming friendships with mainstream children. Confrontation, where it occurred, lay largely in the clash of values between Alternative parents and the school system, though sometimes the children themselves were directly implicated, as the following example illustrates.

The Haircut

This concerned a boy of about eleven who attended the local state school. He had doodled down on a piece of paper an idea for a hair style, and a friend offered to do it for him: the boy started to attend school with a new hair cut. The style was indeed slightly unusual, but it was short and involved no hair dye. His parents were happy with it and thought it would cause no problems. However one of the school teachers noticed it, and the boy was challenged: 'What made you think you could get away with that haircut?' He was sent to the headmaster. *The Glastonbury Times* chose to write up this story as an example of the problems of the Alternative Community with the state school structure. The story was reported in the newspaper under the heading, *Community Education Haircut*,

> He found himself in the Headmaster's office. The Headmaster, who seems fearful of any hint of individuality lest it reached epidemic proportions, pronounced the haircut 'ostentatious'. The boy, therefore, was unfit to socialise with other pupils during breaks and mealtimes. Three options were offered. He could be taken by a staff member to have his

tonsure cut off, be segregated, or go home. He was delivered home that afternoon by the deputy head, to think on advice from the Headmaster 'to score a century at cricket if he wanted to do something different, and laudable.'

The boy's parents were upset with the reaction of the school and chose to support him. They felt the school was being hypocritical since it allowed highlights, perms, and other fashion creations with the aid of hair spray, and yet did not allow creative design. The boy took the situation a step further; as it was reported in *The Glastonbury Times*:

> He had felt vulnerable, that his individuality was threatened and his creativity at risk. He felt in need of protection and wanted to express that symbolically.
> Coming from an enlightened family he knew about runes, and that the rune symbol of protection is the C.N.D. symbol inverted. This was the symbol he chose to use, and decided that the only possible place it would be seen [and thus have the necessary impact] was on his head . . . A C.N.D. symbol was bleached into the back of his head.[6]

But this time he had broken a school rule by bleaching his hair, and the school followed with the predictable authoritarian response. The boy was very upset, and in turn the parents became angry and brought their opinions to the headmaster's attention. At this point the dispute had developed into one between the parents and the school, rather than directly involving the boy who by this stage had dyed his whole head brown. The headmaster suggested that if they did not agree with the rules the parents should consider sending their child to another school.

Afterword

In some respects, New Ager children in Glastonbury, particularly adolescents, were very similar to those in the larger British society. Most households in the Alternative Community had television, so the children were subject to the same mass-media influences as in any other family. Thus during 1990 'acid house' music was generally very popular among British youth, and the Assembly Rooms hosted regular acid house discos. Equally, adolescents in the mainstream commonly explore elements of an 'alternative' identity. For all this, some teenagers in Glastonbury from the Alternative

Community were definitely still further removed from mainstream youth culture, such as the sixteen-year-old who told a woman not to worry about her miscarriage because the spirit would just reincarnate. Moreover, in their distinctive community, New Ager children benefited from the high status placed upon children generally, and from the emphasis upon personal freedom, autonomy and individuality. These were privileges which many mainstream youngsters might have cause to envy.

Reincarnation?

The idea of the 'child within' is a particularly compelling, and fundamental, New Age concept. The question is how it relates to other cosmological ideas. The notion of reincarnation appears to be presumed in the idea that the child is born with inherent wisdom and an already-existing personality. But reincarnation itself is a complex idea, associated with concepts of a transcendent universe and ideas relating to some non-physical human essence that circulates between universe and the human world. In Chapter 9 we will attempt to describe these other New Age notions. Rather than preempt an understanding of how these latter notions are linked with the New Age idea of the child, we have preferred, in this chapter, to remain closely with what New Agers have to say about children and their socialisation. Chapter 11 will indicate precisely how all these ideas may be related.

Notes

1. Pan Books edition, 1980, p. 20.
2. 'Hal Stone and Sidra Winklemen, Originators of Voice Dialogue', interview by Philip Rogers. *Kindred Spirit*, Autumn 1990, Totnes, p. 23.
3. 'A Voice of Youth'. James Bloom. *The Glastonbury Times*. Spring Equinox 1990, p. 16.
4. ibid., p. 3
5. ibid.
6. 'Community Education Haircut'. *The Glastonbury Times*, Summer 1990.

9

Cosmology and Charisma

Is not religion all deeds and all reflections,
And that which is neither deed nor reflection, but a wonder and a surprise ever springing in the soul, even while the hands hew the stone or tend the loom?
Who can separate his faith from his actions, or his belief from his occupations? (Gibran 1980: 90)

For its part, anthropology has not completely resolved what religion is or is not. So far in this study we have mostly preferred to talk about cosmology. This is a neutral term by which we mean the model of the world, or worldview, which people, as members of a society, are socialised into respecting, as providing a more or less coherent account of the universe, including the place of human beings within it. Thus respected, such a 'picture', or representation, takes its place as an aspect of the people's culture.

Whether a particular cosmology is religious, scientific, or whatever, depends, in our opinion, on how one investigates it. From discussions in previous chapters it is implicit that we regard New Age cosmology as a religious cosmology. We shall present the analysis that confirms this in Chapter 11 where, with non-Western shamanism as the exemplar, we lay the groundwork for understanding cosmology as a 'constructed' social phenomenon. We shall argue, in this analysis, that cosmology, because it amounts to a *considered reflection* on the relations between humans and the universe, has an ideological function: thanks to cosmology, knowledge is available by which people may both interpret and rationalise profound aspects of their social affairs, particularly aspects that are in some way contradictory. In this chapter we evoke the religiosity in New Age cosmology.

There is a clear point of departure. 'New Age' (as we shall see) is a broad notion, such that many, somewhat differing views of the world can qualify under its heading. But one notion, common among all such views, is that the spiritual is, or should be, a central part of people's everyday experience. For example, the New Agers that Ruth Prince met in Glastonbury emphasised over and again that in mainstream society people had lost contact with an older and intrinsically spiritual part of themselves; from this loss, they maintained, stems many of the problems of modern living. A major theme in the New Age is of the outer reflecting something inner and of the inner as being influential on the world, and a prevalent opinion in Glastonbury was that there would never have occurred such circumstances as the abuse of the environment and human beings exploiting one another had people properly been 'in touch' with spiritual values and, above all, with the spiritual aspects of their own character. In this chapter, it will be seen that, in New Age thinking, everything relevant in the universe – the animate and the inanimate, the visible and the invisible – is imbued with spiritual essence.

The quotation above, from Kahlil Gibran, epitomises the belief that spirituality touches all aspects of a person's life. Thus, rather as the Shakers taught 'Let every breath be a continual prayer to God', people in the Alternative Community in Glastonbury upheld as their motivation for being in the town the enjoyment of a lifestyle where one's spiritual beliefs were all-pervasive: on this basis the 'religion is for Sundays' attitude sometimes associated with the Christian church would get strongly criticised. A corresponding way by which New Agers often express this is by invoking the idea of Experience. One person in Glastonbury said:

> I have had these powerful experiences in my life which are really beyond words; indescribably sweet, just feeling myself bathed in interconnectedness to everything. Now I am trying to bring those experiences into the rest of my life and to find a way of being where I can operate in the world from a spiritual space and also enhance the opportunity for more of these intense revelatory experiences.

In Glastonbury, the acknowledgement that there is something sacred in the totality of everyday living is very much encouraged. Bearing witness to this was a section in *The Glastonbury Times* called Holy Housework. Here the home, like the body, was seen as somewhere to be honoured and cherished. Some people took this a step further and saw the 'household' as imbued with its own energy. One person, looking round a prospective house for renting, said he felt the house's strongest point to be the energy by the cooker. Others were aware of the presence of spirits at nearly all times, as intimately connected with the moods and events of the home. One booklet, about moving house, advised on a ritual to invoke the devas[1], or angels; the symbols of the four elements were to be placed in the four corners of every room – incense to represent air, salt for earth, a candle for fire and a bowl of water for water. Thus,

> Today, one can still have an overshadowing angel who tends to the home's atmosphere, adjusting energies so as to aid a more attuned and beautiful life. A conscious effort, however, must be made to invoke the help and ongoing presence of an angel of this kind. First one must be aware for several weeks of one's intention to call such an angel to one's home. Second, one's home must be thoroughly cleaned. Then at a quiet and serene moment sit and light a candle for the angel. Remain quiet and sense that an angelic presence may come to the home.[2]

The omnipresence of angels and spirits – in trees, in people, in living spaces – is the basis for it being considered important in Glastonbury to maintain a lifestyle and a way of being which is consistent with 'spiritual energy'. Thus many within the New Age movement hold in enormous esteem non-Western peoples who practise ancestor worship. When people, anywhere, declare that the spirits of their ancestors are continuously beside them, and explain events that occur as the work of spirits, New Agers generally admire their 'spiritual consciousness'. Conjuring a tribal idyll, members of the Alternative Community in Glastonbury often commented that in isolated non-Western societies people maintained a connection with their spiritual selves which nearly all of us, in the West, have lost.

In previous chapters, we introduced the basic New Age ideas relating to spirituality and energy – which are tied in with notions about the mutuality of human persons. In the present chapter we shall describe the wider body of New Age cosmological knowledge in which these ideas are incorporated. Cosmological practice and cosmological content are the two relevant perspectives here. In its broadest sense, the New Age movement encompasses a number of (rival) subdoctrines. Cosmological practice refers to the choices that are exercised as to what particular subdoctrine to embrace, and the strategies pursued in respect of sustaining the option chosen. Cosmological content deals with the particular knowledge of which a given option consists. One notes that individualistic and holistic principles figure strongly in both such dimensions.

Individualism, Holism and Cosmological Practice

Contradictions between individualistic and holistic principles underpin the character of cosmological practice in the New Age arena. On the one hand, cosmology, declaring a 'considered view' of the world, implies submission to a particular conception by the relevant human population, and as such is inherently holistic. But, on the other hand, individualism is a pre-eminent feature of the New Age lifestyle, and, as occurs in Glastonbury, this amounts to an obligation that people should not be required to subscribe to any one particular view. The key social value in this latter respect is acceptance of the other person's (cosmological) preferences. The result, we have noted, is a proliferation of different versions about the 'nature of the world' (i.e., the different New Age subdoctrines). Cosmological practice, connoting choice and strategy, implies the existence of a distinctive social context. The task of this section is to illustrate this with ethnographic material. Such social context will almost always include deeply contradictory elements.

In Glastonbury, a group of friends, and friends of friends, had talked of forming some kind of spiritual community that would meet on a regular basis, so that, in a stable social environment, they might share their spiritual experiences. The impetus to form such a group came mainly from two sources: people who had been involved before in specific religious groups or practices (but then had left, or abandoned, them), and people with, or planning to have, children, who wanted them to be brought up in some kind of spiritual community but did not feel sufficiently sympathetic with the views of the mainstream church to have them baptised or become regular churchgoers. (Of course, some of these people fell into both categories.) The idea had been discussed for many months and there had emerged a consensus about what people wanted. Eventually a meeting was arranged to take things further and to try to sort out a kind of procedure and pattern for the meetings to follow. The meeting was explained to Ruth beforehand as a group of people looking for a sense of family. One person said,

> You know what it's like, when you meet some people – it's as if you know them immediately. There's some kind of commonness there; this is just a group of people getting together to explore this.

At the meeting itself, however, it quickly became clear that those involved had very different expectations. Differences arose over whether the group should be 'closed' or 'open': thus some wanted to develop a group where they would always know who was going to be there and so could feel comfortable to open up, whereas others felt that the whole point was to go beyond the level of personality, to recognise the profound communality of humans everywhere and to accept that sometimes one could have one's most powerful experiences with a total stranger. Another point of contention was over children. Some people felt that it was perhaps appropriate to have children around more at some times than at others, whereas other people, particularly two sets of parents, said it was appropriate to have children there at all times. Eventually it was suggested that some games be played so that people would become more relaxed with each other. However, during this first evening a series of polarities had clearly emerged.

The next meeting was the following week. Some members from the previous week were missing, notably the two sets of parents. In both meetings there had been a sense of awkwardness about how to proceed; people were trying to 'evolve' a procedure, and although a number of those present had experience in co-ordinating groups they were hesitant about imposing their ideas on the rest of the group. Their numbers having shrunk, people played 'trust-building' games and then sat around talking. During the evening the conversation turned to the fact that nearly all the people there had been involved in either a new religious movement, or a more traditional one, or had closely followed the teachings of one particular teacher. People talked about how, in these experiences, they had felt too confined, and had felt compelled to take on a whole body of beliefs, not all of which they could accept; their individuality had been threatened, and now they preferred to select from diverse teachings, as they pleased. Jokingly at first, one person suggested that that was what the group had in common: a mutual dissatisfaction with teachers, 'the guru syndrome', and the discipline of a group. Soon everyone was exchanging experiences on this theme, deciding that what they shared was their reluctance to embrace 'one faith' and jeopardise their individuality by doing so. This continued on for a number of weeks, with similar routines of trust games and 'sharing'. However, the group slowly became smaller and met more irregularly. It certainly never became a spiritual community.

A juxtaposition of two ideals is reflected in this case study: a desire for community, with an emphasis upon shared understanding, connectedness, and a sense of family; and a strongly individualist ethos and the acceptance of dissenting opinions. In the Alternative Community in Glastonbury, conflict relating to the opposition between holism and individualism may therefore be expected when the attempt is made deliberately to construct in-common perspectives on the world. It is one thing for people (as individuals) to drift towards one another on the basis of coincidentally sharing the same beliefs; it is evidently quite something else for a group to oblige its members to sign up to a common body of perspectives, standards and practices.

Cosmological Content

Cosmologies, as systems of knowledge, famously display a holistic bias. They generally provide descriptions of the universe which specify a relatively coherent, or integrated, picture that explains how the various relevant elements (including human beings) relate to one another in an ordered manner (but see Brunton 1980). But from another point of view a cosmology may be mapped along a relative scale of holism and individualism; this is in accord with its description of the place of the human individual within the total universe. Thus in the case of New Age cosmology, many elements have a definitely holistic quality: they amount to broader entities that subsume the human individual. But an individualistic dimension is very evident as well, corresponding with the considerable space afforded in New Age conceptualisations to the individual as an existential (as opposed to practical) being. For the remainder of this chapter the broad cosmological elements which the New Age evokes will be examined in turn, beginning with those whose qualities are clearly holistic.

The New Age notion of cosmos (Chapter 5) expresses cosmological holism in its most general terms. Its content varies, as will be seen, but cosmos very broadly refers to transcendent spiritual force. Turner's idea of communitas, in its 'ideological' or rhetorical sense,[3] depicts the cosmos notion quite well in analytical terms. It also permits a link between New Age ideas and the evocations of both mainstream and non-mainstream poets. Thus communitas refers to the abandonment of roles informing the individual's daily routine and their replacement by some sort of communal transcendence (e.g., Turner 1974: 46). Correspondingly, T.S. Eliot, in *Four Quartets*, spoke of an 'inner freedom from practical desire'; and in the poem, *Jerusalem*, William Blake describes 'being mutual in love divine'. More recently, Allen Ginsberg wrote of 'angel headed hipsters burning for the ancient heavenly connection to the starry dynamo in the machinery of night'.[4] Turner, for his part, acknowledges his indebtedness to Martin Buber, from whose *I and Thou* our favourite passage goes as follows:

> Community is . . . the universal relation, into which all streams pour yet without exhausting their waters. Who wishes to make a division and define boundaries between sea and streams? There we find only the one flow from I to Thou, unending, the one boundless flow of the real life. (Buber 1937: 107)

The Alternative Community in Glastonbury consciously constitutes a 'movement of people' with a common overall goal, such that this enhances the possibility for transcendent spirituality. Once Ruth explained Turner's ideas to a New Ager in Glastonbury whom she knew well. He considered, nodded slowly, and assented: 'Ideological communitas – that's where I live'.

In New Age cosmological thinking there are a number of important holistic tenets, which we shall detail over three subsections.

Notions of Common Essence

Closest to the literal idea of cosmos, and to the analytical notion of (ideological) communitas, is the New Age belief in a common essence among all living forms, particularly among human beings. Most usually spoken of as a common 'spirit', this is sometimes expressed in terms of a common divinity, and at other times in terms of a higher or common self, which the individual is usually suppressing. The key understanding is that at this higher level the idea of separation – of individuals from one another, or of individuals from the world beyond – is illusory, and a movement away from the 'truth' or 'spirit':

> A mind that conceives of itself as fundamentally separate from all that it perceives is an instrument of division. It can do nothing but divide, analyse, compartmentalise, and dissect. Everything on which it turns its attention is reduced to disconnected segments, while the spirit, the life of the whole, is forgotten. With the fictitious premise that it is fundamentally distinct from both 'others' and nature lying at the root of its thinking, the ego is not capable of reason, for its premise is a lie.[5]

Ken Carey, the author of this quotation, maintains that the 'lonely ego' is something isolated, and lacks the strength and power of the spirit, or truth. His statistic is that 'without the spirit, the ego is capable of using only about ten percent of the brain's capacity'. The spirit is what is common to all, and what links all to all.

One of the most ardent, and famous, proponents of such a theory was Sir George Trevelyan, the founder of the Wrekin Trust. Sir George was a regular visitor to Glastonbury, until he died in February 1996, and had close contacts with people there, having participated in many local events as well as giving lectures in the town. When Ruth was in Glastonbury during the Harmonic Convergence, she met Sir George a number of times; a tall, craggy man with piercing bright blue eyes, his agility, charisma and vivid, sweeping gestures belied his older years. The thrust of his teaching lay in people becoming more aware of the oneness of life, to realise that each human being is part of a wider life-force: to their detriment, human beings are divided each one from the other, similarly to the *Ancient Mariner* ('and no one told pity on my soul in misery'). Through knowing the oneness of all life, it is possible to move beyond the transitory states of personality. He writes,

> This consciousness includes the capacity to be one with any other human being. Normally you and I experience separation: we are separate beings, which is the essence of Newtonian thinking. When I look into your eyes, however, I realise that it isn't just two chaps. The divinity in me is the same as the divinity in you. Obviously: the holistic viewpoint implies it. I can look through your eyes and it is the divinity in me looking at itself through you. In this sense we are one. (Trevelyan 1986: 15–16)

To exemplify these ideas, Sir George practised a ritual, which he described as an experiment. Participants were told to stare into someone's eyes and look beyond the outer faces of personality so one didn't feel the need to visually respond to that level of communication. At that point what you saw in someone's eyes was the same thing and part of the same whole as yourself: that which you see and that which is in yourself is a little droplet of divinity. When Ruth participated in the ritual, during the time of the Harmonic Convergence, it was to welcome the 'energies' of Sun Ray as they came down to earth. As Ruth recalls it:

> Firstly ten of us stood round an oak tree holding hands to give thanks, some of us with flowers to celebrate nature. Then we moved to a circular rose garden to 'appreciate the beauty of creation'. At that point we branched into pairs and I, the participating observer, found myself

staring into the eyes of Sir George himself. We were to look into the soul in each other, and then say, 'I wish you the beauty of the rose and the strength of the oak'. Then he gave me the Essene blessing by putting his hand on my cheek and saying 'Blessings be with you', and I replied, 'And with you'. Then we exchanged a hug.

Thus was apparent the holistic principle – a communality on both a higher and deeper plane than the individual entity.

Gaia

Gaia, for New Agers, externalises ideas of common essence, for it identifies and describes a system of which all entities (humans and other things) are a part. What inspires it is

> the hypothesis that the entire range of living matter on earth, from whales to viruses, and from oaks to algae, could be regarded as constituting a single living entity, capable of manipulating the Earth's atmosphere to suit its overall needs and endowed with faculties and powers far beyond those of its constituent parts. (Lovelock 1991: 166)

As a spiritual notion, the Gaia concept underwrites the New Age movement's environmentalist ethic.

James Lovelock elucidated Gaia from the standpoint of mainstream science (Lovelock 1979). The hypothesis, that the planet Earth may be viewed as an independent living organism, he named Gaia, after the Greek Earth Goddess. Yet Lovelock drew an unexpected body of supporters – the New Age movement. Thanks to its comparison of the elements of the earth with a nervous or communication system, many people in the movement hailed the Gaia idea as recognising the integral interconnectedness of all things: New Agers celebrate the Gaia hypothesis, along with its feminine connotations, as the symbol of the holistic vision.

Many people in Glastonbury, embracing the idea of wholeness, interdependence and interconnectedness in nature, construed the Gaia hypothesis as acknowledging the earth as having a spiritual consciousness – as being alive. At a night-time vigil on the Tor during the Harmonic Convergence of 1987, one man, who lived in a tent in nearby woods, explained to Ruth how he felt about Gaia,

> When I look up at the sky now and see the stars twinkling, I feel the aliveness of the earth, I can feel her breathing. We are part of it all, we are the communication system of Gaia's body. When I realised that I

knew it didn't matter who I was or where I was, I knew I could never feel lonely.

Others in Glastonbury attributed to nature a corresponding moral quality of 'goodness'. Following a violent storm in which a number of trees were blown down, one woman told Ruth, 'it's a message, she's expelling herself at the roots, the fallen trees are there to teach us a lesson'.

Many New Age commentators concord with this view, that the problems facing the 'human race' today are caused by our misplaced arrogance towards the earth. Thus, Sahtouris, in her article, *Gaia's dance*, states:

> Our ability to be objective, to see ourselves as the 'I' or 'eye' of our cosmos, as beings independent of nature, has inflated our egos – 'ego' being the Greek word for 'I'. We came to separate the 'I' from the 'it' and to believe that 'it' – the world 'out there' – was ours to do as we pleased, telling ourselves we were either God's favoured children or the smartest and most powerful naturally evolved creatures on Earth. This egotistic attitude has been very much a factor in bringing us to adolescent crisis. And so an attitude of greater humility and willingness to accept some guidance from our parent planet will be an important factor in reaching our species maturity. (Sahtouris 1991: 161)

But not that Lovelock himself attributed a consciousness to the earth as an intelligent being. Strictly, such an interpretation of his ideas is misleading:

> Sentience, the possession of senses, suggests some level of awareness, and awareness suggests consciousness. Gaia begins to resemble an intelligent being.
> It is hardly surprising, therefore, that given a very brief and simplified outline of this new view of the way the planet works, together with a name to attach to it, that some people may come to regard Gaia as a god. Not only is this incorrect, it is potentially harmful. The apparently persuasive line of reasoning that leads to this interpretation is false. Gaia, or the Earth, is not intelligent, does not think, and most emphatically is not a god. To this extent the name Gaia is perhaps unfortunate. (Allaby 1989: 111; see also Milton 1996)

To New Agers, however, this is beside the point. For them, the Earth, the one giant *living* organism, includes human beings as an integral part. New Age environmentalist ethics play precisely on this: this wider living organism is supremely vulnerable to human practices, which, for fear that the totality be destroyed, must be closely restricted so that the organism's limits and tolerances are fully respected. As people in Glastonbury explained it, Gaia, as a spiritual idea, serves to further the notion that human beings have a place and connection in relation to each other, beyond individual needs and perceptions.

Rituals of Community

Ritual is important in the Alternative Community in Glastonbury. This was particularly so during the Harmonic Convergence, itself a very major ritual event. Then the efflorescence of ritual was consistent with the large numbers of people gathering together to celebrate. But in 1990 ritual enactments remained common, including, in everyday life, singing grace before a meal. Among New Agers in the town the clear purpose of these acts was to celebrate the holistic vision and sustain a sense of community, and also to consciously build upon the symbolic construction of the Alternative Community in relation to the outside world. To cover the variety of New Age ritual happening, we shall describe a number of particular instances, some quite short, others longer, that Ruth encountered during this period.

A Meditation and Healing Ritual

Meditation is commonly something individuals conduct alone, but in Glastonbury people would often meditate together and 'share the energy'. Then the holistic dimension was patent: through collective effort energy in the world beyond, greater than that which an individual could achieve alone, might become available to everyone participating. The following example, of a meditation meeting, exemplifies this.

The event began by people finding somewhere to sit around the outside of the room. People picked up cushions and sat either cross-legged on the floor or on chairs. In the centre of the room was a candle and a bunch of flowers. The meditation leader sat at one end, and people chatted quietly amongst themselves waiting for the meeting to begin. First the leader welcomed people who had not been before; people were invited to go round the circle and introduce themselves. Then he started to talk about how the energy is building up in the world, citing the end of the Berlin Wall and the revolutions in Eastern Europe as examples. He said the people present were lucky to be in Glastonbury because that was the heart chakra of the energy and it was getting more and more powerful. He then began a guided meditation. Everyone was told to breathe in the light that was coming down, to fill their bodies with white light, and then to start passing the energy from left to right, to receive it from the neighbour on their left and to pass it on to the neighbour on their right. Then with 'out breaths' participants were to breathe out the light and form a common pillar of white light in the centre of the room. The pillar of white light was described as infinite – 'in the way we all are'. This was followed by twenty minutes of individual meditation and then three 'oommms', which were called 'earthing' sounds, to 'ground' the light and bring the session to an end. Opening their eyes after this individual meditation participants beheld a woman sitting in the centre of the room, holding a crystal. Crystals constitute an important part of healing rituals since, by their structure, they connote harmony and peace: they are believed to receive and transmit 'pure' waves of energy. Unlike the soul, energy represents a power beyond people and is available for people to harness.[6]

A Christmas Party

The ritual focus here was likewise a candle in the centre of the room. After participants had performed a number of circle dances and other games, the candle was lit and the lights turned off. The only other form of light in the room was an open fire crackling in the background. Twelve people sat cross-legged in the centre of the room around the candle. Some music was put on and those present were told by the person leading the ritual to start singing, 'how I love you, how I love you', along to the tune. At first people were to sing this all together, and then look at each other person in the group in turn, stare deep into their eyes, and sing to that other person; this was to continue until everyone had sung to every person in the group. Again, a concentrated white light served as a key symbol for social harmony and communality.

Lunar Meditation

A candle was again the focus of this ritual. Upon entering the room people arranged themselves in a circle around the candle and burning incense, and commenced silent individual meditation. Once significant numbers were present the leader began a guided meditation. Evoking the cycles of the moon, he suggested striving towards one goal, and then as soon as it was reached, striving towards the next. He told participants to let the light and peace fill their bodies, and then let it out into the world; north, east, south, west, up and down. In front of participants on pieces of card was 'The Great Invocation', which those present read out together,

'From the point of Light within the Mind of God
Let light stream forth into the minds of men.
Let light descend on earth.

From the point of Love within the Heart of God
Let love stream forth into the hearts of men.
May Christ return to Earth.

From the centre where the Will of God is known
Let purpose guide the little wills of men –
The purpose which the Masters know and serve.

From the centre which we call the race of men
Let the Plan of Love and Light work out
And may it seal the door where evil dwells.'

Let Light and Love and Power restore the Plan on Earth.

The Aquarian Cross

Following a spiritual message a golden cross had been brought from Jerusalem to Glastonbury. In this ritual, the cross was carried in procession from Wearyall Hill to the top of the Tor where it was received by a large crowd. There, a blessing ceremony on a couple was also taking place. Four people dressed in white held the cross in the centre, and then people began to chant,

To you I give
From you I receive,
In this we share.

They turned and repeated the vows to their neighbours, with whom they then exchanged a hug. Following this, a group of people started playing the bongos and guitar, chanting,

We are from the Goddess,
Unto her we shall return,
Like a drop in the ocean . . .

Silent Sharing

Retreats were held regularly at the house where Ruth lived. Over the Christmas period, there was an extended retreat, and during this time a gong would be sounded twice a day to invite people to come and participate in a period of silent sharing and meditation.

In form, substance and context these rituals differ. In some the participants remained separate, with 'energy' mediating the contact between them. An example is the meditation group engaging with a common essence ('breathing in the light coming down'): the energy one person received might be passed on to the next. Moreover, within such a group, energy could be created which might be manipulated and controlled. At the end of some of the meditation sessions, the 'light' would often be dispatched ritually over the whole of Glastonbury. In contrast, in other rituals, such as the Aquarian Cross and the Christmas party, people were directly in contact, and the significance of the ritual lay in expressing interdependence and sharing between two or more individuals. Yet in all the rituals the common theme of communality and holism was upheld. Thanks to ritual performance, the bonds between the participants were celebrated and their relationships transformed. In the Alternative Community in Glastonbury such bonding was intended to reflect a sense of commonality, firstly with respect to fellow participants, and secondly throughout entire humankind.

Cosmological Content and Individualism

Let me merely say that it is plain, particularly to us, that there has never existed a human being who has not been aware, not only of his body, but also at the same time of his *individuality* both spiritual and physical. (Mauss 1985: 15, our emphasis)

In New Age cosmology very considerable attention is given to the elaboration of the individual person as an existential being. The Alternative Community in Glastonbury used the term 'individual' widely, both to refer to the separate physical body, and also (as in the quotation from Mauss) to convey the sense of an entity having a distinctive form of expression. At the cosmological level such a perspective celebrates the self as primary. In this context New Age individualism places emphasis upon self-development, as part of a necessary personal philosophical and spiritual quest. Here the New Age argument is fundamentally about a change of consciousness, amounting to a new world view and a spiritual awakening, which must take place separately in each person before there can be change in the collectivity or in the societal structure. A major public face of the New Age as a social movement or philosophy is of a therapy-oriented group of individuals striving to change and develop themselves and their approach to life. In this the ambitions, desires and separate paths of each person are fully acknowledged. The mystical resonances here are marked:

> No one can know God who has not first known himself. Go to the depths of the soul, the secret place . . . to the roots, to the heights; for all that God can do is focused there.[7]

Thus spirituality, as with many aspects of New Age belief, starts with the inner self. This is for two reasons. Firstly, one must work on the inner as a precursor to influencing the outside world, and, secondly, the inner is a reflection of external divinity. We should look at both these dimensions.

Spirituality and the Self: Start from Within

Recall what one person in Glastonbury said of the New Age:

> I associate it with the period of time following the Harmonic Convergence. Before everyone was dreaming death and now we are dreaming life. There is a new ecological vision where we are suffering from an environmental sickness or cancer. Ecologists focus on the outer rather than the inner, but change needs to come from the inside to the outer. You have to look for solutions inside yourself and then start taking responsibility.

Taking responsibility for, and changing oneself, then, is a precondition for concentrating on the 'outer' world. Since the process of personal transformation is partially about developing a spiritual awareness of being, it follows that this is intrinsically a spiritually-oriented process; therapy and spirituality interpenetrate, and it is difficult to differentiate between the two. Most people in the Alternative Community in Glastonbury would consider they have undergone such a process.

One centre in Glastonbury, 'Shambhala', tells in its advertising how it creates a space for people to come 'with trust' to get to the heart of their spiritual malaise so that the healing process might begin. Such spiritual malaise, the centre's leaders believe, is caused by a lack of love in humanity, which they feel they can counterbalance:

You have always been part of Shambhala by loving yourself. You have always been in the heart. This Trust is to remind you of this. There are many who suffer on this planet, many thousands who are unhappy and many millions who are lonely and confused. These are but the symptoms of the disease. A disease caused at its very roots by the lack of love within humanity and it is only by working at the root cause that any lasting change takes place. The Trust acts like a sword to clearly cut through illusion. It acts like a cradle to catch you in moments of distress and in your darkest hour. It acts like a catalyst and a signpost to activate and guide you back to your home in the heart. For this is the centre of love and this is the centre of peace. If the soul does not have this nourishment, it will wither and die'.[8]

It is suggested that in such an environment the person will be able to relax and let go of a lot of their fears, experience their true selves and climb back onto the path of spiritual well-being. Such an experience changes the perception of the world. The self *is* spiritual.

Spirituality and the Self: the Sacred Within

The inner self is often seen as a reflection of a divine element: there is the sacred within everyone. This is often discussed, both in New Age literature and by people Ruth talked to, in terms of a particular, enhanced level of self, enshrined variously as 'higher intelligence', 'higher self', 'inner teacher', or 'God-within'. With respect to this fundamental essence, individualistic and holistic ideas clearly condense together: we noted earlier that transcendent (holistic) ideas are expressed in it; yet spiritual individualism shines through. In the magazine *Kindred Spirit*, a woman describes her different levels of being, which she becomes aware of during moments of heightened spiritual consciousness.

At such times I am aware of myself – flesh and blood, heart and still. It is as if an 'inner observer', or higher intelligence, surfaces out of my usual unconscious activity, expands my awareness, sharpens the listening ear and enables me to witness my everyday reactions with a benign indifference.[9]

In New Age thinking, the sacred within must be in balance with the physical, emotional and mental aspects of the self. Gabrielle Roth, calling herself an urban shaman, argues that it is only in such conditions of harmony that the soul makes itself manifest,

When the body, the heart and the mind are in unity, when we are thinking, feeling and doing as one action, then the soul can manifest. The soul can only manifest through unity, it cannot manifest through contradiction or separation. Normally we're walking around in a state of what I call 'trizophrenia', where we're thinking one thing, feeling another and doing a third. Each of us needs to feel that state of power, that unity, that 'yes', that totality of Body, Mind, Heart, Soul and Spirit.[10]

Spirituality and the Self: the Individuality of the Soul

A person's soul is something special. In New Age thinking it is viewed as having existed before a person's birth in another form and as continuing on in another form after their death. The soul is not often seen as subject to any higher control or deity; it is part of the 'life-force' which is present in every animate being. Usually the preceding and following 'other forms' are other human bodies, but souls can also exist as disincarnate spirits. Although the soul is seen as distinct from the personality, some people are able to recall memories and experiences from their past lives. 'Regression therapy' exists to help people relive such past life experiences, especially those which might have left a negative impact and be hampering in the present life. The New Age idea of soul invites a number of distinctive elaborations, which are discussed in the following three sections.

Spirituality and the Self: the Soul and Death

To die is different from
What anyone supposes
And luckier.
(Walt Whitman)

You have squeezed yourself into the time span of a lifetime and the volume of a body, and thus created the innumerable conflicts of life and death. Have your being outside this body of birth and death, and all your problems will be solved. They existed because you believe yourself born to die. Undeceive yourself and be free. You are not a person.[11]

One strand of thinking in the New Age movement is physical immortalism, which proclaims 'the Christing of the flesh' (Chapter 5). Accordingly, it might appear that the movement is not particularly 'into' death. On the contrary, many people in the Alternative Community saw death as part of nature's cycle, and part of their own cycle of reincarnation (Walter 1993). Thus in the Glastonbury area courses were run to promote a loving acceptance of death. The facilitator felt that the fear of death or bereavement inhibited many people's lives. Ruth had several discussions with people about death, and ideas about the human soul emerged as very prominent. For most people, indeed, it is merely the human soul which perseveres in an individual form; *physical* immortalism is therefore a minority creed. One person commented,

> When I die I can visualise myself going towards a bright and warm white light and all my fears and worries drop away; I can leave that all behind and join my mother on the other side. She is standing there waiting for me and smiling.

In Glastonbury, the thinking about death inspired by the medical practitioner, Elizabeth Kübler-Ross (who died in summer 1997), was widely known and influential – though Kübler-Ross' work and ideas go far beyond the New Age movement as such, and into modern medical practice (Kübler-Ross 1995). Kübler-Ross worked with the terminally ill for more than thirty years, most recently with people suffering from AIDS, and she gives strong credence to 'out of body' spiritual experiences. To exemplify her position she uses as examples the often very clear and unsceptical thinking of children, as evidence of how the individual soul passes onto the spiritual realm,

> We have had children mention next-of-kin who died ten minutes earlier miles and miles away, and we have never had a mistake. Many times, I would say almost all the time, children who die slowly are given a glimpse of what it's going to be like. Once they have experienced and seen that, they are no longer afraid. Anyone who has seen the light, whether it's an out-of-body or near-death experience, will never again be afraid of death, it is not possible once you have been in that spiritual realm.[12]

In New Age thinking, the soul, in its individual consciousness, maintains memories from previous lifetimes and recognises relationships from these lifetimes – with, for example, dead parents. By reference to the soul – the immortal soul – the individual human being is honoured as a separate entity.

Spirituality and the Self: Channelling

Complementary to the human being's soul continuing on independently of the physical body, and building up a memory, New Agers
also considered it possible for disincarnate spirits, or souls, to exist,
and to enter the body of a living individual. The spirit takes over
the body and imparts *its* personality. The process in which this
occurs is called channelling, where the spirit is thought to enter a
particular person in order to communicate a message to people at
large. The person who is the vehicle of communication in this way
is known as a channeller. Channelling is a form of spirit possession, which bears resemblances to shamanism in non-western
society.

In 1990, channelling appeared to be increasingly common in the
Alternative Community in Glastonbury. Its popularity was
explained both in terms of people jumping on a bandwagon, and
also to an atmosphere of increasing acceptance, so that people felt
confident to come forward and announce themselves as channellers. A number of people in the town presented themselves as
channels, and also many channellers came to Glastonbury to 'give'
channelling to groups of people. Channelling is something highly
individualistic, in terms both of who it is that finds themselves to
be a channel, and of the character the disincarnate entity assumes.
Thus much channelling literature starts with the ubiquitous, 'This
is the last thing I ever expected to happen to me, I was leading an
ordinary life . . .' One channeller in Glastonbury described how she
had been interested in psychic phenomena since taking up yoga in
her early twenties. Then, sometime in 1988, she had been in Spain
on holiday and had had the experience of being entered by the
spirit of one of Jesus' disciples. At the time she had been feeling
emotionally upset after an argument with her lover, and said she
felt as if her own soul had been taken away for healing while
another stepped in. Apparently her voice had changed to a deep
gruff and masculine manner, and her hand and face gestures had
altered accordingly. The woman has channelled regularly since
then. She said, 'Being channelled through is like having a torch
shone on your third eye'. Through channelling she would provide
people with advice, either in person or through tapes; she was
even able to start spontaneously channelling over the telephone.
She would fast regularly and try to eat raw foods, saying that in her
vocation it is very important to be as pure as possible in lifestyle.
Consequently she could not sleep with a man who was not himself

undergoing purification, otherwise resistance would be lowered: it would be possible for a 'walk in' to occur, where another lower form of soul entered her body and took her over. She described how, after she had drunk a pint of cider, an amoeba-like entity had entered her, and it was a few uncomfortable hours before this lower being left her body.

In Glastonbury, Ruth attended a public channelling in the Georges Rooms of the Glastonbury Experience. Long and airy, with big windows, and at one end a visionary, many-coloured painting of the Tor, the room held about thirty people, who had paid £3 or £5 for admission, depending on their income. They were there to welcome the Reverend Joy Ballas-Beeson, of New Thought Science, Boulder, Colorado. She channelled the apostle Bartholomew. However she was quick to mention that she was not the only one to channel Bartholomew: a man in Florida received him, in addition to an employee of the Pentagon who had since changed his name to Brother Snowflake. Joy Ballas-Beeson said she had been interested in psychic phenomena since childhood but it was only later in adulthood following a divorce, losing her job and developing rheumatic arthritis that she had fully 'surrendered to the Spirit'. Having introduced herself and her background, she paused for a moment, dropped her head, closed her eyes, and then looked up and began to channel Bartholomew. 'Bartholomew' took the audience through a guided meditation, focusing upon throwing one's negative thoughts into the purple flame. 'He' said that this method of meditation was originally only available to masters who chose to be on Earth without incarnation. Since the Harmonic Convergence, however, it had become available to all light-bearers. A question and answer session followed, whereupon the spirit of Bartholomew left, and Reverend Joy Ballas-Beeson returned.

Spirituality and the Self: Rebirthing and Regression

'At the moment of your birth, you formed impressions about the world which you have carried all your life; these impressions control you from a subconscious level. Many of them are negative:

> Life is a struggle.
> The Universe is a hostile place.
> The Universe is against me.
> I can't get what I need.
> People hurt me.

> There must be something wrong with me.
> Life is painful.
> Love is dangerous.
> I am not wanted.
> I can't get enough love.'
> (Orr and Ray 1991: 141)

The rebirthers' credo is that the moment of birth is for the most part hostile and traumatic, and the rebirthers' therapy consists of re-living this experience. In California, Leonard Orr developed a technique involving a snorkel, a nose plug and a tub of water in which the rebirthee would float face down so that he or she might re-stimulate the initial birth in a pleasurable way, removing the association with trauma and challenging the negativity. This technique has later been modified into what are mainly a series of breathing exercises called 'dry re-birthing'. In New Age thinking such self-development is integral to the existential enhancement of the individual person.

Though initially concerned with birth, re-birthing is also used to stimulate people into regression, that is, the remembering of past lives. One person in Glastonbury described a visit she paid to a rebirther – not that it was particularly successful,

> I lay on the floor and Sarah told me to breathe in and out regularly, then quite fast and then to stop. Then I was told to start again. Eventually this was meant to take me into a remembrance of a past life or some other event which is acting as a block in me. Sarah told me to let it out and experience it. It didn't really do very much for me, I even noticed Sarah writing in her notes 'finds it hard to let go'. She backed up the session however by giving me lots of affirmations including one about physical immortalism.

Another person had a more powerful experience:

> I was doing my breathing exercises when I was taken back to another life where I was in a church being raped by a group of monks, these men were taking away my power. To me they represented my father, my boyfriend etc. Then suddenly I rose up onto the crucifying cross of Christ and became like a female Christ. My stomach swelled up like a pregnant woman. The men below were overcome and gave me my power back.

In Glastonbury, mainstreamer critics of the New Age community would sometimes ask, about reincarnation, 'How come people always find out that they were Egyptian Princes, or raped by Italian Saints or Tudor Kings? Why aren't they ever serving maids or English peasants?' In reply, one rebirther explained that when people remember things from past lives they retain important and spectacular events, not the mundane details of domestic living; correspondingly, from among many past lives one recalls the ones which had the most impact.

It has been noted already that rebirthing and regression, together with the concept of the individual soul, presume notions of reincarnation. In *Dancing in the Light*, Shirley MacLaine's account of her life and spiritual experiences, the actress recalls a conversation with her healer and past-life therapist, Chris Griscon, who explains how a soul consciously chooses the body it wants to enter and thus (individualistically) has responsibility for its fate:

> If we taught our children that they choose us as parents, the child would learn early on to take more responsibility for its fate. That is why enlightenment is so crucial. We are not operating with enough knowledge in our society. This way the child either gives up because of the authority he experiences, or becomes rebellious. But his soul intuitively knows that he can't legitimately blame the parents for his situation, whatever it might be. A damaged child CHOSE to experience that. (1986: 307)

Shirley MacLaine writes in long and vivid detail of her experiences tracing past lives, to explain personality patterns and conflicts in her present life. This she achieves with the aid of spirit guides present close by:

> I shut my eyes again. The crashing storm persisted. Why was I seeing this?
> 'Ask your higher self why it's showing you this image' commanded Chris.
> I did. Instantly I got back: 'Because you had mastered the knowledge of weather control in this particular incarnation, but abused your power, you were insensitive to the consequences of your manipulation'. The words came in English but it was the thought behind the words that I felt more deeply. I had mastered the knowledge of weather control?
> My conscious mind raced to my appreciation of wild and stormy weather conditions today. To be in the centre of crashing lightning, rolling thunder, and pelting rain gave me as much pleasure as anything I could think of. Could this feeling be related to a former existence? (ibid.: 317)

The Charismatic Presence

New Age cosmology, like any cosmology, is closely associated with the existence of specialist practitioners who enunciate it. In the case of the New Age movement, as with the new religious movements in general, this typically has a charismatic character: gurus, healers, shamans, special texts (etc), by inspirational endeavour, prominently express the supreme worth of the cosmology and make claims for its pertinence in the lives of ordinary people.

Academic work on religious movements has explored the significance of the charismatic presence intensively, particularly work on the new religious movements, where institutional structures to support organisation, recruitment and belief have not yet fully been laid down (e.g. Wallis 1982). In Weber's terms, charisma refers to a relation of authority based not on social rules but around the devotion and emotional commitment that the (charismatic) leader inspires. The dynamics of the relationship between charismatic leader and follower is a fascinating, if elusive question. Because charisma is often destructive, much general anthropological discussion on the topic has focused on the putative psychological dimensions of this relationship. Thus Lindholm, in an excellent account that attends to the charismatic impact of the likes of Hitler, Charles Manson and Jim Jones (of the Jonestown massacre), makes much of the presence within everyone of a deep-rooted desire to escape the limits of self, a very basic psychological tendency in relation to which, he argues, entering into charismatic communion may be readily understood (Lindholm 1990).

The prevalent assumption in the academic discussion is that the charismatic impact is crucially responsible for such religious movements existing. There will, of course, be other factors as well. For example, cargo cults, the millenarian religious movements that during this century have ubiquitously sprung up among indigenous peoples in the southern Pacific, may be examined in terms of the economic and moral disruption wrought by colonialism (e.g. Worsley 1957; Burridge 1969). Also relevant will be the circumstances of ordinary folk, since for a religious movement to be successful charismatic leaders may not fail to address such people's troubles, and promise alleviation and relief (e.g. Lawrence 1964). Yet inspirational leaders (prophets, messiahs, shamans, gurus, or whatever) remain the central cause, because, so the assumption goes, failing this sort of leadership such movements would never get under way.

But important questions remain unanswered. These are basically about the legitimacy of the charismatic presence (as a response to peoples' troubles, etc). Mainstream society is unlikely to supply this legitimacy because mainstream settings are generally disdainful of charismatic display. Therefore the charismatic relationship must be legitimised in terms of social relations within the movement. Psychological explanations of charisma only exacerbate the question, for an appeal to something deep-rooted in the human psyche inevitably implies that there exists a charismatic dimension in all human social relations – indeed, Lindholm seems to propose this when he suggests that charismatic processes, or something very similar, are evident in, among other things, people's attachment to the nation-state, to the consumerist ethic, and even to romantic love (1990: 176–85). This hardly helps with the task of tackling the particularities of religious movements, and so cannot be satisfactory.

Chapter 11 responds to what we consider are the crucial issues. Religious movements, especially in their early historical phases, seem to be equated with compelling and dramatic individuals. But it remains that such people occupy a social position. Maybe an individual's peculiar psychological sensibilities have drawn them to such a role, yet 'social position' implies 'acceptance within the community at large'. What is this 'community at large'? Logically it is the community of the ordinary members of the movement at hand. Therefore charismatic leadership is dependent on the movement existing (and therefore cannot be responsible for bringing it into existence). From this, two vital questions arise. First, are all cosmological ideas of a religious movement the consequence of charismatic leadership, or are certain cosmological ideas preconditions for such leadership's existence? Second, if charismatic leadership is dependent on the community of ordinary members, might charismatic inspiration, which implies (opposite to this) the dependency of ordinary people, have to be reconceived?

Notes

1. Devas are low level spiritual forces, typically concentrated in plants.
2. *Devas, Fairies and Angels. A Modern Approach*. William Bloom. Gothic Publications, Galstonbury, 1986, p. 30.
3. See Chapter 1 for Turner's own description of different senses of communitas. Note that existential communitas, the profoundest type of communitas, which is the cornerstone for analysis in this book, is not being referred to here.

4. 'Howl and Other Poems'. Allen Ginsberg. *The Pocket Poetry Seri*es, 1978, San Francisco, City Light Books.

5. 'Instinctual Living – the Path Beyond Language'. Ken Carey. *Global Link-up*. April/May 1991, Gloucester, p. 7.

6. Luhrmann, in her study of contemporary witchcraft in London, describes similar currents which magicians elicit and direct (1989: 115–6).

7. The words of Meister Eckhart, translated by Raymond Blackney (Ferguson 1980: 382).

8. Shambhala Charitable Trust, introductory literature. Coursing Batch, Glastonbury.

9. 'My body is the wind – the Call to Non-Separation'. Chloe Goodchild. *Kindred Spirit*, Winter 1990/91, Totnes, p. 12.

10. 'On the path of the urban shaman'. Gabrielle Roth, interviewed by Patricia Yates. *Kindred Spirit*. Winter 1990/91, Totnes, p. 4.

11. *Grim Reaper or Happy Harvester?* Nisargadetta Maharaj. From selection of quotations on death. The Manna House, Greinton, Somerset, England.

12. 'Elizabeth Kübler-Ross Interview'. *Part Two. Kindred Spirit*, Spring 1990, Totnes, p. 34.

Part Three

The Construction of a Social World

10

Towards a Framework

Why does Glastonbury hold such appeal for New Agers? Why have people settled in the town such that the Alternative Community there has a membership? Why does the New Age in Glastonbury take on the social and cultural character that it does? We shall attempt to answer these questions in the following three chapters. In this chapter we will examine some rival explanations both of religious movements in general and of the New Age in particular, and we also delve into the logic of tribal society. The intention is to lay down the framework for our own novel account.

Most existing explanations of religious movements attend to what we called, in Chapter 1, the movements' surface appearance. That is to say, they consider a movement as if it was a completed entity, and its elements fully formed components of social organisation or cosmology. A typical enquiry examines how the fully formed components relate to, or mutually support, one another, in the context of the completed entity. For example, in a published article separate from this book we explain the New Age idea of the holistic person as existing because of New Age individualistic practice (Prince and Riches 1999a). New Age individualistic practice is not dissimilar to mainstream entrepreneurialism, yet the New Age sees itself as opposed to the mainstream. Accordingly, the holistic person functions in order that the New Age individual (the author of individualistic practice) may be conceptualised as radically different from the mainstream individual.

This book follows a quite different approach. Neither the movement nor its elements are tackled as completed, or fully formed, but rather are treated as immanent in relation to levels of social processes. By virtue of these social processes, the movement and its elements are understood as the accumulated results of deep-rooted principles and contradictions. The result is an alternative account of the holistic person. In Chapter 11 we argue that the holistic person emanates from a foundation social process, which then permits the generation of further social and cultural elements in other, superimposed social processes; New Age individualistic practice is one of these further elements. Discussion at the level of 'surface features' legitimately dwells on how the holistic person reinforces other elements through positive feedback. But discussion in terms of social process emphasises that its presence is a *precondition* for the other elements existing. As regards the holistic person, this book focuses on how such presence comes to be. In Chapter 2, calling on the metaphor of 'construction', we presumed such social process to be the work of individuals. Our individualistic analysis, we maintain, stimulates a perspective on the New Age movement that is enormously suggestive.

Four introductory points remain, which highlight matters that the next three chapters will address. First, in this book we elucidate the social and cultural features that one recognises as New Age in relation to the basic experiences of people interacting with one another at the level of the local community. But this raises the question, which we shall address, of the New Age movement as a global entity. Second, the Alternative Community in Glastonbury is found attractive by many people (who join it). So it should be compared with other 'alternative movements' on offer, and with the mainstream. This requires that we establish some fundamental 'common denominators' of experience that imply variability as between different alternative movements and the mainstream. Then the question arises as to whether the sociological patterns reported about New Age membership (for example, that New Agers are largely middle class) may be understood in terms of such a common denominator. Thirdly, as mentioned in Chapter 1, Glastonbury's mystical allure is not something given, to which New Agers respond; the special meaning Glastonbury holds for New Agers as a place is something New Agers (in Glastonbury) construct. We now add that the explanation for why this is so should arise naturally from the consideration of all the other matters to do with New Age society and culture.

Finally, when we elucidate the New Age social and cultural features, we shall presume, with regard to the people concerned, that New Ageism entirely pervades their lives. As we indicate in Chapter 12, this is the simplest scenario by which the New Age exemplifies religious movements generally as constructed phenomena.

But, of course, a greater majority of people, in Glastonbury and elsewhere, uphold New Ageism in aspects of their lives (say, just in health and education). However, one may not say, in the case of such people, that the analysis applies only with reference to the respective particular activities. The fact that they uphold New Ageism in aspects of their lives makes a difference to how such people experience these activities (people for whom New Ageism pervades their lives will experience the selfsame activities differently). There is a further point. In the Western world these days, many people briefly or just occasionally consume New Age products. For example the mainstream business world is interested in New Age ideas of personal transformation and empowerment (Roberts 1994), and many people purchase 'alternative' health remedies from time to time. The question is: do such instances qualify for inclusion in this study? It is a fine line, yet we are interested only in people who, with regard to the New Age have 'gone native'. When the New Age is merely an 'experiential holiday' (Heelas 1994: 107), we consider that the people concerned remain rooted in mainstream understandings.

New Age social organisation and cosmology is a complex phenomenon. Where analysis is concerned, as with any complex phenomenon, the perennial problem is where to start. One could plunge in, permitting some especially alluring element to set the discussion in train, and then proceed from there. Our preference, instead, is to establish a basic framework of explanation and some first principles of social organisation, and show that from these it is possible to deduce New Age social organisation and cosmology in their full glory. The second half of this chapter is devoted to laying down this framework and some of these principles. Meanwhile, with the framework in mind, the rest of the first half of the chapter considers what other sociologists and anthropologists have had to say.

Analysing the New Age Phenomenon

As a new religious movement, the New Age movement is sociologically distinctive in that it is relatively open to the outside world, and relatively less secretive about its customs and practices. Yet the New Age has in common with very many such movements two rather interesting features. Its recruits seem mainly to be supplied by the mainstream middle class, and there is a very strong spiritual, or mystical, element in its practice.

Given that the new religious movements have emerged within Western urban–industrial society, many commentators find such a juxtaposition intriguing. A 'middle class critique of the mainstream' voiced in the rhetoric of spirituality is something definitely worth investigating. Educated Westerners should surely be able to articulate their dissent from mainstream assumptions and practices in secular and rational terms, the mode of reasoning with which, so it is said, the mainstream majority generally feels most comfortable. Yet this does not occur. The environmental movement, at the more instrumental end of the new movement spectrum, is commonly cited here. Its arguments invariably make excellent sense in terms of orthodox science. Yet very many environmentalists, ranging from politically orthodox Greens through to Deep Ecology communards, enthusiastically uphold Gaian mysticism or 'Green spirituality' (Milton 1996).[1]

We are sceptical about labelling the New Age movement as a 'middle class phenomenon'. In this chapter we want to establish this scepticism, leaving it to Chapter 12 to resolve more fully matters to do with the social complexion of the movement's membership. We shall critically examine several broad interpretations of social and religious movements, where one frequently discerns the variable of class-based recruitment. A first batch of interpretations evokes the middle classes as carrying forward ideas of spirituality latent in Western culture; a second batch evokes the middle classes as reclaiming spirituality that Western culture has completely lost. Some theories of religious movements, especially those relating to globalisation and secularisation, include both these strands; but we shall leave these until Chapter 13.

Carrying Forward Spirituality

The first type of explanation is that the new social and religious movements reflect something more generally occurring in late twentieth century Western society; they exemplify Western culture in evolution. David Hess, in 'Science and the New Age' (1993), puts one version of this. In his stimulating opinion, orthodox science and non-orthodox mysticism (such as the New Age movement and parapsychology), even as they stand as doctrinal opponents, mobilise much the same cultural concepts to uphold their respective positions. It follows that one is witnessing in the West today the emergence of a broader, transcending para-culture, which overarches both science and mysticism, and presages the shape of Western culture into the twenty-first century. For example, Hess suggests that science and mysticism alike invoke what might be termed scientific canons of verification: each side justifies its preferred version of the world in terms both of reason and of up-to-the-minute standards of empirical validation. In this regard, many New Agers, while they consider that orthodox Western science is wrong-headed, believe that a new synthesis based around (among other things) quantum physics, humanistic psychology, the anthropic principle and lost archaic wisdoms, heralds the truth. New Agers in Glastonbury would certainly find favour with Zohar and Marshall's scientific treatise, *The Quantum Society; Mind, Physics and a New Social Vision* (1994), which effectively integrates many of these dimensions (see also Badone 1990, Hanegraaff 1996).

Hess may or may not be right about an all-embracing Western para-culture, but we have reservations about his treatise. It is not the case that in the New Age all advocacy and practice respects the force of, for example, empirical rationality: in Glastonbury, most New Agers would maintain that many human experiences, especially those founded in emotion and intuition, are precisely beyond reason. Lurhmann's work on witchcraft and magic in present-day England is instructive in this regard. Granted that the Neo-Pagan magicians of her study, though they saw themselves as dealing with a mystical world incommensurable with the ordinary and the mundane, declared that (scientific) falsification was appropriate as a criteria by which their techniques might be judged (1989: 115–6). But, on the other hand, since these magicians' purpose was to grasp the ineffable, and a world where words do not apply, this suggests that they were engaged in a domain of activity that science, by definition, cannot reach (ibid.: 233).

Within his 'cultural discussion', Hess elucidates what he sees to be the key social dimension of the New Age movement. In his view, the New Age (and also parapsychology) reflects the restless individualism and optimism of the broader contemporary (American) society, in which middle class baby-boomers find particular appeal (Hess 1993: 14, 174). This is similar to the opinion that aligns the New Age with the New Right, whose ideological cornerstone is 'freedom' for the individual, in particular with regard to a person's entitlement to determine their options in life untrammelled by interference from others.[2] But this perspective is not totally convincing. The explanation of the New Age must in our view be true to the central fact that, in Glastonbury, the Alternative

Community, by its name, signals 'anti-mainstream'; moreover, there would be no New Agers if people in some manner or another did not turn their backs on mainstream life. Indeed, it might be better to say that the New Age movement is founded on an accumulation of idiosyncratic personal discontentments (with the mainstream). In which case, the analytical challenge is to finesse the relationship between the fact of such myriad discontentments and the overall character of New Age society and culture. We attempt this in Chapters 11 and 12 via the notion of communitas, where, intrinsic to the discussion is New Age individualism understood as a distinctive type of non-mainstream individualism.

Where Hess summons individualism, Klaus Eder, in a quite contrasting argument, upholds the question of human relations with nature as the pervasive theme of the new social and religious movements. According to Eder, unlike in the mainstream, where nature is treated as mere object, the counter-cultural currents in the West celebrate a social relation between humans and nature. Thus in the late twentieth century mainstream, class struggle relates to matters of the *exploitation* of *nature*. In this context the middle classes, since they are peculiarly sensitive to environmental issues, function as the chief bearers of the counter-cultural point of view, whereby 'exploitation' equates with morally inappropriate behaviour (Eder 1990). But like Hess, Eder identifies a deeper cultural logic, which subsumes both mainstream and counter-culture. In the case of human relations with nature, the West since the early nineteenth century has generally embraced an ambivalent attitude, upholding an antithesis between (on the one hand) a pure state, that of living within nature, and (on the other hand) a polluting state, that of imposing force on nature from the outside. With present-day religious movements such as the New Age movement, the former perspective is merely writ large, spirituality being the vehicle of expression for purity.

One may question Eder's thesis, paradoxically because new religious movement ideology makes much of environmental themes (Gaia, for instance). When Eder ascribes analytical priority to human relations with nature, may he have been seduced by the movements' representations of themselves? When we examine the construction of the New Age movement, in Chapter 11, it turns out that environmental themes are not so fundamental. To the extent that the New Age and other religious movements have anything in common culturally, more plausibly it is the idea of the holistic person – which is something that the mainstream seems definitely *not* to share. However even this common factor has its origination in some deep-rooted social experience.

Recent academic discussion on postmodernism offers a further perspective on the New Age movement, which again sees it as something intrinsic to the contemporary Western scene. Here the New Age movement is considered to be part and parcel of a general Western condition associated with global developments at the close of the twentieth century (e.g. Danforth 1989; Heelas 1993; Lyon 1993; Hess 1993: 36–40; York 1994: 15). The hallmark of this condition, according to many commentators, is consumerism's domination of economic and cultural life, such that everything, even that which is spiritual, is available for purchase (e.g. Baumann 1988; Jameson 1991). Consumerist morality is most thoroughgoingly upheld by the broad middle class. Postmodernism describes the cultural character of the West during this historical period, in such a way that the efflorescence of the new religious movements, along with the consumerist ethic, makes sense. Its interpretation is a controversial one.

Postmodernism's particular advocacy is that truths or 'underlying logics' about the social and cultural world cannot be exposed because none exist. Therefore, academic disciplines, since their raison d'être is precisely to uncover such truths and logics, embrace a false agenda. The general cultural 'fragmentation' in the West in the late twentieth and early twenty-first century encourages this apparent heresy. In this period, contrasting markedly with the 'modernism' that has gone before, 'orthodox' tastes or fashions no longer hold sway. The disappearance of restrictions on taste, it is noted, is highly appropriate to the pervasive consumerist ethic.

In postmodernity, differing cultural styles flourish simultaneously and intermix tolerantly. This occurs in many cultural domains (e.g. in architecture, art, music), and fragmentation is also evident in the social world. People from once-separate classes and social categories (e.g. owners and workers, young and old, men and women) now jostle culturally together: distinctions between them, in terms of their respective identities and what is socially expected from them, are becoming increasingly less clear, all the while that, in a relaxed way on all sides, one finds experimentation with an increasingly wide range of social practice. Meanwhile, academics (be they architects or anthropologists), the boundaries between their disciplines now extremely fuzzy, have had to develop radically new approaches. Over a wide span of cultural and disciplinary arenas, the prevalence of pastiche exemplifies all these trends, whereby insight and invention no longer come from authoritatively novel pronouncements, but instead from re-combining and juxtaposing elements available in the cultural domain that various existing genres have already supplied (echoes of Greek, Tudor and Art Deco will be included in the one postmodernist building). Side by side, thanks to the burgeoning televisual media, a hegemony of images with no real meaning and an essential shallowness has been imparted to people's sense of the world (e.g. Baudrillard 1988). Does the New Age – given its individualism, its doctrinal liberalism, and, above all, its apparently sparklingly eclectic mix of themes from a wide variety of cosmologies and religions – amount to postmodernity? An affirmative reply is tempting indeed.

The postmodernist perspective does not enthuse us. Already we have indicated that we believe our task is precisely to uncover some logic underlying New Age culture and society. Moreover, if 'postmodern' in general characterises the West today, then due respect suggests that the New Age, which labels itself anti-mainstream, exemplifies an anti-postmodernism. As much is indicated in the way New Agers in the Alternative Community determinedly oppose the consumer ethic: in Glastonbury people considered that objects and work and services were generally imbued with spiritual energy, and so were keen that they should not be blatantly bought and sold according to the principles of the impersonal market. For us, Hess's opinion, that in the New Age commodity production is turned into cultural production, summarises this state of affairs very well (1993: 38–9).

In any event, as modernists, we do not feel that the condition of late twentieth century culture and society in the West corresponds at all well with the descriptions of life that the postmodern label depicts. Indeed, the present-day West might better be described in a way that is opposite to what 'postmodern' conveys. The point is, each of the distinctive 'fragments' into which the overall Western way of life has separated *considers itself* as an orthodoxy: compared with rival styles and ways of being, whose various tastes it calls into question, each regards itself as in some sense exclusive and superior. The New Age movement would constitute one such fragment here. It passionately – and deeply – upholds its way of being, not least as the mainstream's superior (Dawson 1998a). If, ideologically, it takes in a broad range of beliefs and practices (bar those of the mainstream) this is part of its *orthodoxy*. For us, the so-called cultural fragmentation in the West is best described as the proliferation, within the Western fabric, of a multiplicity of dogmatic ethnicities, each one amounting to a determinedly distinctive way of life associated with a particular body of people. (It is true that traditional social divisions such as 'middle class', 'the elderly', 'men', etc., may be inadequate to describe such groupings.) The needs of consumerism should not explain this state of affairs. Rather it is the consequence of the weakening of the unifying authority of the nation-state (and probably of the community and the family as well), stimulated by enhanced educational levels, and by the greater personal security enjoyed in the late twentieth century by individuals in the West. In short, when one declares that the late twentieth/early twenty-first century West is marked by tolerance (as between the cultural fragments), this, at best, is tolerance in a negative sense, born of the fact that the proliferation of other ways of conduct is barely in anyone's power to prevent. When New Age orthodoxy takes in a broad range of beliefs, this amounts to its *acceptance* of these beliefs. 'To tolerate is to put up with someone or something, not to sympathise or understand' (Mestrovic 1994: 4).

In this context, one may review the notion of an opposition between mainstream and New Age. The mainstream must be acknowledged as something culturally heterogeneous. But the label 'mainstream' may be retained, because in the West there is overlap of lifestyle among the very many dogmatic sub-groups: 'mainstream' embraces such overlapping sub-groups. Meanwhile, the New Age construes these overlapping groups as a whole, and against this collectivity determinedly sets its face.

From this discussion something may be said about academic practice, past and present. If academics have felt obliged to seek out truths about the world, as something relevant for all citizens, this may be attributed to the very considerable power of the state, the academics' sponsor. But now, with the power of the state relatively diminished, this fruitless search is something from which they are released. But theirs is still an important task, namely to reveal that the visions of the world that their many audiences (corresponding to the many mainstream 'sub-groups') sustain are not the last word either. To do this requires systematic and logical thought, and the presentation of such thought in reasonably accessible language.

Reclaiming spirituality

We shall consider here academic research that treats social and religious movements as reactions *against* mainstream Western society. The key notion is that in present-day Western society people experience disenchantment with the world, such that the material success that they currently enjoy has been won at a terrible social and spiritual price (Weber 1958). This particularly applies to the middle classes. Postmodernism apart, mainstream orthodoxy upholds the rational and the calculated, which includes conceptualising the human being in terms of specialised, and compartmentalised, fragments (the individual separate from the social, the mind separate from the body, illness as an array of particular symptoms). Meanwhile, tradition, emotion, intuition, and the mystical – things which afford human social experience feeling and depth – are decried. For Weber, bureaucracy is the epitome of this state of affairs (Weber 1947: 329). In this context, religious movements function to counter this trend and to 're-enchant' (by being the handmaiden of disenchantment mainstream Christianity is seriously compromised in this regard). Paul Heelas, in one strand of his interpretation of the New Age movement as a re-enchanting phenomenon, considers the mainstream 'de-traditionalised', which implies the human individual's pervasive separation from institutional controls (Heelas 1996; see also Heelas, Lash and Morris 1996). Other writers comment that the New Right governments in 1980s' Britain and America failed to respond to the developing trend of single-parent and dual-income families, as well as continuing to regard motherhood as an unpaid and mechanical method of supplying the worker to the factory gate. With large sections of the population thus disenfranchised in terms of their value, religious movements supply the opportunity to reclaim meaning. Roy Wallis sums up this perspective well:

> At the same time as the emergence of a market for recipes for worldly success, there has emerged a need for methods of escaping the constraints and inhibitions usually required in order to achieve that success. Methods are sought for overcoming the effects of a lengthy socialisation into the Protestant Ethic, in order to explore the private self, to buttress a deinstitutionalized identity, and to indulge hedonistic impulses in an affluent advanced industrial society in which consumption has become as much an imperative as production. (1978: 18–19)

In sociology, such themes are elaborated under the heading of social movement theory. We should briefly explore its principal conclusions.

Social movement theory enshrines various purposes. For example, not all approaches under its heading focus on the origination of particular social and religious movements, and how they assume their distinctive social and cultural features – though, that said, virtually all social movement theory bears implications for this sort of question. Our interest in social movement theory concerns the way it construes a social movement. In most approaches, a 'social movement' is reified as embodying a collective will, and as ranged against the mainstream. We dislike this conceptualisation, for it implies that a movement somehow exists independently of the members who go to make it up. Also one grants that to understand social movements, matters to do with the rejection of the mainstream are going to be pertinent in some way. But reification begs the key question, as to precisely how the rejection of the mainstream is pertinent.

The key observation here is that most social movement theory evokes *contrast*, both in substance and political intent, between movement and the mainstream (seen as completed, and rival, entities). Thus the mainstream is variously characterised as modern, secularised, technocratised, bureaucratised, authoritarian, patriarchal, Eurocentric and rapacious (and much else), whilst social and religious movements are variously awarded correspondingly opposite properties. By way of a supplementary theme, particular social or religious movements are sometimes considered in contrast to yet other movements. For example, according to some commentators, the New Age movement should be explained as arising from the failure of the 1960s' American Hippy movement (Hippies are culturally nihilistic and economically parasitical on the mainstream, New Agers are the opposite). Our criticism of much social movement theory refers to two main types of account which follow from such a postulation of contrast (many particular theories of course combine both types).

The first type of account considers the relation between social and religious movements and the mainstream, both treated as wholes. Thus the new religious movements either affirm or reject the mainstream world (Wallis 1984). Or, social movements' role is to provide the mainstream population with novel (non-mainstream) frameworks for understanding and meaning (Eyerson and Jamison 1991). Or, religious movements are instruments for the religious conversion of mainstream people. As to how social or religious movements come to have such effects, emphasis is usually placed on the activities of movement intellectuals, or 'cultural entrepreneurs' (Bainbridge 1997: 260), who themselves can be transformed by the movement's momentum (Eyerson and Jamison ibid.: 119). In this vogue, a related question enquires into the particular features that dispose a social or religious movement to remain viable as opposed to collapsing (Stark 1996). One notes that these approaches are chiefly functionalist, dealing as they do with the consequences of a movement once it exists, and saying little explicitly about what brings the movement into being.

The second type of account relates social and religious movements (as wholes) to the circumstances of individual people, such that movements are explained as arising to meet such people's needs. For example, movements exist to satisfy interests not provided for by the mainstream (Scott 1990). Or they respond to feelings, among mainstreamers who join them, of relative deprivation, poverty, loss of status or grievance (e.g. Bainbridge 1997). In this vein, the New Age and related religious movements are broadly explained as relieving people's frustrations, not least (though not only) frustrations typically experienced in the mainstream middle class.

There is a methodological problem with both types of account. Explanations of social and religious movements that evoke contrast between movement and mainstream rest on the supposition that the mainstream is deficient in some way. But the question is how one identifies what this deficiency is (which the movement, one presumes, exists to rectify). Given the mainstream's complexity this is quite a question, which social movement theory is not strong on elucidating. In most of the instances just cited, something compelling about the movement at issue seems to supply the answer. Simply the fact that a new religious movement is highly unusual culturally, highly religious, or highly optimistic, is, in some social movement theory, sufficient to delineate what it is the mainstream lacks.

But to establish what explains the social or religious movement from the movement's own properties is misleading (the reasoning is circular). A preferable procedure is to establish the basis for the movement independently of the movement's properties. This is attempted in Puttick's account of women in the new religious movements, where such movements are explained in terms of meeting basic human needs (Puttick 1997). Such needs (for example, survival, safety, love, esteem) are postulated as psychological universals (via Maslow's 'hierarchy of needs'). One has reservations over this case as well, since what it is that humans 'need' is arguably something religious movements, in their pronouncements, *produce*.

Social movement theory definitely advances suggestive explanations of particular social and religious movements. Yet we believe that social and religious movements are better considered not as completed entities, but rather (to use another metaphor) as pieced together. Indeed, what appears as a completed entity is undoubtedly composed of components manifest at different levels, overlapping one another, and in general reflecting varying degrees of fundamentality. The explanatory factors that social movement theory offers will only be understood in this sort of theoretical context. This being so, it is more productive to understand a social or religious movement as being generated from certain assumed first principles. This, in any event, is the procedure we shall favour.

It is also true that many commentators recognise that social and religious movements exist because of the work of individuals (who piece them together); some writers have provided excellent descriptions of this occurring, normally focusing on the contributions of movement leaders.[3] Yet such a perspective is rarely carried through to the heart of movement theory itself. For example, Bainbridge promisingly announces his account of religious movements as based on a game theory approach, but in the event analytically attends merely to individuals choosing between different types of (completed) movement, or between movement and mainstream (1997: 53). We prefer to reveal the accumulating processes in relation to which individuals construct each such movement, and not to mention the fact that the emergence of a social movement in this way ultimately lies in the hands of ordinary people. Let us turn to anticipate this model, in particular its description of how 'contrast between movement and mainstream' may figure in our understanding.

In this book, we accept that the New Age movement is in essence anti-mainstream. Moreover we acknowledge that New Age ideology emphasises the ethical difference between the New Age and the mainstream – it would be incredible if this were not so. But what fundamentally underpins the New Age movement as a social and cultural phenomenon? In this regard the model attends to the difficulties and dilemmas experienced by people who come to be movement members. These crucial difficulties and dilemmas do not refer to specific discontents with the mainstream (though this is not to say that such discontents do not exist). Rather they relate to people's experiences once the mainstream has been abandoned. Moreover, these latter experiences certainly have less to do with intellectual anxieties, such as worry about what the philosophically

213

correct principles for living might now be. Instead they revolve more around how, given that the mainstream has been rejected, people come together in the organisation of daily affairs. The spirituality which marks the New Age and other contemporary anti-mainstream movements reflects less an anguished struggle by the mainstream middle class for re-enchantment, and more the difficult predicament of people once they find themselves in the liminal commitment of being not-mainstream. We shall shortly describe how this difficult predicament basically refers to matters of reconciling egalitarianism and individualism in the experience of practical social conduct.

In order to reveal the relevant social processes, we propose to draw on some remarkable parallels between the New Age movement and tribal society. Anthropological analyses of particular tribal societies will inspire a framework for understanding the New Age. In the case of tribal society, we shall see, it is evident that such social processes are patently religious processes, so we can be confident in saying that with the New Age we are addressing an inherently religious culture.

The New Age and the Tribe

The New Age, by its name, looks forward. But it is young, experimental, and still a minority way of life. It is also subject to scepticism from the outside, though, that said, it commands large numbers of peripheral sympathisers who will defend its perspectives on life from within the mainstream. Thus the New Age strengthens its case to the extent that it shows that, far from being parasitical on the mainstream, the lifestyle for which its membership strives has been achieved already in vibrant and fully independent glory. This is one reason why the New Age, in Glastonbury and elsewhere, eulogises the tribal world. For many New Agers, the tribe is a living example of what human society ought to be. Thus even as it looks forward, the New Age also looks back (historically) and sideways (geographically) – at Celtic society, at the North American Indians, at Bushman hunter–gatherers in the Kalahari. And the historical and geographical perspectives are often mixed, for when New Agers refer to the tribe, their descriptions generally evoke an idealised period prior to contact with European colonial powers, before such people came to take up aspects of Western values and practice. Normally it is tribal society's social and cultural wisdom that is celebrated, less so its technological capacity: New Agers call for a scaled down technology, appropriately adapted to use within a local community, but rarely advocate that the techno-logical advances of the industrial and post-industrial age should be surrendered altogether – witness, in Glastonbury, the prevalent use of computer technology. In the Alternative Community in Glaston-bury, virtually all major aspects of the tribal lifestyle were praised, from its practical routines to its broader conceptions of the world; there is the New Age school, described in Chapter 8, whose cur-riculum importantly includes just such themes.

New Agers, and New Age literature, are mainly interested in the spiritual and ecological dimensions of tribal society. People in Glas-tonbury enthusiastically supported contemporary non-Western peoples in their local struggles over environmental threat and degradation. The magazine, *One Earth*[4], which is widely in read in the town, epitomises this concern when it declares:

> Compassion is not the only reason to support [such] people in their struggle. The ecosystems of the forest are unbelievably rich and also very fragile. The Indians believe that they are guardians of the forest. They know how to live in it and how to use its many gifts without destroying them . . .
>
> If traditional cultures are destroyed such knowledge will be lost. These people have much to teach us and perhaps the most important lesson is that the Earth can provide for all our needs if we approach it with humility. Our technological culture does not like to admit its ulti-mate dependency on Nature but if it does not 'recall its memory' we may not see the 21st century.

Among New Agers in Glastonbury favourite non-Western people were the Kogi, the ecologically-minded people of Colombia, who, as 'elder brother' guardians of their region, contrast themselves with the 'younger brothers', the White and Mestizo society that despoils the earth through deforestation, mining and drilling. The New Age journal, *Kindred Spirit*, refers to the Kogi priests' pro-found traditional learning, secured through contemplation and meditation. The Kogi regard the world as a 'single living harmony, a single Mother . . . their society, then, is based on divination and a submission to the unknowable[5].

The New Age movement most frequently invokes Native North Americans as a way of life with the perfect ecological/spiritual bal-ance. The Hopi of New Mexico would be an example. Thus in *Global Link-Up*, Nancy Becker states[6],

We can learn from the wisdom of the Hopi to revere all of nature and to honour those exceptional places that move people with their unique configurations, beauty and energetic properties. We too can become custodians of the Earth by our reverence for sacred sites.

Comparable New Age ideas refer to the 'ancients' (Badone 1990). Thus *One Earth*[7] writes about Igor Tcharkovsky, the Russian underwater prophet:

Interestingly, in all ancient cultures, which were much advanced in comparison with our present state, the relationship between humans and water was more beneficial. We have received a lot of striking evidence, empirically, and our experience reveals that all this knowledge which we thought we discovered was already known to ancient cultures. They were much more advanced spiritually around such things as collaboration with other species during pregnancy, dolphins assisting delivery, and telepathic communication between the foetus and whales and dolphins.

In general, the New Age regards present-day tribal peoples as a beacon of enlightenment in the face of Western colonialism and depredation. Even when subject to Western pressures their traditional values continue to shine through.

Now the New Age movement romanticises tribal society, especially with respect precisely to the issue of environmental ethics (e.g. Milton 1996: 109). For example, while it is true that tribal societies sustain many traditional values, these days they have to come to embrace a very good deal of Western materialism and consumerism as well. Also, Roy Ellen is right when he observes that if, in traditional times, tribal society lived comfortably within environmental limits this was as an unintended consequence of the fact that they had small populations and low energy technology, and not – as New Agers would have it – as the result of some overarching spiritual plan. Accordingly:

It is less the conscious wisdom or the superior mental abilities of such societies, or even some superbly adjusted system which has evolved over the millennia, which leads to the maintenance of a state of environmental relations which we describe as 'balanced' . . . There are many ecological lessons to be learned from an understanding of the structure of small-scale societies, but they are not necessarily those which some influential Green guru would draw attention to, or even approve of. (1986: 12)

But there are valid parallels between New Age and tribal society. These, we believe, are highly suggestive for understanding the social dynamics of New Age culture. New Age descriptions of tribal environmentalism in fact fairly accurately describe tribal *cosmology*, which is similar to New Age cosmology (Albanese 1990). Moreover New Age daily practice and the daily practice of some tribal societies is likewise highly similar, as we shall see. Cosmology and daily practice are two quite separate domains of life, whose relationship, it is well known, is problematic. With respect to the New Age movement we may elucidate this relationship precisely by focusing on these similarities.

The term 'tribe' needs to be clarified. It is a convenient label to describe a certain type of non-Western society. By 'tribe', one refers to a way of life (or components of a way of life) not much changed by Western impact, where the human population is low-density, technology is low-energy, and social arrangements display relatively little by way of complexity or hierarchy. By this reckoning, 'tribe' clearly covers a wide variety of human societies; its pejorative connotations apart, its potential as an analytical category is low.

In fact, New Age practices and beliefs would seem to compare quite closely with a rather narrow range of 'tribal societies'. In our view, Glastonbury New Agers, in their social organisation and cosmology, sustain a way of life which is in many respects similar to the social organisation and culture one finds among nomadic hunter–gathering peoples, such as the Bushman, or the Indian peoples of the coniferous forests and tundras of northern North America, including the Eskimo (Inuit) of Arctic Canada and Alaska.[8] We shall argue that from the study of these particular societies, one may draw both facts and analyses that very usefully help elucidate the nature of the New Age movement (Riches 1995). Very broadly, such societies have egalitarian and highly flexible social organisations (for example, they lack corporate groups), and individual members correspondingly enjoy very considerable autonomy in the routines of everyday life; meanwhile, their cosmologies uphold a holistic relationship between human beings and the natural environment. In addition, by consideration of these particular societies anthropological analysis claims to have discerned certain fundamental and general principles of human organisation, for example contradictions associated with egalitarian social organisations and values. In the following three sections we provide our own analysis of hunter–gatherer society, and draw the relevant parallels with

New Age society and culture; this prepares the ground for Chapter 11, where the New Age is explained.

The Nomadic Hunter–Gatherer Society

Many anthropologists have held, and some continue to do so, that societies such as the Bushman of southern Africa and the Indians of the northern Canadian forests exemplify the very first human way of life (Lee and DeVore 1968). Such peoples take their food from the wild, as did the first humans, and their social organisations are not elaborate. Recently, however, opinions strongly dissenting from this view have been voiced, particularly with regard to the Bushman, and the whole issue has become a major area of controversy. Thus one group of scholars insists that in the case of the Bushman and other nomadic hunter–gatherers we *do* glimpse some sort of pristine human social organisation – or, at least, a social organisation unchanged since times preceding the dawn of agriculture and pastoralism (Solway and Lee 1990). The other side, meanwhile, observes that, within their geographical area, the Bushman for centuries have been surrounded by politically powerful cattle-rearing neighbours: in the past at least some Bushmen may have engaged in cattle rearing themselves. It is also noted that during the last two centuries there has been substantial disruption within the Kalahari following incursions of European colonial powers, bringing increased opportunities for wage employment and trade in its wake, and not to mention the curse of slavery. This 'revisionist' side insists that the Bushman's 'simple' social organisation may be *the result of* this sort of culture contact, which has had a fragmenting effect on the social structure (e.g. Wilmsen and Denbow 1990). Similar debates could be produced with respect to hunter–gatherer societies in many other parts of the world.

For our part, we reject revisionism's dogmatism, and note that during the last few years academic work on the Kalahari refutes it on the basis of detailed empirical evidence (e.g., Barnard 1992; Kent 1996). In our view, the social organisation exemplified by the present-day Bushman is a highly versatile social organisation (e.g., Woodburn 1988; Kent 1992), so it should be adaptive and viable both in circumstances of disruption by neighbouring peoples and colonialists, and also, in the opposite situation, where hunter–gatherers stand alone. Leaving history apart, we conclude that the Bushman, today, illustrate the simplest viable hunter–gatherer society.[9] If the New Age, in its basic social organisation and cosmology, is similar to the nomadic hunter–gatherers, it is also reminiscent of the 'first human society' (Prince and Riches 1999b). We wish to compare New Age society in Glastonbury with the Bushman and the Inuit (Eskimo) whose similar social organisations one of us elsewhere has labelled the Inuit/Bushman type (Riches 1995).

Inuit/Bushman society displays four key features, which together reflect the social ethos of flexibility, individualism and egalitarianism (Riches 1982). First, in daily life people are associated with quite small groups, seldom exceeding one hundred members. Each such group identifies itself with a tract of territory within which its population normally confines its activities during the annual foraging round. Such identification does not imply a right to exclude outsiders from a tract: there are no notions of ownership over the territory and its wild animals and plants. Rather, each group considers itself as the 'customary occupant' and guardian of the territorial area, by some prominent part of which it names itself. Second, in some seasons the entire group may forage together, but in other seasons it may split up into several smaller subgroups, which go their respective ways for several months at a time. When this happens, individuals (or, more exactly, married couples and their dependent offspring) are free to choose which subgroup to join. Through the years the membership composition of such subgroups is very fluid since, over time, people tend to shift allegiance from subgroup to subgroup. Also, people may move right across into a neighbouring territorial tract if they can find kinsmen there to help them. Third, in this type of social organisation, the idea of leadership (such as it is – it is often very weakly elaborated) lacks a developed concept of authority. Leadership, among these hunter–gatherers, essentially implies exemplary behaviour in some walk of life that others acknowledge. As Silberbauer puts it, referring to the Bushman, hunter–gatherer leaders are 'authoritative' but not 'authoritarian' (1982: 29), and owe their position to the fact that others, impressed by their superior performance in some area of social affairs (usually hunting), have elected to follow them. Overall, hierarchy within and between social groups is absent. Fourth, this kind of social organisation incorporates a system of pervasive sharing of food and assistance (Riches 1982). Kinship relations are important here. In these hunter–gatherer societies, kinship ties invariably relate everyone within the overall territorial group and, indeed, link people with groups beyond. Kinship implies mutual trust, and it is through this idiom

that the altruistic morality dominating the culture of all these hunting and gathering societies is expressed. A final point is that in
hunter–gatherer sharing systems, some sort of formal recognition
(i.e. esteem or prestige) normally goes to anyone who contributes
disproportionately to the greater good (Riches 1984).

The religion of nomadic hunter–gatherers is particularly interesting, and it is striking that in virtually all such societies it is very
similar. This religious type is shamanism, which flourishes among
Amerindians, as well as in Siberia and central Asia, and which
many writers either have explicitly associated with a flexible, egalitarian social organisation (e.g. Bourguignon 1977), or else have
cited in connection with the evolution of human society (e.g. La
Barre 1970). The most famous study of shamanism is that by
Mircea Eliade (1964), for whom shamanism, though not primordial, is certainly archaic.[10] His book, subtitled 'archaic techniques
of ecstasy', concentrates on Old World shamanism, notably among
the Northern Tungus (now known as Evenks), the reindeer-herding
people of northern Siberia from whose language the word
'shaman' derives. For Eliade the central focus in a shamanistic religion is the religious expert (the shaman), who vocationally prac-
tises the techniques of ecstasy, and who, thanks to the intensity of
his or her religious experience, stands out as a quite exceptional
person (1964: 8). Our interest is in shamanism in the Inuit/Bush-
man context, and, beginning with the Inuit (and taking inspiration
from Eliade), we start the description with the shamans themselves
(in Inuit society most shamans are men).

The term 'shaman' marks a prominent social position. In Inuit
society it is a social position the incumbent will have chosen to
assume, the initial decision to do so normally having been
prompted by the experience of being possessed by a particular
minor spirit. This spirit will subsequently come to support the
shaman (as a 'helping spirit') in all mystical endeavours. Once a
shamanistic career has been settled on, the novice shaman enters
an apprenticeship with an experienced older practitioner, which
includes, as well as intellectual instruction, submission to
extremely demanding physical and psychological ordeals. The particular skills an Inuit shaman masters relates to the existence of
several highly powerful 'major spirits', which are believed to exercise control over the unfolding of all significant events that affect
human well-being. Good health, good weather, good hunting: such
fortunes are all in the hands of these spirits, who dispatch them to
the human domain from their realms beneath the sea, in the sky,

and elsewhere. For example, the sea spirit sends out animals from her underwater lair with instructions to surrender themselves to waiting hunters, in their kayaks or on the ice. Accordingly, the shaman's essential task is to intercede with the spirits supposing misfortune strikes (when the weather turns foul, the animals become scarce, and so on); misfortune is understood as arising from the spirits taking offence because humans have disregarded their religious duties, most particularly by neglecting the taboos (such as the rule that caribou meat and seal meat should not be mixed into the same cooking pot). The spirits must be persuaded to look kindly on human beings and grant them good health and abundance. Alone in the community the shaman can deliver the spirits' forgiveness. All humans are believed to be animated by spiritual essence reincarnated from past ancestors, and all humans are considered to have an extra-physical identity, or soul, which upon death departs for ever to the spirit world. But the shaman is unique. Even as he continues to live, his soul may leave his body: it journeys to the spirit's lair, there to cajole the spirit to accept the people's promise, that from now on they will better respect the taboos. Such soul loss is achieved, in a public forum, through the technique of ecstasy. In the ambience of music and dance, the shaman enters a trance, his bodily writhings indicating his soul in desperate pleading with the spirits. Then the shaman declares that the people's pleas have been heard: emerging from the trance, he tells them they can expect better times providing they attend more assiduously to their religious duties. Among the Inuit, around two or three people within the broader territorial group can expect to command such skills.

Among the Bushman, the trance state occurs in respect of similar purposes, though it may be achieved by a far broader sector of the community. According to Katz (1976), around fifty percent of Bushman men and thirty-three percent of women are thus 'masters of the ghosts'. But the Bushman religion is definitely shamanistic: some of these people are renowned as much more religiously powerful than others, it being said that the Gods directly provided their superior capabilities (ibid.: 295–6).

Nomadic hunter–gatherers and the New Age

The parallels between the nomadic hunter–gatherers and the New Age in Glastonbury are, in our view, striking. At the level of cosmology, New Agers likewise subscribe to the notion of a mystically animated environment that incorporates humans as an integral spiritual component. Also, they invoke the idea of spiritually-blessed individuals (gurus, teachers, and so on) able uniquely to deliver enhanced insights into the spiritual realm. The term, shaman, is indeed often summoned by New Agers to denote these special individuals. For example, Gabrielle Roth (1990), questing to uncover increasingly deeper levels of personal spirituality, describes herself as an 'urban shaman', who is undertaking a 'journey'. On the social level, New Agers, like hunter–gatherers, uphold egalitarianism, and celebrate flexibility and individuality in daily social arrangements. The mutuality in New Age social relations compares directly with the kinship organisation of hunter–gatherers, especially those hunter–gatherers who summon the metaphor of family when describing sharing with others in common activities in the immediate locality (Myers 1986: 112; Bird-David 1994). It is significant that, among New Agers, the metaphor for mutuality is love.

The Glastonbury ethnography indicates that there are differences between hunter–gatherers and the New Age. Firstly, New Age cosmology is heterogeneous. For example, between Deep Ecology and the various therapy-oriented branches (such as regression therapy or crystal healing) there are very particular, and quite contrasting, interpretations of this cosmology. Hunter–gatherer society, meanwhile, is marked by cosmological homogeneity – though, that said, it is interesting that some commentators have queried this by drawing attention to what appears to be areas of inconsistency and incoherence (e.g. Morris 1976; Brunton 1980). Secondly, some New Agers are unhappy with charismatic leaders, be these 'gurus', 'teachers', 'shamans', or whatever. Thirdly (and perhaps more importantly), New Agers more usually attribute misfortune *directly* to human misdemeanour and inappropriate action: a spirit realm is much less invoked as the mediator of misfortune. Finally, hunter–gatherer cosmology is devoid of a revolutionary component. As a 'mainstream' cosmology it lacks ideas heralding sea changes in human experience and societal organisation; there are no notions of personal transformation in hunter–gatherer cosmology.

Hunter–Gatherer Cosmology and Society

With many other anthropologists, we believe that examining a people's social organisation and daily practice yields profitable insights into their cosmology. The critical relationship between social organisation and cosmology reflects, in our view, certain social processes common among all human societies – including Western mainstream society, where a major cosmology is called 'science'. Elsewhere one of us has labelled these processes 'religion' (Riches 1994). New Age cosmology, it follows, *is* a religious cosmology.

Cosmologies exist because they relate in some manner to people's practical interests. In the case of hunter–gatherer shamanism, one should investigate why, in relation to everyday social affairs, it is worthwhile for people to uphold the idea of shamanic power, and the related ideas about the universe which are implied from what a shaman does. The notion of interests invites an investigation of people's purposes and choices, and about how people justify, or legitimise, these purposes and choices in the face of fellow members of the society whose concerns may be different. For example, with respect to shamanism, the particular individuals incumbent in the role will be different, in terms of their interests, from ordinary people. More than this, to understand shamanism properly, ordinary people's interests should be treated as paramount: were their role not valuable to the population at large shamans would not exist. In sum, cosmology exists because people – different types of people – have worked to produce it (Riches 1994). The 'religious processes' which underpin cosmology consist of the strategies that this work necessarily implies.

In this section, we show that hunter–gatherer cosmology, in all its key elements, may be explained by reference to the egalitarian and individualistic character of hunter–gatherer social organisation. In doing this, we importantly take in the notion of communitas, along with discussion on the relationship between individualism and holism. We shall proceed logically. We demonstrate how the strategies of shamans ultimately reduce to the strategies of ordinary people, and how the strategies of ordinary people relate to fundamental contradictions concerning, firstly, egalitarianism, and, secondly, communitas. By way of illustration, we confine ourselves to the Inuit ethnography.

The shaman, then, is the starting point of the analysis. Initial focus should be on the *rewards* that accrue to people who are incumbent as shamans: rewards constitute a first element of religious process, for without rewards people would be unwilling to be religious specialists. We attend here to the fact that it is through the shamans that the Inuit vision of the universe is sustained, for shamans alone visit the spirit world where the form of the universe is revealed. Immense social and intellectual endeavour goes into producing a compelling vision of the universe; also, when it comes to the interpretation of ordinary people's everyday experiences in terms of such a vision, there will be competition among a number of shamans within a particular social arena. In short, making a success of shaman-ship – of intellectual guardianship of a cosmological system and of social watchdog over conduct in the Inuit community – is demanding indeed. So, for people to be prepared to undertake such duties there should be compensation, both tangible (in the form of material payment) and intangible (in the guise of prestige and renown). Thus Inuit shamans receive special gifts of food, and sometimes they demand sexual favours akin to *droit du seigneur*. Given the generally egalitarian social setting of Inuit society this not infrequently results in shamans cutting controversial figures within the local community. Some who have exceeded the mark in exacting such payment are known to have been killed.

That the shamans' competitive endeavours are creative endeavours is evident from their performance in the seance. Following trance, the shaman's soul having grappled with the spirits, the shaman sometimes 'returns' to the ordinary world to announce the existence of a social misdemeanour that is completely new: hitherto acceptable everyday behaviour is now causing the spirits offence, and this is why people are so sorely afflicted by misfortune and illness. Alluding to this, Knud Rasmussen, the Inuit's foremost ethnographer, comments: 'should the shaman have nothing definite to go on, he will keep to matters of ordinary everyday life in which he can be sure that all the women offend the taboo' (1929: 132). Such creativity results, in Inuit culture, in an incredible proliferation of religious rules (taboos), which bear upon virtually every area of daily life, including cooking, eating, sewing, and also impinging on all the main life-cycle occurrences, such as birth, coming of age, and death (and not excluding the death of animals in hunting). The point, of course, is that when it comes to identifying human miscreancy (which has given the spirits offence), the shaman must be found plausible by ordinary people, and this will be so to the extent that such miscreancy could actually have occurred. Therefore it is in a shaman's interest that there are rules in profusion. In short, one may say that in Inuit culture all such rules' exist because the shaman – their creator – keeps them relevant and in the public eye. But sometimes it is a struggle. This is illustrated in Rasmussen's dramatic account of an Inuit seance among the Iglulik people of northeast Hudson Bay, in which a shaman interrogates a patient as to the taboos she has broken. The patient willingly confesses to numerous transgressions, but the shaman is still not content, invoking more, and yet more, breaches of religious rules (in the end he mentions around thirty taboos in all). But the audience is sceptical. Even as the shaman summons his authority on behalf of the truth of the rules, the audience cry out: 'We will not take any notice of that [breach]'; 'It is such a slight offence'; 'Oh, is that all?'; 'Oh, such a trifling thing'. Occasionally, the audience remarks, 'That is very wrong . . . a great and serious offence' . . . but let her be released nonetheless' (Rasmussen 1929: 133–41).

The shaman is only encouraged to greater heights of invention by such exchanges. It is a cumulative matter, such that the analyst may conclude that the cosmology, in its full elaboration, originally arose, and is presently sustained, through the shaman's doings. This chimes in with Joanna Overing's assertions, about Amazonian shamans, that they are truly makers of the world; and with Barth's descriptions of secret cults in New Guinea where ritual leaders subtly alter the religious cosmology, such that religious change slowly accumulates (Overing 1990; Barth 1987). In both Amazonia and New Guinea, rivalry ensures that each religious specialist produces his own unique version of the respective religious cosmology.

There is a further dimension of this. Why do *particular* cosmologies – with their particular accounts of spirits, souls and rules in all their particular detail – get 'made'? Why does Inuit cosmology have the specific content it does (of a complex spiritual realm which controls the availability of animals, the state of people's health, the weather, etc.), and not some other content? The reply, given that the shaman elaborates the cosmology, is that the cosmology has the content it does because of the shaman's *choice*. Choice-making amounts to the second religious process. As to the direction of such choice, the major constraint relates to matters of power, of shaman over layperson. The point is, the cosmological world, which is the shaman's vision, should be one from which shamans alone may receive practical reward. Inuit cosmological ideas clearly reflect this. The notion of a spirit world that controls human fortune effectively declares that it is vital that there be exceptional intermediary figures (linking spirits and humans), their potential validated by some sort of initial spiritual sign, and whose special skills will have required years of training. Capitalising on human vulnerability, such cosmological ideas lay special emphasis on ordinary people's misfortunes. In short, the cosmology that the shaman elects to uphold (in all its detail) permits the shaman to present himself as someone essential and exclusive: a spiritual sign that it is in one's capacity to achieve extraordinary tasks relating to intercession with the spiritual world is something that few human beings receive, and fewer still are able or prepared to take on the rigours of apprenticeship with its painful and troubling ordeals.

The final question pertinent to the construction of cosmology follows on from this. It relates to matters of *legitimacy*, and amounts to a third element of religious process. Thanks to a cosmology's existence, benefits in the form of material reward and power flow exclusively to the religious specialist: but why should ordinary people, with their different perspectives on life, allow this? In short, so that the shaman's cosmology can command confidence in the population at large, it must be experienced by ordinary people as directly responding to their particular concerns as well. The shaman's vision of the world must include ideas which relate to this. Thus one turns, in this analysis of Inuit cosmology, to the standpoint of ordinary people.

Ordinary Inuit willingly submit themselves to ideas concerning the shaman's exclusiveness and power because their personal well-being depends on it. In Inuit cosmology, what crucially underwrites this is the notion that extraordinary and exceptional events are a central part of human experience. The point is, for ordinary people exceptional events effectively mean either unexpectedly good or unexpectedly bad fortune (relating to hunting, the weather, illness, and so on). One concludes that, accruing to ordinary people, the *reward* from submitting to the shaman's exclusive powers is that the shaman, by interceding with the spirits, alters human fortune (for the better). With reference to this context, the shaman is commonly described, by analysts, as charismatic, with the implication that inspirational personal qualities are intrinsic to what he does, both in interceding with the spirit world and in convincing ordinary people that he has achieved it. This is interesting since what the shaman delivers (better fortune) can be understood simply as a practical accomplishment (successful intercession with the spirit world). In our view, if the shaman is deemed to be inspirational, this may correspond with ordinary people reflecting on the shaman's accomplishment. Rather than as an objective instrument for success, charismatic inspiration may better be understood as an idea summoned up by ordinary people; by this idea ordinary people make sense of extraordinary achievements, especially when, in the absence of institutional support, these result from behaviour that is impressive.

But why are ordinary people content to construe extraordinary events in this particular way? Why are they comfortable with the idea that supreme forces exist whose entities (spirits, souls, etc.) are different in kind from ordinary folk, and cannot easily, or at all, be reached through average human competence? Here the questions, once again, are about matters of *choice*. The nature of unexpectedly good or bad fortune supplies the answer. Exceptional (mis)fortunes are occurrences that run directly counter to ordinary people's routine expectations: people experience – unpredictably experience – exceptional fortune the while that they anticipate the mundane and the routine. In short, exceptional fortunes are out-of-control experiences. One suggests that Inuit are content to comprehend such fortunes in terms of entities which cannot be 'reached', because this expresses, more appropriately than any alternative way, the sense of events being beyond one's control.

The focus, in this analysis of Inuit cosmology, is on individuals throughout. Ultimately, the spiritual system may be understood in terms of desires on the part of individual people to make sense of the especially good, and to reconcile themselves to the dreadfully bad. Put very generally, Inuit cosmology exists by the fact that individual men and women, in relation to highly personal circumstances, find it to their advantage that it be present. But talk of personal advantage raises, once again, the spectre of *legitimacy*, for an advantage that accrues to one person can imply disadvantage for another. Accordingly, all religious cosmologies include ideas which reveal that while particular individuals better themselves through engaging, directly or indirectly, with supernatural powers, others may rest content whilst they do so. Crucial holistic notions supply these ideas, specifically that such powers are in some essential way omniscient and omnipresent. These notions, in Inuit cosmology, are manifest in the central belief, with respect to human fortunes, that the spirit world commands overarching control, such that in some essential way responsibility for what happens to people in their daily lives lies with the spirit world, *and not with people*. Relating to matters of legitimacy, this powerfully guarantees that everyone, in time (indeed, sooner, more likely than later), will require to engage with the spiritual world. Therefore if, for the sake of personal well-being, that is what some particular individual is doing now, others may have no cause to object.

Thus interpersonal acquiescence lies at the foundation of the

Inuit cosmological system. This confirms that cosmologies, even as they are constructed by individuals, exist in a definite relation to the broader social fabric. This relation may be explored. With respect to the nomadic hunter–gatherers we argue that one should focus here on the pervasively egalitarian ethos of these societies, such as is notably evident in respect of many key social values, for example non-authoritarian leadership and kin-based food sharing. As regards the link between an egalitarian ethos and cosmology, it would appear that one key cosmological idea is central, namely that when human hunters meet with exceptional successes and failures, the spirit world (which controls and dispatches the game) has caused it.

The link between a shamanistic cosmology and egalitarianism may be demonstrated by reflecting on each in turn. Starting with cosmological ideas, we recall that these, in Inuit society, pervasively explain the practical successes and failures of ordinary people as not their direct responsibility. The spirit world, by dispatching animals to be killed, or by withholding them, ultimately decides whether hunters will make the kill or come back empty-handed. In this regard, an important observation is that, in cosmological terms, whether the hunter brings home the animal or not, technical competence does not come into it. Also, one notes that arising from these ideas is the particular way by which hunter–gatherers construe the human being as a holistic person. In the case of the Inuit the intellectual context for this is the tension between the spirits (who control the animals) and humans (who physically eliminate them). The spirits' supremacy in this regard must be upheld, and Inuit ideas achieve this through the notion that when the animal is 'killed' the spirits reclaim a crucial part of it: thus a non-physical essence – the animal's *soul* – returns to the spirit realm (there to animate a fresh batch of animals). We suggest that this underpins the idea that humans, too, reincarnate: if an animal incorporates such a mystical capacity so also should the human being. (For further elaboration, see Riches, 1994: 388.)

As to the egalitarian ethos, the key point is that this betrays social instability. A number of writers have commented upon this (e.g., Brunton 1989), most recently Helliwell (1995), who demonstrates that egalitarianism sits uneasily beside another central social principle, also embraced by hunter–gatherers, namely individualism (or 'personal autonomy'). With societies such as the Inuit, the conundrum is that the egalitarian ethos, because it is antithetical to authority, licenses individualism. Yet individualism may subvert egalitarianism, for individualism legitimates individuals in making strategic choices that may have authoritarian intentions. Deliberately to achieve an egalitarian state of affairs, Helliwell shows, there needs somehow to be restrictions on people's autonomy. Among the nomadic hunter–gatherers generally, this tension clearly prevails. On the one hand, in the name of egalitarianism people emphasise that social differences regarding both wealth and power should not develop within the community. Thus on a practical level there are a number of 'levelling-down' procedures, in which, by such methods as 'rough good humour, put downs, teasing and sexual joking' (Lee 1988: 262–6), persons blessed with superior skills in some significant walk of life are hindered from capitalising on the fact and entrenching themselves in formal hierarchical positions. Draper, writing about the Bushman, captures this very well:

> Pride and boastfulness are particularly devalued; for example, when a young hunter returns from a hunt and announces to no one in particular, 'I killed an eland!' he is greeted by indifference . . . If the young man persists, an older person will remark in a voice designed to carry across the camp clearing, 'Why only one?' (1978: 41)

On the other hand, there are other social conventions where individuals who stand out from the rest seem explicitly to be acknowledged as important. Running counter to egalitarian values, Inuit hunters whose catches rank consistently above average, and whose decisions about moving camp prove to be most effective, will come to exercise influence and be designated in the wider community as 'thinkers' (the Inuit term is *isumataaq*). The notion of prestige captures the quality of the relationship between such individuals and others in the community (Riches 1984).

The salience of the shamanistic cosmology in the nomadic hunter–gatherer society is that it functions to sustain the social principle of egalitarianism in this context. Here one attends to people's exceptional practical successes and failures in the conduct of everyday affairs, especially hunting. The point about practical successes and failures, in particular consistent successes and failures, is that they bespeak of inequality, and so jeopardise egalitarian social principles. But hunter–gatherer cosmological ideas, by invoking a non-human realm, declare that such successes and failures do not arise from a hunter's practical (in)competence, but rather from the decisions of spirits. Thus the egalitarian ideal in human social relations is strongly underpinned. In short, in a

determinedly egalitarian society the fundamental basis of shamanistic cosmology lies in ordinary people's efforts to deal intellectually with anti-egalitarian practical trends.

Thinking ahead to the analysis of New Age cosmology and society, the hunter–gatherer discussion may be pushed a final stage
further. We remain with the egalitarian ethos and observe that
egalitarianism is a holistic notion connoting distributive justice.
Among hunter–gatherers, this is particularly expressed through the
idiom of kinship: in kinship relationships people experience the
mutuality present in virtually all social relations in the community.
As Bird-David puts it, in the hunter–gatherer community everyone
considers themselves as 'family'; indeed the environment is
included here as well, such that the relation between spirits (con-
trolling animals, the weather, and so on) and humans is thought of
as one between parent and child, or husband and wife (Bird-David
1992; 1994).

But egalitarianism may not be the starting point for understanding hunter–gatherer social organisation, for it, too, must have
a social source. One of us (Riches 1982) has argued that this source
relates to the very intensive social interaction that obtains among
the small numbers of people who make up hunter–gatherer communities. Living cheek by jowl, often during lengthy foraging seasons, such people cannot but be voluntarily involved with one
another in a multiplicity of essential daily tasks. Egalitarian and
altruistic ideals for social interaction may arise from the severe
social pressure that such a state of affairs brings. So intertwined are
people in the small, intensively interacting hunter–gatherer community that the demands individuals inevitably put upon one
another, regarding requests for assistance and resources, simply
cannot be resisted. The predicament is: refuse someone's demands
in respect of one aspect of life and one stands *to be* refused in
respect of another. Riches proposes that intellectually the way to
cope with this most effectively is for people to construe the hand-
ing over of resources and assistance as something done keenly and
willingly – without thought for the self. In short, the social principles of egalitarianism and altruism exist in order that there be a
positive gloss on the experiences, of individuals, in the 'intertwined predicament'.

In this book we have made much of the relation between
individualism and holism. In this regard, the revelation, with
respect to hunter–gatherers, that behind the egalitarian ethos
there is individualist strategy, is helpful, since, as we have noted,

egalitarianism is a holistic idea. Our general view, indeed, is that in relation to every holistic expression there are strategic, individualistic underpinnings. This is the obverse of Dumont's thinking (see Chapter 2), which basically declares that transcendent (holistic) ideas are a condition for strategic action. 'Culture', 'customs', 'social norms' or 'social values' are the labels generally given to such ideas. However, for us, rules, values and so on, are better seen as concepts that people invoke in order to lend weight to what they want to do; thus they are creations authored (over and again) by individual human beings (Holy and Stuchlik 1983). Likewise the notion that such ideas are 'transcendent' is something that people (individuals) strategically attribute to their creations in order to lend them credence. The ultimate here is that even as a given social rule is conjured up to justify a particular course of action, the individual(s) concerned must creatively hold in mind other, broader social ideas which might appropriately be summoned to 'justify the rule' should fellow members of the community decide to challenge its veracity.[11] By this latter process a particular rule finds 'acceptance' – or, as it is often said, gets 'shared'.

The logical conclusion is that, for there to be social interaction, all that is required is that individuals recognise one another as human beings with whom dealings are possible. Concerning such a primordial mutuality, communitas is the term, in our view, that best describes it. Communitas, in short, is the sole condition necessary for individuals, in strategic endeavour, to generate the full range of human societies and cultures.

Turning to the New Age, communitas, which undergirds human society, is particularly manifest in the Glastonbury situation, and therefore the study of the Alternative Community in the town is ideal for examining the social processes that occur in the construction of human society generally. Communitas, in the case of Glastonbury's settled New Agers, exemplifies itself in the fact that these people, in their whole beings, are likemindedly not-mainstream. Analytically, one may think of the New Agers' communitas as a *tabula rasa*, upon which an enormously rich social organisation and culture comes to be written – by themselves. Here we note that communitas is in essence an egalitarian circumstance: in communitas people experience an elemental social equivalence. Such existential egalitarianism is not quite the same as the egalitarian morality of the hunter–gatherers, yet there are parallels which are surely enlightening. In connection with the New Age we shall argue that communitas admits of instabilities and contradictions rather similar to those associated with the 'egalitarian ethos'. It is arising from instabilities and contradictions relating to communitas that the construction of New Age society and culture begins.

Notes

1. Luhrmann poses the complementary question, about witchcraft and mystical magic in present-day England: why do middle class people practise magic when they should know it does not work (1989: 4).
2. For reviews, commentaries and analyses of the New Right, see Bosanquet (1983), Green (1987), and King (1987). These take in a number of versions of New Right thinking, including their social dimensions, ranging from monetarism through to the more thoroughgoingly individualistic ideologies of the anarcho-libertarians.
3. As good an example as any here is Balch's account of the development, by Marshall Applewhite, of the Heaven's Gate movement whose UFO-related beliefs led to mass suicide in California in March 1997 (Balch 1982).
4. *The Journal of the Findhorn Foundation*, 1989, vol. 9, Forres, p. 3.
5. *Kindred Spirit*, Summer 1991, Totnes, p. 33.
6. *Global Link-Up*, 1991, issue 6, Gloucester, p. 24.
7. *The Journal of the Findhorn Foundation*, 1989, Vol 9, Forres, p. 18.
8. The discussion on hunting and gathering societies does not include either the Australian Aborigines or the Northwest Coast Indians, hunting and gathering peoples whose social organisations and cosmologies are, for reasons considered elsewhere, very different from those discussed in this book (Riches 1995).
9. One acknowledges that, thanks to substantial social changes, Bushman society as a nomadic-hunter society is evident in only limited areas of southern Africa today (Barnard 1982).
10. Eliade insists: 'nowhere in the history of religions do we encounter "primordial" phenomena; for history has been everywhere, changing, recasting, enriching, or impoverishing religious concepts, mythological creations...' (1964: 11). This is an important observation. Yet we shall argue that with hunter–gatherer shamanism we *do* 'glimpse' the primordial.
11. Holy (1979) offers an excellent example of this occurring. Among the Toka of Zambia, a rule that sons should inherit from fathers was introduced so that sons could take over the animals that they had helped their fathers rear. In the face of those who objected to this rule (which superseded a matrilineal inheritance principle) a broader idea was summoned. This idea amounted to a principle of natural justice, namely that people who work together, in whatever task, should be entitled to share in the rewards.

11

Foundation, Vision and Representation: Levels of New Age Culture

Beginnings: Contradictions in Communitas

New Age culture may be treated as consisting of levels of knowledge, some more fundamental than others. In terms of the construction of New Age culture, the more fundamental levels are logically prior to the less fundamental ones. As to the substance of New Age social organisation and cosmology, either a particular element is evident at one particular level, or alternatively, hitherto thought of as an undifferentiated entity, it turns out to be a composite from more than one level. In any event, social and cultural matter manifest at a more fundamental level functions as preconditions in the construction of social and cultural matter of less fundamental levels. We theorised this overall position in Chapter 1, where we announced that we shall focus on three principal levels of knowledge. 'Cultural foundation' is the most fundamental level: this consists of knowledge generated by ordinary people. 'Cultural vision' is the next most fundamental: knowledge at this level, generated by New Age teachers, is broadly shared amongst all New Age subdoctrines. Finally, 'cultural representation' is the least fundamental in terms of generative potential: knowledge at this level, which functions in relation to the communication of New Age ideas, generally differs as between different subdoctrines.

Theorisation in Chapter 1 also indicates that people's communitas experience of being 'not-mainstream' underpins and makes possible the construction of all these levels: this in-common experience is present at a still deeper level of knowledge. In Chapter 10 we reasserted such a perspective via the hunter–gatherer analysis. In this chapter we shall deduce New Age social organisation and cosmology as being based on this communitas experience, using the hunter–gatherer analysis as the template – for example, with respect to religious process, we frame the New Age discussion in terms of reward, choice and legitimation. (But in this chapter we shall be less explicit about such process, so as not to be pedantic.)

The interpretation of New Age society and culture in this chapter is in relation to the 'questions' about this society and culture that the Glastonbury ethnography invites; these questions were discussed in Chapters 5 to 9. The deductive model will be successful to the extent that, on the basis of reasoning from first principles, it provides stimulating replies to these questions; contradictions relating to communitas constitute such basic premises. From time to time, the 'questions' that the deductive model is answering will be recalled by interposing earlier chapter numbers in brackets. The aim in the present section, with regard to the construction of the three levels of knowledge, is to elucidate the basic premises. It will be noted that, in this chapter, compared with the hunter–gatherer analysis in the previous chapter, the order of exposition is reversed. The New Age analysis starts, rather than ends, with the idea of communitas; it is informed not by the position of shamans or other religious specialists, but by the circumstances of ordinary people present in Glastonbury full of expectation for something different in life. This reversal of exposition is because, as noted in Chapter 10, the hunter–gatherer parallels are not exact. Indeed, when we come to analysis, the difference between New Agers and hunter–gatherers provides an immediate point of departure.

The main thing about this difference is that hunter–gatherer societies amount to a mainstream society. Hunter–gatherers may be knowledgeable about neighbouring societies, which these days will most likely be agriculturalists or pastoralists, but other ways of life do not normally present themselves as realistic or preferable alternatives. With New Agers it is the opposite. For them the larger British society, of which all but the youngest were once members, and to which they could correspondingly return, continually stands as a viable and welcoming option. The wider world remains something one turns oneself against.

Communitas corresponds to a deep level of experience, and is not directly available to the anthropologist from the surface features of society and culture which, in a sense, overlay it even as they are conditioned by it. This is not to say, however, that ethnography cannot inspire an understanding of the communitas experience and the contradictions that relate to it. In Chapter 12, with reference to different religious movements we pin down the nature of this experience in terms of the variable 'space-time', such that one may say that different religious movements have different communitas experiences, which are different again from mainstream society. For the moment, with reference to the fact that New Agers are not a mainstream community, we note that what communitas connotes is different as between Glastonbury New Agers and hunter–gatherers. The Glastonbury communitas experience is distinctive in that it is a highly reflexive experience: we describe New Age as 'not-mainstream' in order to grasp, at the level of communitas, people's consciousness that they are turned against the mainstream.

As to the contradictions relating to communitas, the hunter–gatherer discussion is instructive. The social organisational egalitarianism of hunter–gatherers is analogous to the profound, deep-rooted egalitarianism of communitas (see Riches 1994, for further elaboration). The contradictions regarding hunter–gatherers refer to the relation between egalitarianism and autonomy, and the parallel contradictions regarding New Age communitas may be expressed as between the experience of communion and the experience of practical action (individuality). Thus New Age communitas implies undifferentiated social positions, to which the closest analogy at the level of observable features is the notion of love, denoting the unreserved acceptance of one another by all in the Alternative Community. On the other hand, communitas includes doing, as well as being, as we pointed out in Chapter 2. Thus 'unreserved acceptance' requires that practical action be unrestricted. But unrestricted action's outcome may constitute a departure from what communitas, as a profound egalitarianism, ideally specifies.

We are theorising this contradiction, yet the Glastonbury ethnography makes it plausible, as the discussions in Chapters 5 and 7 make clear. In the field of health, the cosmos, in which all humans are essentially incorporated, and from which all in like manner derive benefit, expresses well-being as something in which everyone deeply shares; yet individuals, precisely by becoming ill, frequently fall below its egalitarian standard. In the field of wealth, distributive justice is the key value, yet not a few people in the Alternative Community make considerable sums of money by selling New Age practices and insights as specialist services. As to Glastonbury communitas, New Ager residence in the town is a whole-life situation, such that in an essential way practical action (keeping healthy, doing work, educating children, etc.) is intrinsic to the experience of being there. Thus in the Alternative Community, communitas, the essential communion relating to being not-mainstream, stands to be confounded, at the deepest level of the social formation, by the individuality which it licenses.

New Age Cultural Foundation

Our thesis is that human beings construct 'social structure', and distinctive 'societies' emerge, in order that contradictions relating to communitas might experientially be resolved. Thus New Age cosmology and social organisation in Glastonbury may be explained in terms of contradictions relating to the Alternative Community's distinctive (i.e., reflexive) communitas experience. In this section we consider how a foundation level of New Age cosmology and social organisation might emanate from such contradictions; this foundation level consists of ideas relating to the holistic person and the social position of the charismatic presence. The inspiration for the argument is the basis of hunter–gatherer cosmology in the contradiction regarding egalitarianism and autonomy. The New Age model imagines the construction of cosmology and society, at this foundation level, as the work of ordinary people.

The New Age concept of the holistic person, since it relates directly to New Age experience of communitas, may be considered the 'first element' of New Age society and culture. The holistic person may be deduced in relation to how, in the New Age context, individuality jeopardises communion. The relevant principle here is that, when such experience occurs, human strategic will may not be held responsible. The analogy with hunter–gatherers refers to circumstances when exceptional success or misfortune fall to particular individuals. But the difference between New Age and hunter–gatherers is immediately relevant.

For hunter–gatherers, circumstances of exceptional success or misfortune denote autonomy undermining egalitarianism. The construction of the cosmological idea of non-human spirits and animal souls occurs in this context: thanks to the notion of non-human spirits, which dispatch the sentient animals, when hunters enjoy successes beyond those of their fellows the spirits may be held responsible. Accordingly egalitarian values within the human community are sustained by being experienced as being uncompromised by human will.

Turning to the New Agers, we predict that contradictions relating to communitas will be construed in parallels terms, but yet contrastingly. When New Agers, as individuals, experience success and misfortune, this will be understood, like the hunter–gatherers, as not resulting from deliberate strategic action. But the specifically self-reflexive nature of New Age thinking means that New Agers will conceptualise such circumstances differently. Such reflexive thinking will invite a quite distinctive cultural expression of what causes especial success and failure. The cause of success and failure will be symbolised in terms of something forceful, but uncontrollable, *within people themselves*. People may do exceptionally well or else be extremely unfortunate when they involve themselves in practical social life. But something inside – something ineffable – is ultimately responsible. Quite opposite to Western mainstream ideas of chance or luck, the New Age understands human fortune by summoning up specific non-physical agencies; but distinctively for the New Age such agencies are condensed on the human individual. The result is that the New Age 'person' is constituted as an indissoluble admixture of observable body and non-observable essence – in short, as a holistic person. As to how one should label this forceful non-observable essence, it is tempting, as New Agers do, immediately to use the term, 'spiritual'. Yet the 'spiritual holistic person' appears to be a composite idea: according to the deductive model, the construction of the specific idea of spirituality occurs at a less fundamental level (whereupon it becomes available as the label for 'forceful non-observable essence'). So, whilst discussion remains at the foundation level, we should properly label the non-observable essence with a less committing term – perhaps 'mind' would be appropriate. However, even at this fundamental level, to talk of a person's spirituality does not seem unreasonable, and this, with qualification, we propose to do (in this section, at least).

In New Age conceptions, the idea of the holistic person interprets misfortune comfortably, but it construes success rather less well, especially where this is material success. When someone falls ill the diagnosis is plain: the balance within the person as between the physical, the emotional and, above all, the spiritual, is wrong. For New Agers, then, wellness is effectively a matter of internal spirituality, as the Glastonbury ethnography has related (see also Burrows 1993: 19). As to especial success, New Agers can find this discomfiting. Thus, with regard to material success, it is accepted that people must make a living – but perhaps not too good a living. Discomfiture often relates to circumstances when wealth accumulates unintentionally, by a process rather similar to how Weber described the Protestant ethic leading indirectly to the emergence of capitalism. A case in point would be members of the Alternative Community making money by running an Alternative shop on Glastonbury High Street. In this context, prosperity consciousness, discussed in Chapter 7, may well be an idea whose time has come. In prosperity consciousness, wealth is construed as accumulating through the individual having achieved a correct personal balance, especially relating to the spirit and to emotion.

There is a final comment about the holistic person. A reflexive understanding of the human person, as a physical entity imbued with a non-physical potency, is complex and somewhat abstract. One therefore expects, in New Age cosmological thinking, that this notion finds its expression in something more concrete. Paradoxically, the domain which most promisingly conveys the importance of the holistic person is the physical body: certain attitudes to the physical body symbolise rather well the worth of the person in his or her non-physical dimension. In New Age cosmology – as, indeed, in other religions as well – this seems to occur. As discussed in Chapter 4, New Agers uphold the purity of the physical body, for example in relation to the foods they eat. The salience of physical purity as representing the integrity of the holistic person has indeed been remarked upon by others, both commentators on the New Age and New Agers themselves. For example, Hess comments that by New Agers the body is seen as inherently natural and as having an innate wisdom of its own (1993: 116); for Roth (1990: 29), the body is the ground metaphor, the elementary site of spiritual exploration.

Among hunter–gatherers, the notion that departure from everyday equality is caused by an external spirit world legitimises the role of the shaman, whose task is to intercede between the realm of spirits and the realm of humans. In the case of the New Age, the salience of the guru (or teacher, or shaman) is going to be different, and in some respects less central, since, in New Age thinking failure and success are essentially (self-contained) matters of personal responsibility. Yet New Agers have another, quite different intellectual concern: the difference between the New Age and the mainstream. Such a concern is invited precisely by differences relating to the nature of the human person: the holistic person established in the New Age contrasts dramatically with the fragmented person upheld in the mainstream, where the mind, soul and body are considered to be operationally entirely distinct, such that, according to the situation, the human being is basically understood as something *either* physical *or* mental. This contrast, it will be seen, paradigmatically expresses the opposition between New Age and mainstream. But first New Agers must reflect upon it. We argue that in the New Age movement the existence of the charismatic presence – teachers, gurus, sacred texts, and so on – is constructed so that this occurs. In later sections in this chapter we shall discuss at length the teachers' work in this regard.

Here context is provided for the points made elsewhere in this book about the charismatic presence in the New Age movement. The presence of teachers etc. does not relate to the fact that they inspire people to abandon mainstream routines. The construction model shows that, thanks to the ordinary New Ager's independent decision, such departure can be considered to have occurred already. The teacher's worth instead stems from the value to the ordinary New Ager that certain basic meanings about being non-mainstream should be reflected upon further and rationalised. We have indicated, in this respect, that a primary function of New Age teachers, gurus and texts will be to elaborate upon and develop the notion of the holistic person as a dominant symbol of the New Age. The model helps make a further point. The fact that a movement's membership pre-exists the movement's leaders puts a perspective on the inspirational character of the New Age teacher/guru. Movement leaders exist because of straightforward interpretive tasks needing to be done, and their value, to ordinary New Agers, is in relation to the effectiveness with which these tasks are discharged. We suggest, in line with our remarks about Inuit shamans, that the inspirational dimension associated with the New Age teacher comes to be attributed as *a consequence* of the job done well. Far from impacting on ordinary people, charismatic inspiration is an idea that ordinary people construct. Finally, one may understand the critical significance, in New Age thinking, of *healing* and *therapy*, in which gurus, teachers and other charismatics engage. Such activities are focused around *care* for the holistic person. Via holistic healing, we suggest, ordinary New Agers appropriate a vibrant metaphor of their decision not to be part of the mainstream world.

To summarise what the construction model has yielded so far, responses may be given to several questions, posed in the Glastonbury chapters. First, the notion of the holistic person does seem to be more fundamental than other holistic ideas in New Age cosmology: the holistic person appears to be a root cosmological idea, whilst holistic ideas relating to, for example, the universe, evidently emerge at some other, subsequent level of construction (Chapter 5). Second, the charismatic presence, which, as will be seen in the next section, is responsible for the formulation of the bulk of New Age cosmology, is itself dependent on specific elements of cosmology. Failing the idea of the holistic person, the charismatic presence would not exist (Chapter 9). Third, the anthropologist should not construe charisma as a causal relation. The New Age idea, that charismatic inspiration has an impact in making things happen, should not be treated as an explanation for why things happen, but rather as a representation of the fact that, because of exceptional practical competence on the part of a certain individual, things have happened, which ordinary people want to reflect on (Chapter 9).

New Age Cultural Vision

Properly to grasp the significance of what teachers, healers, shamans and gurus 'do', one should take their activities literally. (From now on, following Chapter 5, we shall mostly use 'teacher' as the generic term to cover these various categories.) Declaiming wisdom or writing a text is an activity and, that being so, all that is said and written in this regard should be treated as the teacher's construction. This is important, since this study is concerned with how the social organisation and cosmology of the New Age movement in Glastonbury is constructed through people's endeavours.

Theoretical matters are implicit here, relating to the fact that the approach one takes to understanding cosmology differs very much according to whether one thinks of it as a 'finished' whole, or whether it is viewed as something 'in the making' (Barth 1987). The role of teachers should be understood correspondingly. In the first alternative, one treats a cosmology as a completed understanding of the universe – a universe which teachers and texts 'deal with', both intellectually and through action (for example, by journeying to a spiritual realm). In this perspective, the 'world of gods and spirits' is taken as something given, and the teacher's function is seen as helping ordinary people make sense of it and come to terms with it. Following this stance, cosmology as something ready-packaged becomes the starting point for analysis. This is not satisfying. It resonates, to be sure, with the way Westerners generally think about cosmology; yet it ignores the fact that where cosmology exists it does so as a *human product*. The second alternative is therefore preferable: that cosmologies, as bodies of knowledge, result from human endeavour. Thus the more pleasing metaphoric image is 'cosmology as pieced together'. As to the teacher's seminal role in this, Luhrmann's account of witchcraft and similar groups in England stands as the paradigmatic example. With respect to the groups' rituals and ideas, Luhrmann vividly describes how, just like non-Western shamans, adepts in these well-established groups uphold their prestige in relation to their inventiveness and creativity (1989: 26, 72–3).

The 'cultural vision' of the New Age refers to the social and cosmological knowledge that New Age teachers establish as the essential religious, moral and ethical principles of the New Age: these include notions of the holistic universe, of personal transformation, of spirituality, of the mystical world, along with the key social values by which New Agers should live their lives. The thrust of this section is, again, to predict these elements through the construction model. Such prediction is based on the premises, established in the previous section, that New Age teachers exist in order to cogitate on the difference between the New Age and the mainstream. It will be seen that the holistic person, which this duty is based on, very much influences these cogitations. The value of the following discussion is again to respond to questions posed in the Glastonbury chapters.

To analyse the New Age cultural vision, the ethical standards of the New Age are an appropriate point of departure. Listed in Chapter 2, and returned to from time to time during the Glastonbury chapters, these especially include ideas of non-aggression, environmentalism, communalism, emotionality and intuition (the idea of spirituality will be examined later). Particular New Age subdoctrines, it was noted, incorporate at least two such ethical standards; each such subdoctrine includes a description of how the respective standards intermesh and are of apiece. In the New Age 'vision' the various ethical standards, which are held to be generally available for humankind's general betterment, imply social practices to which individual New Agers in their personal commitment bear witness. Such a personal commitment implies, for the individual New Ager, a radical transformation in psychological and experiential attitude to which all who embrace the New Age vision must submit.

In line with the New Age's conception of itself as 'alternative' (to the mainstream), these standards seem rather obviously to be reversals, or opposites, of what the mainstream holds dear. New Age subdoctrines, the construction model presumes, result from the teacher's endeavours: they are the teacher's creations – the product of teacher ingenuity. But even as they pursue their own exclusive interests, teachers must, alongside, address the agendas of ordinary people. The fact that the ethical standards they uphold are reversals of the mainstream might reflect precisely the legitimacy of teachers, which, it has been shown, relates to certain concerns, on the part of ordinary people, about the difference between the New Age and the mainstream.

But such a conclusion begs two issues. First, 'what the mainstream holds dear' reflects the New Agers' stereotype of the nature of mainstream society. It may be close to what the mainstream actually is, yet such a stereotype is logically also a construction of the New Age – or, more exactly, the construction of New Age teachers. Second, New Age ethical standards do not *have* to be opposites of the mainstream; to symbolise a difference from the mainstream they might simply be different. Since the New Age and mainstream *are* established as opposites, these two observations indicate that, in the case of the New Age ethical standards, there is occurring a double construction: the mainstream stereotype and the New Age ethical standards are being elaborated simultaneously.

It may be argued that the idea of the holistic person underpins this elaboration. The key matter here relates to the fact that the holistic person specifies the non-corporeal as inextricable from the corporeal (it is important, in this section, not to specify the non-corporeal as 'spirit'). One predicts that reflections, within the New Age, on the difference between the New Age and the mainstream, will examine the mainstream in terms of its understanding of the non-corporeal, and find this understanding in the belief of a power external to the individual, which mainstreamers generally render as God. When it comes to elaborating the New Age ethical standards, together with the contrasting nature of the mainstream, New Age teachers will infer the ubiquitous association between God and morality. Thus morality becomes the metaphor to construct the difference between the mainstream and the New Age.

This elaboration of difference is of course done in the name of specifying the New Ager as in some sense superior to the mainstreamer. We can say two things from this. First, thanks to the metaphor of morality, New Age superiority comes to be expressed precisely in terms of pervasive *ethical* standards. Second, when the mainstream is considered to be not just different, but inferior, *opposite* ethical standards most appropriately counter mainstream's worth. This leaves the final issue. Why is the mainstream stereotyped in a particular way, such that the ethical standards listed for New Age indeed qualify as opposites (Chapter 7)? Again, one appeals to the New Age idea of the holistic person, and specifically its contrast with the mainstream fragmented person. We described in Chapter 2 how the New Age ethical standards amount to opposites in relation to the central value of material accumulation. We suggest now that the mainstream is stereotyped in terms of this particular value in relation to the notion, allowed by the idea of the fragmented person, that the human being can be construed as something purely physical. To stereotype the mainstream in terms of its obsession with physical objects is symbolically appropriate to a mainstream person stigmatised as consisting essentially of physical attributes.

We may resolve questions about New Age social organisation within this context (Chapter 6). Egalitarianism, autonomy and the down-playing of formal roles may recall communitas, yet this is not how this constellation should be understood. In these social features, far from glimpsing primordial 'not-mainstreamness', one sees constructed, in the realm of social organisation, a New Age counter-culture. Mainstream material accumulation implies, in New Age eyes, a certain social fabric, which, as related in Chapter 6, is represented by New Agers as a sort of hypocritical individualism, where capitalist needs restrict the goals individuals may entertain. In Glastonbury, by contradicting or refining parallel mainstream practices, the respective social features symbolise individualism running to its 'proper', unfettered conclusion.

The various New Age subdoctrines display an integration of ethical standards into relatively coherent bodies of knowledge. We suggest that this poses a separate issue for investigation. We mentioned in Chapter 5 that New Age discourse commonly imitates standard sociological discourse, especially so in the charismatic texts. To the Western mind, thanks to the legacy of the Enlightenment, this makes eminent sense, but it is not logically inevitable. As noted in Chapter 10, many human societies, including some hunter–gatherers, uphold relatively uncoordinated visions of the world with rather little holistic linking as between the respective moral components, each of which is construed as valid in relation to fairly particular circumstances.

That New Age teachers offer relatively coherent philosophical systems may be predicted in relation to another matter concerning the holistic person, namely that, in the face of profound main-stream scepticism, New Agers cannot take the 'holistic identity' for granted. The upshot is that New Age acolytes reflexively experi-ence a heightened sense of this distinctive identity, and this, in turn, means that the ethical standards (which separately express the holistic person) likewise cannot be taken for granted. In short, such moral standards will be subject, by ordinary New Agers, to very careful scrutiny and evaluation. In the context of such scrutiny, New Age teachers elaborate the ethical standards relevant to a particular subdoctrine in such a way that all are mutually rein-forcing: thanks to the system in which all are consequently a part, each one is upheld as *valid*. The careful analysis, in many New Age texts, of the evolutionary processes whereby the West turned to its supposed disastrous social and spiritual course, are clearly an important part of this strategy.

The holistic universe, a major theme in most New Age doc-trines, is extremely pertinent here. We identify it as a major theme because it amounts to much more than the ethical standard of environmentalism and a pleasing account of the natural world and how human beings relate to other entities. Epitomising the inter-connectedness of all things, its presence as a crucial component in New Age thinking is, it may be suggested, as a metaphor for the general relatedness among New Age ethical standards. The point at issue is that 'integratedness among ethical standards' is a rather abstract notion, whilst 'interconnected universe' is more concrete and definitely more compelling. The holistic universe therefore functions powerfully to communicate the validity of the New Age vision in which it is included (Chapter 5).

A further, distinctive component of the New Age vision refers to the acolytes' existential predicament in its psychological aspect, namely that being New Age implies personal transformation and a revolution in consciousness. It will be recalled that New Age practice attends very prominently to techniques, notably involv-ing meditation and healing, in which such transformation is expressed. We suggest that New Age doctrines strongly incorporate such ideas in relation to the fact that in the Western world being non-mainstream is very much a personal decision. (Even in alternative communities outside the New Age, where people are socialised from birth into a closed and highly structured environment, the individual cannot, except possibly by physical force, be prevented from leaving, albeit that social and symbolic barriers may be put in his or her way.) An alternative vision of the world will therefore speak to the *personal* responsibilities and anxieties connected with being non-mainstream and therefore with being 'different'. It has been discussed already how in New Age accounts of the world non-mainstream persons are generally represented as both holistic and moral persons. When New Age teachers ascribe ideas of internal enhancement and transformation to the holistic person, we suggest that these ideas express very appropriately the experience of personal moral crisis that being a New Ager implies. The point is, through ideas such as personal transformation crisis relating to being non-mainstreamers may be read in an entirely positive way. One notes that, in many New Age texts, the connection between moral crisis and notions of personal transformation is legitimated through securing the reader's involvement in the personal tragedies which have led the authors to formulate the correct New Age path.

Nearly all New Agers, it has been observed, in some manner or other, engage in economic relations with the mainstream society – by taking a job within it, by selling the New Age to it, or by using within the New Age techniques learned from it. Yet, many New Agers, in Glastonbury and elsewhere, strive for New Age self-sufficiency; in some places, for example, internal markets are established within an alternative community, with exclusive local currencies of accounting. But total economic isolation seems to be barely possible. However, local New Age teachers may be exceptions to this. By elaborating on the New Age to New Agers in both speech and text, many make a handsome living, and on top of this may additionally profit by putting their particular visions of the world on show to the mainstream, for example to businesspeople who seek the royal road to inner confidence and personal empowerment. This highlights the fact that, in terms of self-regard, prestige and, above all, making a living, being a teacher can bring ample rewards. In her book on women in the new religious movements, Puttick discusses very well teachers' appropriations in this respect, including their sexual predations, which many mainstreamers do not find admirable (Puttick 1997). It follows that, even as they emphasise that there is in everyone the potential for inspired thinking, New Age teachers will foster a vision of the world in relation to which the role of the teacher is in some way indispensable. This brings us to a final major component of the teacher's vision, and here there are very close parallels with Inuit shamans.

This last component refers to the spirituality and mysticism that totally suffuse New Age visions of the world, not exempting even the most banal everyday activity (Chapter 7 poses this last point). One suggests that such a profoundly ineffable quality to the world is imparted, by teachers, precisely so that their visions cry out for (their own) specialist interpretation. By its ineffability the world is rendered elusive to ordinary people – as a domain which, thanks to the possession of insights and skills not readily available to others, only a teacher can effectively interpret. Two observations follow from this. First, only at this stage in the construction of New Age culture is the holistic person fully articulated as a specifically spiritual entity. Healing, in turn, comes to be conceptualised as an inherently spiritual process – as the restoration of balance between body, mind and spirit, and thus a positive opportunity for the sufferer (Burrows 1993). Second, Gaian mysticism, which specifies a spiritually animated holistic universe, seems to have a double function. On the one hand (as intimated already) the notion contributes to the legitimation of the specialist, for whom the exclusive task becomes to make sense of this strange and intriguing world. On the other hand, the notion itself is relatively unchallengeable since, thanks to the concept of the holistic (spiritual) person (to which all New Agers subscribe), the idea that the universe, too, is spiritually infused is something that everyone can quite easily accept (Chapter 5).

New Age teachers, then, uphold a world which, to be interpreted, requires a bridge between the ordinary and the spiritual. Given the generally egalitarian social environment, this facilitates the idea that it is possible to develop such exceptional and indispensable skills only through apprenticeship and exclusive spiritual blessing. This is a second element in the New Age vision relating to the teacher's privilege. Most New Age visions importantly include descriptions of their teachers being taught. Castaneda offers himself as the beneficiary of Don Juan's profound insight (1968); Gabrielle Roth (1990) describes long-standing relationships with several inspirational teachers, especially relating to the field of dance. Some teachers – David Spangler, for example (Sjoo 1992: 117) – come to have their own personal spirit guides. Since the world that the apprentice will come to interpret is a spiritually-suffused world, it is not surprising that in the New Age way of thinking apprenticeship normally involves an enhancement in the (normal) spirituality of the teacher-to-be. So it is that New Age gurus and shamans, people who have completed their apprenticeship and have proceeded beyond, are generally considered themselves to be spiritual beings.

In our view, the New Age vision in its entirety is latent in all New Age subdoctrines. Equally it is the case that the vision's many elements (the ethical standards, the holistic universe, the idea of personal transformation, the notion of spirituality) permits scope for more selective emphasis and combination. Some commentators on the New Age movement have reported on broad divergences among New Age subdoctrines. For example, York (1994), referring to different New Age 'camps', talks of the New Age as a 'three dimensional movement', consisting of the occult camp (which emphasises the spiritual as real), the social camp (which emphasises holistic environmentalism) and the leap in consciousness camp (which emphasises personal transformation). For his part, Greer (1996) distinguishes a 'personal spirituality camp' and an 'ecological therapy camp'. Whilst these writers appraise such divisions in terms of surface features of New Age subdoctrines, our model, from the perspective of deduction, anticipates them rather well. These divisions correspond precisely to distinctive appropriations of the elements making up the New Age cultural vision, even as, as has been shown, these elements are in contingent relations with one another.

From descriptions in the Glastonbury chapters, there remain three further substantive ideas, which most New Age subdoctrines, including several of the above 'camps', emphasise strongly. As to the first two of these, there is the idea of a transcendent cosmic (or universe) consciousness as the seat and means of enlightenment, and there is the concept of the human soul. How may these be understood? We suggest that these ideas reflect substantive combinations of the elements of the cultural vision. Thus 'cosmos' implies the combination of the holistic universe, the idea of personal transformation, and the notion of spirituality. And 'human soul' couples the ideas of spirituality and personal transformation.

A final idea is that of reincarnation, which (in turn) couples the ideas of cosmos and human soul. One returns here to the difference between hunter–gatherers and the New Age, for the cycling of non-physical essence, which reincarnation connotes, is clearly evident in hunter–gatherer cosmology, where it is closely associated with ideas concerning the cycling of animal souls (e.g. Fienup-Riordan 1994). The deductive model reveals that the concept of reincarnation among hunter–gatherers is quite different from New Age reincarnation. The divergence between hunter–gatherers and the New Age, evident at an absolutely fundamental level in the model, is the relevant indication here. The 'foundation level' shows that, in the case of hunter-gatherers, contradictions relating to egalitarianism, brought on by exceptional practical success or misfortune, invite the idea of mystical forces *external* to the human being. The idea of a spirit realm (cosmos) independent of the human realm, between which both animal and human essence recycle, is implicated in this, as explained in Chapter 10. Meanwhile, in the case of the New Age, mystical forces *internal* to the human are constructed in relation to similar contradictions. Such forces directly implicate neither a broader cosmos nor notions of reincarnation. New Age ideas of reincarnation are different from hunter–gatherer ideas because, far from being required by foundation cosmological concepts, their existence seems largely as a consequence of New Age teachers elaborating already constructed ideas, namely cosmos and soul, as if in an intellectual exercise.

New Age Cultural Representation

The many and varied subdoctrines conceivably falling under the New Age label effectively consist of elaborations around the basic New Age vision. These elaborations, which play a major part in making such various doctrines distinct, are the topic of this section. Many of these doctrines, it may be noted, contrast or even counterpose themselves to one another, and in relation to this some declare that they are not New Age or even represent themselves as antithetical to the 'New Age'. For our part we prefer to bring all of them under the New Age umbrella since, at the foundation and vision levels, their construction indicates that they are closely related. But this said, our arguments hardly stand or fall on whether the New Age label fits a particular subdoctrine or not. 'New Age' is, after all, an odd job term, as many scholars have intimated, including ourselves. When advocates of particular subdoctrines accept or reject the New Age label, this is, to them, (understandably) of symbolic importance in terms of upholding the respective doctrine's purity and boundary. For us, much more important are the social processes obtaining in the non-mainstream world in relation to which all such subdoctrines emanate. It is these social processes that this section seeks to reveal.

Doctrinal variation, in the context of the New Age vision, develops in relation to social competition among the chief players, the teachers. Being a teacher, it has been mentioned, brings its rewards, and becoming a teacher is something that someone achieves very much on the strength of personal effort. But the art of becoming a teacher above all implies the ability to convince a New Age membership that one has superior insights that they might respect: incumbency in the teacher role ultimately depends on the membership, on the evidence of personal encounters, being impressed by one's brilliant accomplishments. This being so, pretenders to the specialist role strive for recognition, parading their respective insights about the nature of the universe as objects for the scrutiny of ordinary folk. This is the social domain that York (1995) calls the New Age battlefield. Again, there are clear similarities here with the Inuit shaman.

Teachers' success on the New Age battlefield rests on the effectiveness by which they convey the New Age vision (or their version of it) as something that ordinary people may subjectively apprehend. For the members to accept a particular vision, its objective content must be rendered in terms that they appreciate. This process, because of the very many means by which it may be achieved, considerably enlarges New Age doctrinal elaboration and variation, for the chosen means, if it is to be effective, must precisely be represented as in some way intrinsic to the doctrinal vision itself. Yet one metaphor seems to appear in every attempt to subjectify the New Age vision. This is that the (particular) New Age vision speaks to a person's Experience. This is a profound metaphor since, appropriately for New Age individualism, it evokes respect for the membership to whom the teacher appeals. There is the assumption, in the notion of Experience, that the subjective appreciation of the New Age vision is latent in everyone; it merely has to be released. 'Experience' appealingly refers to something perfect, and higher, within the human being, which has come to be contaminated by wrong, mainstream-type social and psychological instincts. 'Therapy' is the appropriate generic term here to refer to the process to which the ordinary individual should submit in order that the 'higher within' may *be* one's existence. When a teacher directly facilitates this, such experiencing importantly includes the dimension of empowerment. In this context, a common New Age idea is that, via such empowerment, the individual merges with a broader cosmic consciousness of which he or she is an inherent, experiencing part.

By teachers, particular New Age visions are offered for the members' subjective experience through various symbolic vehicles. Here, symbols function compellingly to represent the vision so as to convey its meaningfulness. As to the content of these symbols, one may expect this to play on notions which command a basic human resonance, such that the specific elements of the vision for which they stand may be conveyed as 'natural' and so unchallengeable. As anthropologists we would expect what is the case – that New Age symbols draw on such key experiential dimensions as time, space, the human/non-human boundary, sensuality, and gender (one could no doubt adduce more). In the subsections below we explore these symbolic dimensions in turn, nearly all of which play on an opposition between the mainstream and the non-mainstream. By and large, it would appear that symbols relating to time and space convey the New Age vision's ethical standards, the symbols concerning the nature of humanity represent the integration of these standards in a specific doctrinal vision, and the symbols relating to the senses (sight, touch, etc.) represent matters to do with personal transformation; meanwhile, the integration of particular patterns of symbolisation within any one cosmology seems to be achieved powerfully through the symbols of gender. Overall, it appears that in terms of content such symbolisation amounts to quite a significant proportion of any New Age cosmology, and it is typically highly elaborate. Therefore in what follows the illustrations must be suggestive rather than inclusive. However, one does note that many of the symbols are paired as oppositions. Moreover, through these symbols, disagreements relating to doctrine are typically expressed.

Time

Wisdom and utopia, connoting perfect past or future times, are key metaphors in New Age cosmologies. Wisdom, suggesting a link to an admired, already-existing knowledge, is symbolic of a past 'good time', and utopia, suggesting a link to an ideal state to come, is symbolic of a future 'good time'; thus New Age visions incorporating wisdom or utopia make the claim that they are good visions. Accordingly, some New Age subdoctrines orientate themselves to times past, calling upon ancient practice to legitimate the ethical standards that they advocate for today. The Neo-Pagan cosmologies would be an example. Meanwhile other New Age cosmologies relate themselves to times future, defending present-day ethical conduct in terms of events-to-come which prospectively justify it. Doctrines that literally are 'new age' would be included here, such as those that embrace the idea of a just-beginning Aquarian Age. In New Age cosmologies such relationships, between past and present, and present and future, are invariably represented in terms of a continuity of events or ideas – thus some New Agers speak of themselves as custodians of ancient practices. In this regard, prophecy is the key mediator between wisdom and utopia: in prophecy, wisdom anticipates utopia.

Utopia and wisdom in New Age doctrines are best first appreciated via the utopian cosmologies, which promise perfect social harmony once people in sufficient numbers have submitted themselves to the inner personal transformation. Here, the dominant symbol of prophecy, future peace and harmony, may be understood as standing for the correctness of the teacher's (or text's) message for the present-day. But through what process is such a particular symbolic connection achieved? Why, for example, does the New Age look forward to peace and harmony, and not some other utopia (such as untold wealth)? This invites us to explore more basic ideas in New Age thinking where similar notions are upheld.

We introduce a telling parallel here between New Age utopianism and utopian movements more generally in human history, where prophets and messiahs herald perfect times for those who believe. Cargo cultists, for example, famous in the South Pacific islands during the early- and mid-twentieth century, conducted rituals calling upon the gods to dispatch enormous quantities of material goods by plane or ship, which believers constructed airstrips and jetties to receive. As to the significance of such fantastic 'cargo', it is not that it represented the Islanders' desire for a standard of living matching that of the European colonialists – the cultists elaborated no rules on how the cargo was to be shared out once it arrived. Rather the cargo's impending appearance was as a symbol for the correctness of the cult prophet's stipulations for good conduct in the present-day. These stipulations covered the radical reorganisation of Islander social organisation so that, in terms of secular political power, it would come to equal that of the colonialists. Now in these societies cult notions about cargo appropriately stand as a metaphor for future success in this regard, for they draw on ideas, traditional in the Islands, that good fortune (for example in yam farming) directly arises from correct ritual observance (Riches 1979: 24–25). Turning to the New Agers, their utopia, coloured by peace and harmony, is similarly modelled on more fundamental ideas, also connoting perfection. With the New Age these ideas refer to the holistic person: in the holistic person perfection implies an absence of dissonance – harmony reigns amongst its various elements (mind, body and spirit). By this process, then, future peace and harmony are appropriate as metaphors for the ethical standards which the New Age teacher instructs, and so come to symbolise their veracity.

If anticipated future events, by their symbolic power, ratify teaching for the present-day, so also does wisdom from the past. In this way New Age teachers represent their visions as continuations of the moral and philosophical ideas which they themselves once imbibed, or alternatively as developments of inspirational ways of life which (they believe) once flourished among humankind but which now are in abeyance or lost. The old ways for living, as described in the teachers' representations, are (of course) very similar to those that the teachers now keenly advocate for the present. One notes here the popularity of ancient Atlantis in some New Age doctrines, which has, outsiders will want to say, no verifiable empirical counterpart.

How should claims for continuity (etc.) with the past be analysed? May one think of the relation between past and present as one of inexorable unfoldingness? We are inclined to think not – in which case, the relationship must be grasped in a quite different way.

History is, for us, a construction of the present, and so also are notions emphasising a continuity between past and present. We are inspired here by Hobsbawm's and Ranger's concept of 'invented tradition'; their focus on Africa, these authors' interest is in the way social practices introduced by colonialists (such as the idea of the tribe!) have come to be thought of as important customs or practices of an historically indigenous way of life (Hobsbawm and Ranger 1983). The past wisdoms to which New Age teachers refer, along with their claims about present New Age practices emanating from this past, are, in a similar way, one concludes, the teachers' inventions. There are evident parallels, then, with the evocations of utopia by other New Age teachers. Therefore it is appropriate to ask why, in New Age thinking, the past is deemed to be wise (as opposed to having some other quality).

We suggest that the symbolic connection, whereby past moral practice stands as a metaphor for the ideals of the present-day, may be explained by the *idea*, constructed by teachers, of continuity (between past and present). The point is: continuity, with respect to events, activities and teachings, implies durability. The past practices to which the teachers refer are, in short, evoked as having lasted. Even more basic ideas are clearly being summoned here, for, as a general principle, things which last may be considered to be inevitable – and so proper – and (above all) good. Accordingly, past practice is appropriately symbolic of present-day moral conduct. Sjoo and Mor's ecofeminist text, 'The Great Cosmic Mother' (1987), by its insistence that matriarchy remained constant from the dawn of human society right up to the (relatively recent) Neolithic, is an excellent example of such a strategy.

We do not mean to be cynical when we suggest that, in respect of these processes, New Age teachers construct the past. Atlantis apart, the 'ancient worlds', or the older teachings and philosophies, which teachers claim as their inspiration, generally do have some sort of counterpart in an observable reality – human societies documented roughly in the form the teachers describe *did* exist in former times, the older philosophies, more or less as the teachers retail them, *were* enunciated. The point is, New Age teachers draw on such former realities selectively. Thus, order and harmony in social life are emphasised as key features of ancient societies, and disorder and conflict played down. It is the same with the old philosophies: just parts of their messages will be recalled. This is the sense in which New Age teachers construct a particular past. The fact that there are actually available appropriate past realities for teachers to manipulate in this way should not be too surprising. Cosmologies, one notes, have social roots, and there may be quite a bit of similarity between the social foundations of present-day New Age society (as discussed earlier in this chapter) and the social foundations of ancient human societies; so New Age visions of the world and the representations of the world provided in ancient society can be expected not to be hugely different. Much the same may be said in respect of the older philosophical wisdoms which New Age teachers call upon (Buddhism, Druidism, or whatever) – these, too, have social roots. However the central observation is that the existence of a real past world, at least fairly similar to the past world which the New Age teacher desires to conjure, means that the latter can rather easily be represented as if it is a real past world, or a direct development of it. All the while, the symbolic strategy is patent. Together with notions of utopia, the idea of continuity with a past delivers an overarching image of destiny. New Age advocacy for present ethical conduct, as caught up in this destiny, is therefore powerfully justified.

The disjunction between wisdom and utopia is clearly manifest in the central doctrinal cleavage in the broad New Age movement. Taking the lead here are teachers within the Neo-Pagan fold who, celebrating the wisdoms of the 'ancients' (for example in witch-craft, Druidry, even possibly in direct extra-terrestrial contacts) disdain the cosmic focus upheld in the teaching in other submovements. This latter interest, the ecofeminist, Monica Sjoo, avers in her book *New Age and Armageddon* (1992), which strongly criticises the cult of the guru, is ungrounded and pointless, and therefore distracting in relation to proven insights available from (for example) the Ancient Greeks or the Celts (Sjoo 1992). Many in the Neo-Pagan movement indeed thoroughgoingly oppose themselves to the New Age, and, it will be seen, this opposition repeats itself in respect of many of the other symbolic dimensions that we shall consider.

Space

For the communication of New Age visions, symbols relating to time may be the fundamental symbols, upon which other symbolic processes presume and build. That this is so is hinted by the fact that in New Age cosmologies time symbols offer no explicit allusions to mainstream society, whereas symbols relating to other principles definitely play on the mainstream/non-mainstream contrast.

Let us first elaborate on the symbols relating to space. In many particular New Age visions the pertinent symbolic idiom here is 'other countries' (far away from the mainstream): an inspiration from, and an alliance with, such other countries on the strength of a similarity of vision and way of life is strongly emphasised. The famous examples which such visions cite are, it is well-known, eastern societies and philosophies, such as Tibet, and contemporary tribal societies, especially the native North Americans. In New Age thinking, practices and ideas relating to such societies stand as metaphors for good ethics in (Western) New Age conduct.

These examples are interesting because they incorporate definite resonances of the past. Eastern societies and philosophies are frequently emphasised as being of great antiquity, and present-day tribal society is often explicitly upheld as an exemplification of how all humankind once lived. Indeed the fact that witchcraft and magic are practised *both* in other times and in other places may be the reason why 'the occult' is such a prevalent New Age interest. The aphorism that the past is another country in fact suggests that the ancient societies referred to in the previous subsection may provide imagery equally pertinent for the construction of symbols relating to space. However, as has been indicated, 'time symbolising' may be more fundamental than 'space symbolising', so the idea should be preferred that the processes of time symbolising may in some way make the processes of space symbolising possible. In precisely what way is the question we shall consider shortly.[1]

All this suggests that we must view 'other countries', like past societies, as something teachers construct. Such construction is facilitated by the fact that in the contemporary Eastern and tribal worlds there observably are ways of life not hugely different from the images of 'elsewhere' that the teachers have in mind, and upon which teachers may selectively draw as they conjure these images. The contrast between these societies and the Western mainstream is importantly built into the construction of these images. This is because contemporary non-Western societies declare, by their existence, and in a way that ancient societies cannot, that contemporary world circumstances do not inevitably entail the Western mainstream way of life. But (again) the image of the Western mainstream that will be deployed in this respect will be a selective, or constructed one. In sum, New Age teachers deploy an intriguing permutation of the processes identified by Edward Said under the heading of 'orientalism' (Said 1978). According to Said, the Western mainstream sustains world cultural dominance by, in the domains of literature, art, language, and so on, constructing the East as having vastly inferior qualities – for example, as consisting of a timeless, uniform and unchanging world, replete with rickshaws, rice fields and sexuality. In contrast, we note, the New Age constructs the East (and the tribal world) positively, as having enviable qualities, especially relating to its insights into mysticism and healing. Correspondingly, in the New Age the Western mainstream gets stereotyped negatively. Not unlike the process that James Carrier (1992) calls occidentalism, the New Age constructs the West as suffused with imperialistic materialism, and as incorporating a mechanistic attitude to both the human person and to the universe such that it inexorably marches towards deadly crisis.

Drawing on notions of both past and future, this crisis is figured largely in terms of an impending ecological doom – of overproduction, appalling pollution, and the destruction of resources (York 1994).

Contemporary Eastern and tribal societies, represented by New Age teachers as crucially similar to the New Age, validate the New Age vision. The symbolic logic here summons the idea that such contemporary societies, by being extant societies, are viable societies, and that viable societies are good societies. However this is a contestable idea, since simply by existing a society is not invariably viable. Accordingly, if this idea is to hold good, other symbolic processes must be present. Here the symbolic process by which ancient societies validate the New Age may well function as a condition for contemporary societies symbolically validating the New Age. Ancient societies express the New Age vision as a good vision by being constructed as lasting, or durable, societies. The link between society (that exists) and durability is vitally established here. Then, being transferred to the contemporary scene, this link underpins the desired notion that contemporary (Eastern and tribal) societies are invariably viable societies (and so are good societies).

Teachers from both the broad New Age and (more restricted) Neo-Paganism alike uphold the importance of contemporary societies outside the West, yet their emphases tend to be different. Neo-Paganism biases its reading historically, associating, on behalf of its search for extant wisdom, the present-day tribe (for example) with similar societies from the past; whereas teachers outside the Neo-Pagan remit more often bias their reading projectively, for example calling on mystical dimensions relating to the East to inform access to the cosmos and insight into prophecy.

Humans Versus the Enveloping World

In human cosmologies the boundary between the human individual and the surrounding environment characteristically provides potent images for the symbolic judgement of social conduct (Douglas 1966). The New Age and the mainstream offer perceptions of this boundary which contrast starkly and, it will be seen, invite in New Age cosmology the elaboration of what may be termed scientific symbols.

The New Age vision of a holistic universe is the relevant context here, whose chief feature, it has been noted, is overarching harmony and stability. By this vision the human universe is deemed to subsume human individuals along with other living and non-living things, and render them all liable to its equilibriated mode of operating. Here humans are considered to relate to other entities on equal terms, which evinces a basic continuity between the human individual and the surrounding environment: humans may be seen as essentially *of* the wider universe. In contrast, the mainstream way of thinking is quite different, counterposing humans to the surrounding environment in the name of progress. In mainstream thinking, the idea of a holistic universe is played down and humans, seen as pitted *against* other living and non-living entities, are construed as in some manner superordinate and therefore unique: there is discontinuity between the human individual and the surrounding environment (e.g. Ingold 1993). In relation to the New Age viewpoint, one understands the supreme value put, by many New Agers, on Earth as a living entity. Earth functions as the dominant symbol in relation to expressing an indissolubility between humans, as living entities, and their surroundings.

New Agers sustain the correctness of the holistic universe, one is reminded by Hess (1993), by asserting that it is empirically, or 'scientifically' true – that is, by insisting that it conforms more closely to an objective reality than do the mechanistic, fragmentary models and laws enunciated by mainstream science. Thus to uphold their conception of the universe as an entity functioning according to supra-human processes, New Age enthusiastically appeal to the work of the mainstream, if iconoclastic, scientist, James Lovelock, embracing (and changing the meaning of) Lovelock's term, Gaia – as detailed in Chapter 9. It follows that the symbolic means by which the New Age conveys the holistic universe as a valuable idea may call on scientific-type discourse. Mainstream ecology provides this discourse. Uniquely among contemporary mainstream sciences, ecology presumes an encapsulating system where human activity and the activity of all other organisms is deemed to be continuous. Classical ecology considers the system to be marked by an inherent stability, with the system being intrinsically self-regulating through the principle of negative feedback. Now, famously from scientific ecology, 'energy' is the currency in terms of which the elements (individuals, species, other organic materials) are described as relating to one another. Thus the similarity of vision, between scientific ecology and the New Age universe, permits 'energy' to be the highly potent metaphor for the

New Age. Accordingly, the discourse of energy comes symbolically to convey the validity of the New Age vision, firstly with regard to the holistic universe, and secondly, by extension, with the holistic stuff of interpersonal relatedness (Chapter 4). Melded with already constructed ideas about spirituality, energy is available as a highly versatile concept in the New Age teachers' advocacy.

Debates and disputes among New Age teachers relating to the interface between the human being and the environment are generally articulated around the matter of the *flow* of energy – within the person, between persons, and between person and cosmos. The context for this is that, for New Age healers, energy is a powerful symbol of healing (Albanese 1992). Such flow is potentially highly versatile. For example, from the cosmos energy may flow to each individual directly (via chakra points on the body), or through the mediation of other individuals (in channelling), or through the mediation of objects (as in crystal therapy). Different New Age subdoctrines support these various (and other) possibilities with greater or lesser enthusiasm. Ironically, in view of the scientific salience of energy as a New Age symbol, many New Agers dissociate themselves from much energy therapy, especially channelling and crystal healing, on the grounds that it is insufficiently scientific (Hess 1993: 35). Even more ironically, so mainstreamer opinion would aver, is that some New Agers prefer instead to uphold the importance of UFO contact because, compared with, for example, channelling, it is more scientific (Porter 1996: 346).

The controversies in the New Age relating to rebirthing and physical immortality may be understood in this context. Symbolically potent notions, since they refer to the interface, in birth and death, between the human and natural domains, in many texts they are condemned strongly (see those cited by Sjoo 1992: 178–216). In their detractors' view, both, in different ways, smack of human mastery over nature, and therefore contravene the fundamental tenet that human beings are *of* their environment.

The Senses

We attend here to those aspects of New Age cosmology which emphasise sight, sound, touch, taste and smell. The senses, it would appear, are central to those features of the New Age vision concerning personal transformation and related matters to do with healing. The senses refer to the intimate and internal in people's feelings about themselves, and they are highly appropriate as a means to convey the most intimate dimension of people's engagement with the New Age. This dimension is the not fully volitional yet magnificent awakening that accompanies the attainment of a fresh and transcendental wisdom.

From time to time one hears of music described as 'New Age'; New Age tastes are evident from distinctive New Age foods from raw fruits to tofu; and incense is famous among New Age smells. However, in relation to personal transformation, sight and touch seem most compellingly to represent the New Age vision – these are the more manipulable senses from the point of view of symbolism.

The importance of symbolic representation via sight and touch relates to the fact that, of all aspects of the New Age vision, personal transformation is the most ineffable. In the case of a particular person who can say that it has really occurred. Symbolism must therefore have a dual role: first to express the concept of transformation, and second to depict the fact of that transformation in any one woman or man. In New Age cosmology in general, symbols relating to sight particularly convey the first of these, and symbols relating to touch the second. By implication such symbolism also fills out the content of New Age healing. Not a few New Age cosmologies include rituals which permit public witness of transformation and purification in newcomers and longstanding devotees alike.

'Light' is a most pervasive visual symbol in the New Age, and our discussion of visual symbols will concentrate on it. In symbolic activity, light is typically transmitted from the teacher to the New Ager, thus evoking in the latter the possibility of transformation. Maharaj-ji's teaching emanates from the Divine Light Mission, Findhorn is the 'light centre' where Aquarian energy enters the earth, and the Harmonic Convergence of August 1987 was a time, according to the prophecy, when enhanced luminosity relating to the Mexican god, Quetzalcoatl, entered the atmosphere. In rituals in Glastonbury, as described in Chapter 9, light was a central theme; for example, meditation leaders would call for 'light to enter us' (for example, to focus people's collective energies on the work at hand); the lighted candle was a key object in many such group meditations.

But light connotes dark, as its opposite. The Neo-Pagan critique plays on this in particular, upholding dark as the positive symbol, and unflatteringly associating light with values and ethics that most New Agers would, in fact, wish to reject. Thus light is connected with the left, and rational, side of the brain, and (by extension) the masculine principle; by association with the colour of bones and snow, it may also be linked to death. Meanwhile, dark (and the black), according to Neo-Paganism, connotes in particular the nurturing principle and the earth. As the Glastonbury teacher to whom Ruth spoke said, dark is associated, by this way of thinking, with the receptive vessel, with the chalice, with chaos, with intuition – and with the feminine. A major strand in Monica Sjoo's attack on the New Age mobilises the symbol of dark in relation to precisely such themes. Peter Redgrove, in his book 'The Black Goddess and the Sixth Sense' (1987), intriguingly speaks of darkness as 'light not recognised'.

Touch is an enormously versatile sense. It embraces pain and pleasure, it connotes peace and violence, and by extension it includes a person's consciousness of inner muscular movement. More than this, the notion of touch opens up the possibility of violence of a symbolic, or psychological kind (Riches 1991). In the New Ager's experience of personal transformation, particularly in the context of therapy, all these aspects of touch are patent in relation to depicting that such transformation is being experienced.

Of all the symbols expressing the New Age vision, touch is the one in which the individual to whom the vision is directed is the most intimately involved; this being the case a teacher's assistance is invariably on hand. This occurs either in rituals in which an audience is present, to witness and to confirm the individual's symbolic experience, or else in circumstances where the individual is with the teacher alone. In the realm of ritual, firewalking on the one hand, and some forms of psychological therapy, such as gestalt therapy, on the other, represent the New Age extremes here: both are objectively painful, and they are often subjectively distressing as well. The firewalkers significantly represent their ritual as dispelling fear (Danforth 1989). This (may one suggest?) puts a positive gloss on a considerable ordeal; it also brackets the firewalking ritual with pain-related rituals more generally, such as rituals of circumcision (which also mediate personal transformation) (Heald 1986). Meanwhile the psychological rituals imply psychological distress. Their intention, as practised, for example, in the Rajneeshee communities, is to destroy mainstream instincts within the human personality, which is accomplished by subjecting the initiate to considerable verbal assault and emotional barrage. It is interesting that in Gestalt therapy the teachers involved in this sort of ritual are spoken of as 'trainers' (Burrows 1993: 259).

Touch therapy with the teacher alone is generally a gentler matter. The transformative experience here is generally delivered by massage (as in aromatherapy), bodly manipulation (as in reflexology), or pressure (as, for example, in Shiatsu which, through finger pressure, activates the body's self-healing). Finally, one may mention the symbolic potency of muscular control, as evinced, for example, in Tai Chi, where through controlled, sequential body movements the person secures a powerful sense of his or her inner self.

So far as we can see, doctrinal disputes within the New Age are barely at all articulated around touch symbols. Is this because this, the most intimate of symbols, connotes most directly the New Age maxim of 'doing one's own thing'?

Gender

New Age cosmologies famously express a gendered reading of social life. New Age gender symbols appear to encapsulate the essence of the New Age opposition to the mainstream, and so, it may be suggested, effectively function to integrate the symbolic work achieved by ideas relating to time, space, the senses etc. The symbolic potential of gender capitalises on the malleability of gender ideas, such that among human societies there is a great deal of variation as to, for example, the sort of work that is woman's work and the sort that is man's, or beliefs about the distinctive character of a man's personality, as opposed to a woman's. But there is more than this, for the reflexivity in New Age thinking is also strongly evident in New Age gender ideas. The result is the very distinctive symbolic subversion of the mainstream, where such familiar New Age values as emotionality and intuition are drawn out as major components of New Age culture. Let us elucidate the various elements in this argument, beginning with gender in mainstream Western society which, thanks to its potent connotations of sex and sexuality, is blatantly available for symbolic play.

In the Western mainstream gender notions plainly underpin ideas of social hierarchy. This is based on the fact of male domination, whereby men monopolise incumbency in public and political roles. Thus all that is powerful and authoritative in mainstream social life comes to be seen as having distinctively masculine qualities, with controlled aggression thereby coming to pervade such life as appropriate and valued social behaviour. In contrast, New Age gender ideas, as has been noted from Glastonbury, downplay

the importance of male/female difference in respect of the allocation of tasks in everyday life, and at the same time infuse a femininity more generally into all aspects of New Age practice and
persons. With regard to the New Age ideas, it is clear that one
should address the contradiction they seem to imply (in downplaying gender difference whilst playing up femininity). We believe
that the key to understanding New Age gender symbolism is that
this symbolism firstly confronts mainstream gender notions, and
secondly achieves this in a distinctively New Age way.

On the first point, the egalitarianism in the New Age vision is
straightforwardly conveyed by downplaying the association of gender with particular roles. By symbolic opposition this expresses a
rejection of mainstream values: downplaying gender roles clearly
conveys a denial of hierarchy in New Age social life.

As to the second point, we suggest that the New Age *reflects* on
the implications of this. Thanks to such reflection, the contrast
between the mainstream (male dominance) and the New Age (relative gender equality) can be construed, by subtraction, as an
enhancement in the feminine principle. Accordingly, for the New
Age, emotionality and intuition become important values in public
and political process – which subverts mainstream assumptions
just as effectively as does the downplaying of gender roles. But this
is not all, for New Age reflexive thinking invites consideration
along these lines to extend to the very nature of the human person.
Thus everyone in the New Age should acknowledge the presence
within of both female and male principles. Though again, the
importance of symbolic opposition to the mainstream means that
it is the feminine within the human male that gets stressed here –
licensing New Age men to be intuitive rather than calculating, and
to welcome tasks which, in the mainstream, women alone would
normally undertake.

Gender symbols of the New Age vision are alone in depicting
the human experience through a metaphor based around the
human condition. Maleness and femaleness thereby become available to embrace and further articulate the meanings of some of the
other New Age symbols. Gender symbols' potency in this regard
moreover means that they provide ideal material for the New Age
battlefield, and this is particularly so with respect to the division
between New Age and Neo-Paganism. The manipulation of gender
symbols here entails that, as between two 'sides', conflicting
meanings are read into some of the other symbols. Thus, as its
point of departure Neo-Paganism upholds the feminine, and so

dubs the remainder of the New Age as masculine. The oppositional logic from here is that dark (associated with the feminine) is
good, whilst light (by default associated with the New Age) is bad;
and earth energy (associated with the nurturing female) is good,
whilst cosmic energy (by default associated with the New Age
quest for self) is pointless; and that ancient wisdoms (depicted as
matriarchies) are good, whilst guru prophecy (by default associated with 'New Age patriarchy') is a distraction. Through the
famous Neo-Pagan notion of the Goddess, the totality of such Neo-
Pagan ideas are condensed: thus, in terms of this symbol, Monica
Sjoo (1992) concludes that the New Age is essentially fascist. Yet it
is interesting that the Goddess subsumes the general ambiguity,
mentioned above, in relation to the feminine principle in the New
Age more generally. Whilst the term itself is semantically feminine, we are told that the Goddess, as an entity, is essentially
'gynandrous', that is to say, essentially bisexual and/or hermaph-
roditic (Sjoo and Mor 1987: 66).

Conclusion

Competition between New Age teachers, amounting to the selective
emphasis of particular aspects of the New Age vision and of particular symbolic representations of that vision, suggests that the
countless specific New Age subdoctrines basically reflect an array of
niches which each teacher has respectively made his or her own.
This may indeed be in mind where the teachers are concerned, yet
ordinary devotees of particular doctrines may understand such doctrinal proliferation very differently. Ordinary movement members, it
has been seen, legitimise the teacher role, and by implication the
teacher's activities; from the standpoint of such ordinary people,
therefore, what it means to be involved with a particular teacher or
particular subdoctrine needs to be considered very carefully. This
takes us into the whole matter of how we should construe the
apparent techniques which many religious movements devise to
recruit their membership. It comprises the topic of the next chapter.

Notes

1. Intriguingly this reverses the priority set by Fabian (1983). But is not a sense of
   historically antecedent societies a precondition for reading geographically
   remote societies as societies of the past?

12

Transformations in Space–Time

In Western society, people think of 'mainstream' and 'alternative' ways of life as rivals. They conceive of such rivalry above all as being about securing and keeping followers, which they see in terms of 'alternative ways' wooing individuals from the mainstream, and the mainstream resisting or trying to woo them back. This way of thinking is underscored by people's very use of the term 'alternative', and by such expressions, referring to individuals moving from one 'side' to the other, as 'seeing the light', or (from the other point of view) as being 'victims' of some sort of 'brainwashing'. In this context, religious movements' techniques relating to membership command great interest: a movement's specialised recruitment institutions, charismatic leaders and certain compelling symbols (to do with time, space, gender, and so on) will be considered, by all sides, to be highly effective in 'luring' personnel to within its sphere of influence or control.

In this book, we prefer to see matters differently, for we are trying to think about how the New Age and other religious movements are generated. To conceive of the relation between the mainstream and the 'alternative' in tug-of-war terms in our view conceals the creative processes by which religious movements are brought into being, most especially the creative role of ordinary people, who, with regard to an alternative way of life, should be conceived of not as its 'recruits', but as the agents of its construction. Once the focus is put on ordinary people as creative agents, a radically new perspective on religious movements is forthcoming. In the previous chapter, we took as the point of departure the liminal situation of 'being not-mainstream': the deductive model gives an account of how people's experience relating to this situation *causes* New Age society and culture.

When the anthropologists' understanding of religious movements is different from the way the memberships conceive of things, this raises the question of how the latter's perspective should be dealt with. For example, a religious movement's members will claim that the movement is attractive fundamentally because it is pagan as opposed to utopian, or matriarchal as opposed to patriarchal, or dark as opposed to light . . . which is virtually the opposite to the deductive model's priority (see Chapter 11). For us, what the members' conceptualisation amounts to is people reflecting on their movement as a finished product, in the context of a wider world to which this entity must be portrayed as right and good. What is happening is that the movement as a whole is being *represented* to the world as complete and as independent of its members' creative work, all the while that the members are continually engaging in complex social processes through which the movement comes to be sustained in being. In our view, the anthropologist's task is to elucidate the particular interests to which this manner of representation responds. We suggest that when New Agers and mainstreamers alike speak of folk being 'taken up into the New Age', this may well be politically expedient talk, for it implies the existence of social forces which people do not control, and which in some way 'make' people do what they do (Riches 1985). These sorts of notions are helpful the while that people mull over the existence of a non-mainstream movement, and ponder the fact of individuals associating themselves with it. By such notions, the New Age, in the guise of both its practices and its membership, is deemed as not resulting from people's conscious decisions. For all involved, New Agers and mainstreamers alike, a means to deny responsibility for the New Age existing is thereby provided: if social forces prevail which in some way 'operate' on a person, then belonging to the New Age can be regarded as essentially not the New Ager's fault.

This said, the fact remains that religious movements commonly have charismatic leaders who seek to enthuse the world, and recruitment institutions that announce a warm welcome to all comers. The question arises as to how this is compatible with the fact, shown in Chapter 11, that charismatic leadership results from ordinary New Agers' constructions. In the construction model, charismatic leaders elaborate doctrine to express their suitability in relation to ordinary New Agers' needs (relating, ultimately, to the nature of the holistic person). These elaborations, in terms of what they mean to ordinary New Agers, must be consistent with this. In this chapter, we focus on the social processes that inform people's association with a social or religious movement (such that people participate in that movement's construction). These processes correspond with the level of communitas. Discussion in the chapter on charismatic leadership and recruitment institutions will elucidate meanings, valid for ordinary people, whereby these features' pose to the world outside is explained as relating to ordinary members' requirements; with regard to ordinary members' participation in religious movements, this sustains a conceptualisation of such individuals as agents, not victims. Given these various concerns, attention in this chapter will be largely on matters of social organisation rather than cosmology. In this regard we shall argue that it is vital to compare social and religious movements. This is because, for the members, to associate with a particular movement is a matter of choice, not just to be not-mainstream, but also with respect to preferring one form of 'alternative' over another. The first task is to demonstrate the possibility of such comparison.

Comparisons and Transformations

In historical Western society very many 'alternative societies' appear as religious cults or sects, or manifest themselves as a form of deliberate social engineering. Some such social and religious movements are evident as distinctively enclaved communities, such as the Hutterite and Amish colonies in North America, and the kibbutz in Israel, where populations of around 150 people (Hutterite, Amish) and 300 people (kibbutz) submit themselves to varying degrees of communal living. Determinedly upheld in the name of global political or religious ideologies (Christianity, Socialism, Judaism), these particular communities' social organisations are commonly marked by a relative hierarchy, which implies the presence, to a lesser or greater degree, of a relatively authoritarian leadership and a curtailment of personal autonomy. Their cosmologies, of course, are in form far from the New Age, and unlike the New Age the respective ideological directives are very clearly laid down. And yet . . . in the descriptions of these enclaved communities there are clear echoes of the dispersed, egalitarian and heterogeneous Alternative Community in Glastonbury. Kibbutzniks, for example, uphold the idea of the holistic person; Hutterites emphasise the values of love and peace (Shenker 1986).

Communities relatively closed off from the outside world are present in the New Age movement as well, typically the holistic ecology branch of the movement. Findhorn, the New Age commune near Inverness in Scotland, is a famous example, where around two hundred core members along with large numbers of peripherally connected paying 'guests' uphold a highly successful lifestyle based around farming and education. In contrast to the Glastonbury New Age, there are hierarchical and authoritarian tendencies in the social organisation of these communes, with consequent tension and conflict as, all the while, commune members struggle to prevent the social principles of egalitarianism and autonomy from being eroded (Hendershott 1989). In Findhorn, there is 'democratic hierarchy' (ibid.: 89): for example, there is a good deal of regimentation in respect of daily work, yet the commune allows members considerable personal autonomy and 'space', so that, should a person wish to spend time in spiritual contemplation, this is tolerated. Elsewhere, in smaller-scale 'green' communes, people's experience is something similar. Pepper (1991) adds that the richness of social relations in such communes is found by some members too difficult to handle.

These many and varied alternative societies differ markedly with regard to the presence or absence of leadership charisma, and to the quality of their specialised institutions for drawing members in. We propose that comparisons among them should be suggestive for understanding the nature and relevance of these sorts of social feature. Comparisons will also be helpful in view of the fact that such features are not prominent in the Glastonbury Alternative Community, where whether to join or leave is left very much to the individual concerned. The virtual absence of these features in Glastonbury social organisation indeed supports the proposition that generally in alternative communities 'recruitment institutions' may actually concern matters other than securing a membership.

The comparisons may be approached through the idea of transformation. We argue that, in their social organisations and cultural content, all these social and religious movements may amount to logical rearrangements or logical developments of one another. One should be able to relate the different social organisations of various movements in terms of a scenario of social change. Here we shall argue that the New Age analysis provided in this book, in view of the extreme flexibility and lack of hierarchy in Glastonbury social organisation, may be paradigmatic for understanding the other movements. For example, it may be possible to explain the corporate character of the Hutterite communities as a logical development of Glastonbury social organisation.

Our search is for the variables which control this transformation, such that a Glastonbury-type social organisation will transpose into Findhorn type . . . then, eventually, when circumstances become still more extreme, into a Hutterite type. These variables will function at the level of communitas. The relevant variables, it will be suggested later in this chapter, have particularly to do with the socio-spatial and socio-temporal arrangements of the various religious movements, or more exactly, of the social communities that go to make up the movements – for example, whether such communities are dispersed among a mainstream population or spatially closed off from it (or enclaved). Resulting from these considerations will be crucial insights on what involvement in a particular religious movement (as opposed to others on offer) means to its ordinary members.

A movement's recruitment institutions, meanwhile, constitute one of its more prominent surface features. Before attending to deeper social processes, we should first dispense with the nature of such institutions. We shall argue that a religious movement's recruitment procedures are less, or not at all, about the movement's instrumental face towards the mainstream (luring in followers). Rather their purpose, on behalf of the movement's internal organisation, is symbolically to set the movement apart from the mainstream. We make this argument in the following section, where, as in the previous chapter, comparisons with tribal society prove to be particularly helpful.

The Construction of Recruitment Institutions

For ordinary people who 'make' a religious movement (having departed the mainstream), that movement's recruitment institutions is amongst their constructions. We have noted already that such institutions result from ordinary people committed to the common endeavour, so they cannot at the same time be responsible for bringing the ordinary people in. In short, these institutions have significances (for the people who construct them) other than 'recruitment' as such. We may discover these significances by placing the institutions in context, firstly by offering comparisons among a number of movements, and secondly by relating these institutions to other relevant institutions in the social fabric. Some examples of specific recruitment institutions will be mentioned in due course.

One notes that recruitment institutions are especially prominent in movements whose communities are, on the one hand, relatively closed off from the mainstream, and, on the other hand, characterised by a relatively hierarchical organisation. In the case of many such enclaved communities, including the Hutterites and the kibbutz, the institutions most notably direct their attention to the incorporation of the members' children as fully-fledged community personnel. In order generally to make sense of recruitment into social and religious movements, we propose that one should first examine hierarchical community organisation in these particular movements, for such hierarchical organisation frames the recruitment institutions and gives them sense. It is here that the comparisons with tribal society are helpful: the elders of 'alternative' religious communities function in a manner very similar to those in the tribal community.

A simple explanation of hierarchical organisation in enclaved 'alternative communities' is that this arises for reasons of social control, particularly where the communities' memberships are large. Where people live year round, cheek by jowl, and where both they themselves and the respective community are highly reluctant that they should ever leave, problems of social tension and disorder will continually loom, which the presence of community authorities will be necessary to contain. The Green communes which tried to live according to the principles of egalitarianism and personal autonomy, yet collapsed, might illustrate the supposition from an obverse point of view. But there is something wrong with this line of reasoning. For a start, traditional Inuit camps, numbering up to one hundred people, and continuously isolated (from neighbouring camps) for many months in the year, manage to sustain egalitarianism, personal autonomy and non-authoritarian leadership, even as the members engage with one another in often complex economic activities under conditions of considerable environmental rigour. But, more importantly, to account for the development of hierarchy in closed communities merely in terms of problems of organising internal affairs, entirely fails to reckon in that by which such communities take their character: their long-time spatial closure. Thus we contend that it is something to do with the socially enclaved nature of these communities that accounts for the distinguishing features of their internal social structure. But, again, what that something is is not immediately obvious.

In our view, it is the fact that enclaved alternative communities manifest themselves as corporate communities that is the key to understanding hierarchy in their internal social organisation. Here discussion may draw on famous anthropological writing on various types of corporate structure, such as tribal lineages (local descent groups) and, from contemporary developmental economics, cooperatives and collectives. The defining feature of a corporate group is that, in relation to other groups with which its members have dealings, it functions as a single legal personality (i.e., by the rationale of 'all for one, and one for all'). The group (as a whole) represents its individual members' interests against the society at large; and its individual members' behaviour vis-à-vis the wider world implicates everyone else in the group. For example, in some African societies, should people from different local groups get into a dispute, their lineages will assume responsibility for their respective interests and points of view. Correspondingly, the lineage exercises control over its members, and this is upheld in the name of the powerful founding ancestor from whom the current lineage members are exclusively descended. Such lineage responsibility is discharged, on a day to day basis, by the group's administrators, or elders (Smith 1956). In short, within the lineage, ancestors and elders hierarchically exercise some considerable authority over the activities of group members. Something similar occurs with economic cooperatives and collectives. With regard to the particular economic activities which the cooperative is charged with carrying out (for example, farming, or marketing), its elected board of directors enjoys considerable powers, both in representing the cooperative to the world at large and also with regard to the conduct of the members (e.g. Riches 1977). The point is: enclaved alternative communities (Hutterites, kibbutz, Findhorn) are no exception to these corporate principles. The existence of hierarchy in their social organisation is illustrated by such administrative structures as the Hutterite colony's 'council of elders' and the kibbutz's 'adult assembly'. In these communities there is a general group-mindedness (stressed at Findhorn), and an emphasis on social conformity (as in the kibbutz). In the kibbutz, the group provides the individual with his or her principle identity. (For references to these communities, see Bennett 1967, Hendershott 1989, Shenker 1986.)

The explanation of corporate structuring must take into account the social organisation of group economy, for this, in contrast to political hierarchy, commonly manifests egalitarian principles. More often than not enclaved alternative communities are at least to some degree communistic in the economic sense; for example, the members may share land and work it together without regard to notions of individual ownership. This is certainly the case with Findhorn, the kibbutz and the Hutterite colonies, and one may add that economic communism (though not necessarily to do with land) is particularly marked in the small closed communities associated with some of the more recent dogmatic cults, such as Hare Krishna and the Children of God. Similarly, tribal lineages normally have their own landed estates. The relation between corporate administration and economic communism is clearly an intriguing one.

The lineage comparison is highly suggestive for understanding all these matters, because some tribal societies have local groups whose social compositions are lineage-like, but the corporate philosophy is missing. In the highland area of New Guinea, for example, local groups are principally composed of constellations of fathers and sons and brothers and cousins, all related through male ties; but these are not patri*lineages*: there is no distant ancestor to provide for group identity and solidarity, and the members do not subject themselves to group administrators (Barnes 1962). Discussion in the anthropological literature suggests that when corporate structuring in tribal society does occur, what precipitates it is certain qualities in the relations *between* local groups. This is particularly clear among the Northwest Coast Indians of western Canada and southeast Alaska, where systematic alliances between neighbouring local groups, intended to dampen down inter-group warfare, dispose such groups to assume internal corporate organisation (Riches 1979). In the case of the enclaved alternative communities, we shall suggest that economic communism is intimately linked with similar sorts of boundary maintaining processes.

The leads from tribal society invite an examination of the different ways by which members of 'alternative communities' may experience the social boundary with the 'outside' (i.e. the mainstream). The relevant contrast here is between alternative communities where the membership is not enclaved, and those where it is enclaved. In the first instance, where the membership is scattered amongst the mainstream population, or where it exhibits a high level of turnover, the boundary experience is (merely) a conceptual, or imagined, one – as was discussed in Chapter 4 with reference to the Glastonbury New Agers. But where the membership is tightly and spatially grouped and is relatively stable in composition, people's in-common sense of being separated off from the mainstream is much enhanced, to the degree that the social boundary will be construed as concrete, that is, *as the product of intentional and collaborative organisation.*

We suggest that in alternative communities where there is corporate structuring, this exists as a means to express the members' experience of such a 'concrete boundary' (with the mainstream). Through corporate structuring a particular character is imparted to the members' everyday lives such as to convey a sense of the everyday reality of such a boundary. We are proposing that there is a metaphoric relation here, namely that the appropriate way to assert a *common* and intentional opposition against outsiders (concrete boundary) is for the people concerned *collectively* to take responsibility for the actions of one another (corporate structuring). Community hierarchy is thus implicated, as community elders and administrators function to supervise this symbolic pose. This brings us to the matter of economic organisation. In such enclaved alternate communities many daily activities would seem to be organised in such a way as to relate to such processes. (The community's closure will significantly entail that the mainstream world is largely oblivious to the practices at issue.) Economic communism could certainly be explained in these terms. Thus, holding the land in common is not a practical necessity, but symbolically it is highly potent: it denotes the collective responsibility that corporate organisation politically implies. Much the same can be said of other economic tasks. For example, at Findhorn there is a very marked (and un-New Age like) division of labour, such that in daily work the members and guests are assigned to very particular task groups (for example, gardening, kitchen work), albeit for fairly short durations.[1] By such practice, the political interdependence amongst community members is expressed very well. One surmises that only when corporate structuring has in this way been brought into being, that really complex activities become possible, for which, in the name of efficiency, corporate organisation is definitely required.

The central theme in this study, relevant for all religious movements, is the relationship between an alternative community's personnel and its social organisation and culture. This theme is important with regard to the significance of people first associating and then remaining with the community, and, by implication, to the question of the salience of the charismatic presence. This, as has been noted, implicates processes and understandings which are not at all straightforward. It has been argued that to construe an alternative community's social organisation and culture as pre-existing its personnel – as drawing the personnel in and moulding them into correct attitudes and behaviour – is not helpful. What actually is the case is that personnel, sharing with one another a liminal position 'outside the mainstream', shape the organisation and culture. In the case of Glastonbury, even at the point when a person swears his or her dying allegiance to the Alternative Community, we insist that this liminal underpinning remains valid: the Community's members are present only thanks to each one repeatedly making the decision to be 'not-mainstream'. Now, in the case of alternative communities that are subject to corporate structuring, comparable processes must obtain. We shall illustrate them by examining the inclusion of children as community members, in particular to see whether these processes reflect the symbolic significance of corporate structuring (relating to people's experience of the 'concrete' boundary with the world outside).

The context here is a paradox about corporate communities. Such communities represent themselves as if they have lives of their own – as if they existed independently of the specific individuals who make them up. Yet for such communities to continue, they are reliant on a membership. Accordingly, all corporate communities put great emphasis on social mechanisms ostensibly directed towards securing personnel. Among these, the responsibility falling on adults that children be 'incorporated' as community members is prominent. This is certainly the case in lineage society, where the fact of being born automatically links children to a particular lineage ancestor, thereby rendering the child's membership in the parent's lineage as immediate and irrevocable. In the classical kibbutz a similar function is performed by a particularly intriguing institution. Following infancy, children are removed from direct parental control and the community as a whole assumes responsibility for their upbringing, famously in the form of supervising them, during night-time, in small communal dormitories (Spiro 1963). Not dissimilarly, Hutterites almost straight away expose their children to the colony environment (Hostetler 1967: 108); from the age of three, the kindergarten school, where children eat both lunch and dinner, assumes primary responsibility for their socialisation (ibid.: 128). However, in Findhorn and other New Age communes, such as those of the Rajneeshees, institutions specifically signalling the recruitment and incorporation of children seem not to be present.

But 'recruitment rules' relating to children may, in the event, not be about recruitment at all. In general terms, we maintain that the social organisation and culture of enclaved communities should be addressed in terms of *adult* decisions to continue to be 'not-mainstream': the adults are present not because they were brought up in the community from childhood, but because in their adulthood they continually make the decision to remain. Thus the specific matter of the keeping up of group numbers should be explained as an accumulation of such adult decisions. This invites a particular perspective on incorporation rules relating to children, namely that, along with many other community practices, such recruitment rules fulfil the function of metaphorically expressing the community's corporate solidarity vis-à-vis the outside world. Corporate solidarity, it has been seen, is about *adult* members being responsible for one another's actions. Such mutual responsibility, we suggest, is conveyed very appropriately by the existence of community rules directing the inclusion into the group of the child; the image of the child's vulnerability perfectly expresses the value of inter-adult responsibility.

Corporate structures, representing themselves as if they exist independently of the actual lives of their personnel, typically leave little space for the charismatic presence. In the corporate setting, both leadership tasks and the criteria by which such tasks should properly be performed are generally clearly established, such that exceptional character and inspiration are much less attributed to those who successfully take them on. Indeed, discussions of leadership in religious movements whose communities are strongly enclaved frequently speak of a tension between charismatic leadership and community organisation. Either leadership turns inexorably into something more bureaucratic (in Weber's terms, the charisma is routinised), or else charismatic individuals struggle, deliberately and in an unpredictable way, to vary the tasks that a leader should perform – so to say, fighting off the tendency for the community to incorporate. Among excellent examples in the recent academic literature, Lindholm describes this as occurring with reference to Hitler, and Wallis, in his study of new religious movements, with reference to the leadership of David Berg (Moses David) of the new religious movement, the Children of God (otherwise known as The Family) (Lindholm 1990: 103–12; Wallis 1982: 73–134).

What, then, of leadership charisma, and institutional procedures of recruitment and retention in religious movements where relatively fluid or dispersed communities are less, or not at all, corporately structured? In particular, if recruitment rules in corporate communities (relating to children) are not, in the event, about the bringing in of personnel, what of comparable procedures in the non-corporate (or less than corporate) setting? In such a setting, charismatic leaders clearly assume competition with one another, as they do so weaving all manner of different doctrinal elaboration. In many movements, such competition includes intriguing strategies which, in the name of the leader, seem clearly designed to recruit (adult) people in. For example, among the Children of God there was a period when, through a practice known as 'flirty fishing', movement members approached potential new recruits with offers of sexual favours (Wallis 1979: 98). Similarly, Taylor (1982) describes the way the Unification Church (Moonies) make considerable attempts to interest young Americans, for example by inviting them, over brief initial periods, to holiday-type camps. Other religious communities hold out the possibility of altered states of consciousness, either in meditation or through hallucinogenic drugs (e.g., Howell 1997). As to the retention of movement members, ethnographic accounts of religious movements frequently describe the caring, loving and supportive ways in which movement members treat one another, which the members themselves explicitly acknowledge and appreciate (for example, see Thompson and Heelas (1986) on Rajneeshee communes). But the question remains as to the significance of such processes in relation to the everyday understandings of movement members.

We shall argue that, in terms of everyday understandings, the competitive charismatic and recruitment dimension in these sorts of religious movements generally is not about attracting people in, either by seducing them from the mainstream or by subverting rival movements, albeit that this may be how movement members, from time to time reflecting on the movement as a whole and on its activities, may represent things. Instead, in relation to ordinary members' routine understandings, the salience of a movement's competitive pose concerns matters of the movement's internal organisation. To make this argument we shall initially focus on the relationship between the charismatic presence in a religious movement and the situation of ordinary members who find this presence meaningful and worthwhile. The argument is in two stages.

We start by pointing to the fact that a charismatic leader's inspirational character, together with his or her elaboration of a very particular cosmology and distinctive proselytising style, makes the movement with which ordinary people are associated *special*. When a movement's communities are not corporate – where the membership is fluid or dispersed, and where community boundaries are more imagined than concrete – this is particularly important. With religious movements, the issue here, relating to their construction, is about *confirming the correctness* of the social and cultural content that has been generated. This refers very specifically to the predicament of a movement's ordinary members who are ultimately responsible for this construction. In this context, the function of charismatic leaders, on the strength of their accomplishment and imagination, is, by their fantastic elaboration of cosmological styles *different from* other (sub)movements, to create something quite extraordinary. To spectators on the outside, this something extraordinary, along with the leader who fabricated it, may appear as the very stuff of the movement. But for ordinary insiders it is entirely different. For them the salience of this something extraordinary is confirmation indeed that the overall practices and beliefs that they worked to produce, once having come together as 'not-mainstream', are good.

There is a symbolic aspect to confirming the goodness of practices and beliefs which have been produced. This brings us to the second stage of the argument about a movement's competitive pose, and invites us specifically to consider the matter of specialised recruitment practices (flirty fishing, etc.). Practices and beliefs, to be asserted as good, should be *witnessed*, and for there to be witnesses there must be people around to fill the role. In this context, the presence of recruitment institutions in a movement's cultural repertoire signals, from the standpoint of ordinary members, confidence in the movement as a body of practices and beliefs. As ordinary people construct the movement, by announcing (through 'recruitment institutions') that the product of their endeavours is available for inspection, they confirm to themselves that their endeavours are well-founded.[2]

From the ordinary members' point of view, then, the charismatic presence in non-corporate alternative communities, together with the institutions of recruitment which charismatic leaders typically initiate are not about recruitment. But what of the mainstreamer who, experiencing such features, joins up? Are there comparable, 'non-recruitment' experiences for him or her as well?

With respect to all religious movements, this, in many ways, is the final challenge, and our reply must be in consonance with all that has been said until now. We shall focus on recruitment procedures (keeping the example of flirty fishing in mind). We suggest that the incipient member, by associating with others already established in the movement and by participating in the recruitment practices, joins in (re)producing the movement's institutional features (including the recruitment practices). This incipient member, one should suppose, is already departed the mainstream, and his or her participation in the recruitment practices is therefore from an already-established liminal position. For such incipient members the meaning of the recruitment practices in which they engage is not that these procedures have recruited them. It is rather that these practices, because they are highly distinctive, possibly enjoyable and, above all, 'witnessing' practices, confirm to them that, in consort with the other people with whom they are newly linked, they are working to produce worthwhile social and cultural forms.

Space–Time Variables

People's association with a particular religious movement is a matter of choice. To understand such choice, the range of movements presumed to be available must be grasped consistently with how religious movements are deemed to be constructed. The construction of religious movements has been shown to be grounded in the communitas experience. Therefore the range of movements must be understood at a comparable level. The understanding we seek should make it possible to appreciate transformations amongst religious movements as the outcome of change in people's communitas experience. The challenge, then, is to understand communitas as a variable.

Variability relating to communitas should be something that is intrinsic to what communitas is. Communitas amounts to a primordial social aggregation, so the variable at issue should relate to something about social aggregation as such. What is certain is that the variable cannot reflect institutional constraints on social aggregation since this would nullify the idea of communitas. This being so, we propose that variation at the level of communitas consists of variation in social aggregation in terms of space and time. We shall argue, on the one hand, that people's association with different movements reflects different space–time preferences, and, on the other hand, that people's consciousness that they are not-mainstream implies that these various space–time preferences are distinguishable from mainstream space–time. The result, we believe, is that the different social institutional organisations of different movements can be understood as products of such different space–time experiences. In this respect, we shall explain shortly that the Glastonbury New Age, as discussed in the previous chapter, may be treated as the exemplar religious movement. The social and cultural features of this particular movement are constructed on the basis of a space–time experience that is elementary, such that one may presume that the discussion in the previous chapter implicitly incorporates (relating to the level of communitas) this particular experience.

We should like to offer nine ethnographic scenarios to help elucidate the full range of space–time variation. In these scenarios one imagines the construction of different actual religious movements on the basis of people, having abandoned the mainstream, choosing to associate with one another in different, alternative types of spatial–temporal aggregate. Such associations refer to people actually or potentially in direct contact. Surface appearances notwithstanding, television, newspapers and pamphlets do not underpin given spatial–temporal aggregates: the mass media has as its function to link separate aggregates (Chapter 13). (References for the scenarios are given only for significant material not already introduced in this book.)

1. As not-mainstreamers, people can associate with one another in such a way that the Glastonbury New Age is the outcome. They could take up permanent residence in Glastonbury, linking up with 700 or so people there who are reproducing New Age ideas and practices. But, once there, such people will discover that feelings of communality with fellow New Agers are hardly manifest at all in everyday practical activity. In Glastonbury and its immediately surrounding area, New Agers are scattered amongst local mainstream people, occupying a range of accommodation from quite affluent-looking rented farmhouses to decidedly unaffluent-looking benders erected in fields, and with barely any facilities. New Agers in the Glastonbury area pursue highly independent economic lives, some living off the land, others, by selling New Age products from shops in the High Street, quite successfully tapping into the tourist industry. Nobody at all coordinates or oversees New Age activities in Glastonbury, and each person, it would seem, upholds his or her own personal spiritual quest.

2. Alternatively, one could go to North America, and join there with people who all their lives have been reproducing the religious movement known as the Hutterites. Hutterite communities are enclaved communities, that is to say the membership is spatially quite separate from a surrounding mainstream world. Such communities, whose size may approach 200 people, are communitarian: the land is held communally and economic life is directed by community representatives. There is social hierarchy: community representatives, or elders, hold considerable power, which is legitimated in religious terms. Hutterites uphold a version of Anabaptist beliefs which relates back to times of religious persecution in sixteenth-century Europe. Highly distinct in social and cultural complexion, Hutterites regard the modern American world as sinful, and strive for as little interaction with the outside world as possible. Yet they also know it to be intriguing, thanks, partly, to some of their own members who have defected to it and then returned.

3. Or, one could proceed to Findhorn near Inverness, linking into the New Age commune there. Known as a 'Light Centre', a place where, in meditation, people can tap into the new type of energy associated with the Aquarian Age, Findhorn was founded in 1962, and has since grown to over 200 permanent members, plus another 100 or so who are there temporarily, paying not insignificant sums of money to sample the Findhorn experience, and attending courses on New Age and Deep Ecology themes. As noted earlier, in this enclaved community one participates in a democratic hierarchy.

4. Or one could link up with the New Age Travellers, another association whose social and cultural forms people desiring to be not-mainstream could help in reproducing. The Travellers share a similar social and religious philosophy with New Agers elsewhere. They uphold a rejection of consumer materialism, favour living on the land, advocate a non-monetary economy, and celebrate spiritual values; in practical life they are decidedly individualistic. Perhaps more than settled New Ages, the Travellers' appearance, to the mainstream eye, is unkempt, with dreadlocked hair common, and ripped clothes. The Travellers, as the name indicates, pursue a nomadic existence, moving from venue to venue in small groups, seldom numbering a score of people. In Glastonbury, they and the sedentary New Agers rub shoulders at important New Age meeting places such as the Glastonbury Experience and the Assembly Rooms.

5. Or, if one wished to participate only temporarily in a fully-fledged alternative lifestyle, one could associate with the large Rainbow gatherings, frequently numbering in excess of several hundred people, which occur in deliberately inaccessible North American forests at selected times and places during the year (Niman 1997). Those who participate totally suspend the mainstream lifestyle, for a couple of weeks or so engaging in what, to an outside observer, appears to be New Age-type practices and beliefs. Cut off from the outside world, Rainbow People render one another goods and services as gifts, and money is not used. Community decisions are rigorously arrived at through consensus. One gets to know of where the gatherings will take place through electronic communication.

6. One could alternatively proceed to Israel, and associate with those reproducing a kibbutz. In its classical guise, the kibbutz is a large commune incorporating 300 or more people, who, between them, can expect to deploy all the skills necessary for successful agricultural production in the modern world. The social collectivity of the kibbutz is marked; for example, all adult men constitute the kibbutz assembly, which supervises kibbutz affairs. In the classical kibbutz, children are socialised, night and day, mainly not in a family setting, but in small peer groups that particular, trained kibbutz members are charged with supervising. Kibbutniks uphold the notion of the holistic person, but in contrast to the other movements in this list, this celebrates the inseparability of the physical body with a person's social being, more than the physical and the spiritual. Thus kibbutz doctrine represents itself as more socialist than religious.

7. Or yet again, one could link up with people in, say, London or New York, reproducing the Hare Krishna communities. Consisting of at most around twenty to thirty people, the Hare Krishna temples are small in population size, and for the members social and cultural living is strongly regimented and is ascetic. The temple commune is, in Goffman's terms, a total institution, virtually providing for the members' entire life's needs. Under the strong authority of the Temple president, members uphold the mantras of the ancient Vedic Scriptures, and also must desist from gambling, from all intoxicants (ranging from drugs to tea), from pre-marital courtship, and certainly from pre-marital sex; also, they must be vegans (e.g., Daner 1975).

8. Or if that is not ascetic enough, one can turn the clock back and adjourn to North America a hundred years ago, and seek out people, to be found in remote rural parts, who are reproducing a Shaker colony. Shakers are famous for their artisan, especially furniture making, work, and for the celibate relations between men and women members. Secular life among the Shakers is quiet, even silent, but not so ritual life. Under divine inspiration, Shakers engage in ecstatic physical and verbal display, often directed at miscreants who have failed to accede to elaborate communal rules.

9. Finally, one could associate with those who call themselves Jehovah's Witnesses. In the name of apocalyptic Christian beliefs, this relates largely to engagement with exclusive religious texts disseminated by the Watchtower Bible and Tract society whose headquarters are in New York. Their disdain for symbolically significant mainstream practices, ranging from not celebrating birthdays and Christmas, through to refusing to participate in civic elections or military service, signals the Jehovah's Witnesses as a non-mainstream community. Their social association is manifest in frequent meetings which detain them for several hours each week; otherwise they live dispersed among the mainstream population. Their doorstep proselytisation is well-known (e.g., Stark and Iannaccone 1997).

These ethnographic scenarios help us discern eight relevant variables in space–time experience. Every religious movement, we argue, can be plotted in relation to each one of these variables, allowing, therefore, the possibility of at least 40,320 religious movements differing in respect of social and cultural potential! Recalling the definition of communitas, as a primordial social communion, we elucidate these variables in terms of different qualities of social aggregation. With regard to a particular religious movement, such variables are applied to the principal grouping with which members of its 'alternative communities' identify. For example, in the case of Glastonbury, this grouping consists of all New Agers in Glastonbury and the immediately surrounding countryside (that is to say, the Alternative Community in Glastonbury). We shall start by listing these variables in turn, which we do by defining each one's polar values as opposites. With regard to any one variable, most actual alternative communities have characteristics which place them at some point between these poles (though probably nearer one pole than the other). However, to illustrate the variables, we shall mention convenient examples of religious movements where the respective alternative communities lie very close to, if not at, one pole or the other.

1. The first dimension refers to space–time experience regarding social aggregation, as, at the one extreme, spatially discontinuous with the mainstream population, versus, at the other extreme, spatially continuous with it. The former, where there is major space–time disjuncture between the aggregation and its mainstream environment, generally manifests itself as a concentrated social grouping; the latter generally manifests itself as a dispersed social grouping.

aggregation *spatially* *discontinuous* with the mainstream (e.g., Hutterites)	vs	aggregation *spatially* *continuous* with the mainstream (e.g., Glastonbury New Agers)

2. The second dimension refers to space–time experience regarding social aggregation, as, at the one extreme, shifting in relation to place, versus, at the other extreme, social aggregation fixed in terms of place.

nomadic aggregation (e.g., New Age Travellers)	vs	*sedentary* aggregation (e.g., Findhorners [farming communards])

3. The third dimension refers to space–time experience relating to density of social interaction. High density social interaction obtains when members very frequently turn to the same few people in daily affairs, whereas low density interaction is where individuals turn to others infrequently and/or have a wide range of co-members to choose from. Obviously high density interaction is disposed by small social groupings, and low density interaction by large social groupings.

high density aggregation (e.g., Hare Krishna)	vs	*low density* aggregation (e.g., Glastonbury New Agers)

4. The fourth dimension refers to space–time experience which one anticipates will definitely be permanent in relation to one's life's future, as against space–time experience that one anticipates may probably be temporary.

283

non-episodic aggregation	vs	*episodic* aggregation
[long-term/life-long association with the aggregate] (e.g., Hutterites)		[short-term association with the aggregate] (e.g., Rainbow People)

5. The fifth dimension refers to space–time experience where the social aggregation with which one is involved is, at the one extreme, the same as one's natal social aggregation, as against, at the other extreme, completely different from one's natal aggregation. Thus, Hutterites were generally born and brought up within Hutterite colonies; Glastonbury New Agers, by contrast, were generally born and brought up as mainstreamers.

aggregation is *non-natal in respect of members* (e.g., Glastonbury New Agers)	vs	aggregation is *natal in respect of members* (e.g., Hutterites)

6. The sixth dimension refers to space–time experience that detains one in all life's affairs, as against space–time experience that detains one in only a portion of life's affairs. To enjoy the first, one will effectively be participating in a total institution, like the Hare Krishna Temple, whilst the second is illustrated in the case of Glastonbury New Agers who consider themselves members of the Alternative Community but yet hold down a nine to five job in the mainstream.

total aggregation	vs	*partial* aggregation
[aggregation pertains to all life's affairs] (e.g., Hare Krishna)		[aggregation pertains to only some of life's affairs (e.g., many Glastonbury New Agers)

7. The seventh dimension refers to the basis of co-evalness, that is, the sharing of a common time frame. The contrast here is between co-evalness enjoyed in face-to-face encounter, as against co-evalness enjoyed only through people knowing that amongst themselves there is sychronicity. In the latter instance, people are in *personal* contact, but do not experience one another's surroundings (no social or religious movement as such corresponds with this latter extreme).

concrete aggregation	vs	*surrogate* aggregation
[i.e., face-to-face association] (e.g., Shakers)		[i.e., not in face-to-face contact] (e.g., Cyberspace communities)

8. The eighth dimension refers to space–time experience which, at the one extreme, implies the person's direct involvement in an alternative aggregation, as against, at the other extreme, where people identify with such an aggregation even though they are not actually participating in it in their daily lives. By the second instance we have in mind people who identify with a religious movement, such as Hare Krishna or the Moonies, that is commune-based, without actually living in the commune.

experiential involvement in social aggregation (e.g., Shakers)	vs	*vicarious involvement* in social aggregation (e.g., Hare Krishna people who live outside the Temple)

Now we can offer a general conclusion, on the basis of the last two chapters, for why religious movements exist. The reply can be expressed in different, and increasingly complex, ways. Religious movements exist because people, having consciously rejected the mainstream, sustain novel space–time experiences. Or, different religious movements reflect people being not-mainstream in 'alternative' space–time contexts. Or, the religiosity in a given religious movement arises as people, in a preferred, alternative space–time context, resolve contradictions relating to being not-mainstream.

One may add that when people cease associating with a religious movement, either turning their attention to another one or else returning to the mainstream, this should not be treated as the person transferring allegiance, since 'allegiance' implies interaction between the person and the movement as a completed whole. Rather, moving from movement to movement, or from movement to mainstream, may be better understood as reflecting a person's change of preference in respect of various types of space–time experience. People's departure from a particular movement may be *represented* in terms of a discrepancy between what a movement promises and what it delivers. But a movement's promises (for example, material succour) are not things the members appreciate as if they had needs independent of their participation in it (cf. Richardson 1985). These needs the members construct in relation to their particular space–time preference.

The way that particular social organisations and cultural forms of specific movements emanate from distinctive types of space–time remains to be discussed in detail in future research. That said, space–time variation as the basis of transformation as between religious movements is encouraged by the discussion earlier in this chapter, firstly regarding the fact that *enclavement* relating to alternative communities disposes corporate social organisation, and secondly on the fact that leadership charisma is more disposed in relatively non-enclaved communities. Accordingly, when religious movements change their character through their history, for example where the movement leader's charismatic force declines and more bureaucratic authority structures are put in place instead, this should be understood not in terms of social and intellectual trends within the movement, but rather in terms of changing space–time preferences of the members. As to the effect of transformation on the religious movements' social and cultural features, one recalls, from Chapter 11, that religious movements emanate from processes operating at several different levels. One may suppose, with respect to such transformation, that cultural material corresponding with the third (representational) level will be the most vulnerable to elimination or change. Thus one expects that the various 'symbols' of, say, the New Age movement (evocation of ancient society, celebration of the feminine) may well not be evident in other types of non-mainstream social or religious community, even as cultural material relating to more fundamental levels (holistic person, ideas of love, holistic environment) may remain in common. The similarities and contrasts, mentioned earlier in this chapter, between the New Age in Glastonbury and the kibbutz and the Hutterites, would illustrate this rather well.

Space–time variation as a crucial explanatory factor would certainly be endorsed as a matter of principle by received anthropological wisdom. Likewise, the particular space–time variables that we described above would be well recognised as potential constraints on individual human action. The fact that where transformation is concerned Glastonbury New Age can be considered as the exemplar religious movement stems from this. We described the variables in such a way that on the right-hand side of each pair the manifestation is less constraining in relation to group social organisation (e.g. continuity with the mainstream, low density interaction, sedentary aggregation, high turnover of personnel, etc.). With the exception of one variable (concerning the non-natality of membership), Glastonbury New Agers lie at, or close to, these right-hand poles. In short, the Glastonbury New Age is an exemplar because it is almost maximally unconstrained where social organisation is concerned. Accordingly, religious movements that exhibit close to the left-hand poles, where space–time exigencies are highly constraining on social organisation, might be treated as developments (i.e. transformations) of the Glastonbury social organisation and culture.

A final basic observation is suggested from this argument. This is about mainstream society. Mainstream society, no differently from any social organisation, is founded in communitas experience, and, as such, in a given space–time dimension. This suggests that, among mainstreamers, in the same way as New Agers, the relativity of one's communitas experience is tangible, for a particular space–time dimension can be characterised only in relation to something contrasting. One presumes then, that, no differently from non-mainstream communities, mainstream community upholds a sense of an alternativeness relative to (other) communities it considers itself to be neighbouring. In fact, one can make observations from this about the root of all human social organisation. The root of all human social organisation is a sense of alternativeness manifest in space–time terms.

Certain cultural features of some religious movements can, we believe, be explained directly in relation to their distinctive constellation of space–time features. The basis to this is that, for religious movements, the not-mainstream experience is fundamental, such that a movement's distinctive space–time constellation is not only a manifestation of communitas, it also expresses the condition of being not-mainstream. Therefore, at the level of communitas, a religious movement's particular space–time experience must disassociate its respective social aggregate from mainstream aggregates. The interesting instances are where just one space–time variable (from among the eight) functions in this regard. In such instances, where the delineation of the alternative experience is fragile, dominant symbols relating to this one variable crucially articulate the relevant alternative community as a community.

The Glastonbury New Agers are a case in point. What makes them separate, in space–time terms, from the surrounding mainstream is solely the fact that they participate in a social association different from their natal backgrounds. (Otherwise, indistinguishably from the mainstream, the Alternative Community is dispersed, experiences low intensity interaction, has a fair turnover of personnel, and is sendentary; it even involves itself in some mainstream affairs) This surely explains why the location itself – Glastonbury, the town – assumes such symbolic importance for Glastonbury New Agers. Notwithstanding the way New Agers represent it, the town's mystical association is not culturally significant as a lure to draw people to the area. Like all the other social and cultural features relating to the Glastonbury New Age, the town's special quality is something those participating there as non-mainstreamers construct. We suggest that the idea of the town as a mystical place reflects supreme symbolic elaboration being put on the one space–time variable in terms of which the Alternative Community is distinctive. The town as a mystical place perfectly expresses the New Agers' removal, in space–time terms, from their natal aggregations.[3] Something similar can be said about Jehovah's Witnesses. They likewise are fully dispersed amongst mainstreamers, but they cannot point to having moved from their natal locations. Their intensive meetings amount to an episodic association in space–time terms (variable 4). In a weak sense, they are similar to the Rainbow people, or to English Wiccans whose covens assemble during occasional evenings and at weekends. The Jehovah's Witnesses' intensive proselytisation may be understood in this context. Intensive proselytisation is not at all an invariable feature of religious movements, and recruiting mainstreamers in their homes is highly unusual. Such proselytisation may function symbolically to express Jehovah's Witnesses' distinctiveness as non-mainstreamers. Their not-mainstream space–time preference can surely no more strongly be emphasised than by confronting mainstreamers in their homes, the key locus of mainstream space–time. In the terms of this chapter, the Jehovah's Witnesses' striking recruitment institutions 'witness' both their incorporation as movement members (see earlier discussion on recruitment institutions), and also their non-mainstream standing in Western society.

We may review the analysis in this section by imagining a real-life situation where someone joins up with a religious movement. The individual concerned is going to represent what occurs in their own way ('Glastonbury acted as a magnet on me'), but we have argued that it must be elucidated, at a more fundamental level, in space–time terms. Thus the scenario begins where someone elects to be not-mainstream and to associate with like-minded others. There are available a variety of non-mainstream space–time contexts in which the individual can do this, and one presumes that he or she has distinct space–time preferences in this regard. But how do they know where to head in order to find others with like-minded space–time preferences? An obvious reply might be that they hear, from social contacts, about different types of religious community with different types of space–time characteristics, and on the basis of this make their choice. However, it would be unsatisfactory to put it like this since it would amount to falling back into the position, vehemently opposed in this chapter, of treating 'religious community' as some sort of entity independent of the people who make it up. So we are going to have to say that, when choosing 'where to go', people make the decision on the basis of learning about a venue where the preferred space–time characteristics occur. Thus people who head for Glastonbury fundamentally do so because the sole expression of not-mainstream association there is physical removal from the natal location (the space–time experience there is otherwise indistinguishable from mainstream life).

Getting into Shape

So that it exists, a religious movement must have members (who construct it). The question that detains many commentators is whether one can discern distinctive patterns of membership, with respect either to religious movements in general or else to particular individual movements. But the memberships of religious movements are notoriously difficult to characterise. As mentioned in previous chapters, academic literature on the New Age movement in Europe and North America commonly depicts those involved as, more often than not, middle class, female, and babyboomers (who these days fast approach middle age), adding that in their previous mainstream incarnations these people will most usually have worked in domains of life outside the productive sector (e.g., Rose 1998).[4] Somewhat differently, other commentators observe that participants in religious movements tend to have experienced some sort of personal crisis or trauma in their former mainstream lives.[5] With respect to very many people in the Alternative Community in Glastonbury, teachers and ordinary New Agers alike, one cannot deny that these characterisations ring true (see the biographies in Chapter 4). But, as Wallis (1979: 3–4, 102) points out, to consider religious movements like this is going to be misleading. For example, plenty of New Agers have working class backgrounds, and in Britain only a tiny minority of middle class people are New Agers. Not all Glastonbury New Agers have had personal traumas, and not everyone in Britain with a personal trauma has headed for Glastonbury. A few academic commentators, taking such facts seriously, refuse to describe movement members in terms of conventional social categories, declaring that this is impossible (e.g. Luhrmann 1989: 100; Thompson and Heelas 1986).

Yet the general academic literature is clearly pointing to something: certain patterns do seem to be there. Surely it is possible to appreciate the membership of a religious movement properly, *and* in a way that indicates why, for example, New Agers turn out more often than not to be middle class. The problem with most academic discussion, we suggest, is that membership patterns get called upon in two, contradictory ways, firstly as something deserving explanation, but secondly as something that explains (e.g., middle classness leads the New Age movement to emerge). But this contradiction can be eliminated if one resists understanding religious movements in terms of background mainstream factors. Patterns of membership of religious movements may then be considered via meanings consistent with those who participate in them, namely meanings associated with communitas space–time. Therefore, to address patterns of membership, distinctive space–time meanings would seem the promising place to start: different space–time experiences may be found attractive by different types of person. We should like to offer some brief indications.

The most pertinent space–time variable, especially pertaining to the matter of social class, is the opposition between space–time aggregations spatially continuous with the mainstream, and those spatially discontinuous with the mainstream (variable 1). One suggests that aggregations where the alternative community is dispersed, such as at Glastonbury, will be found meaningful more by people comfortable with encounters with a mainstream population on a daily basis. One has in mind people who, in their mainstream incarnations, were socially competent in multi-cultural settings. Such people will more likely be of middle class background and/or of relatively mature (babyboom) age: middle class values state that competence in moving among a broad band of different types of person is a definite social asset, and such competence also increases in relation to adult maturity. For these people, scattered throughout Glastonbury, now it is the mainstream that provides the 'different type of person'. Meanwhile, people with opposite types of mainstream background may prefer spatially concentrated, exclusive associations: very young working class men desiring to be not-mainstream favour the navy.

As to the fact that movement members are commonly afflicted with personal crisis and suffering, the least one can say is that their participation in an alternative way of life presumes a preparedness to assume a liminal position vis-à-vis the mainstream. This being so, amongst Westerners experiencing crisis, one expects that individuals most likely to gravitate to this position will be people who are sensitive, intolerant and imaginative types, and confronted by a restricted choice of opportunities within the mainstream. Hence the preponderance, in New Age communities, of divorced and single women who were teachers or social workers in their 'previous lives'?[6]

Final Comment

We have argued that religious movements exist because people submit themselves to novel space–time experience. In this chapter, we derived the notion of space–time experience directly from the notion of communitas. Variation in space–time experience, which underpins variety among social and religious movements, was, in short, elucidated in relation to deep social processes. However, it is worth noting that members of religious movements commonly express themselves in explicitly space–time terms. We conclude with a New Age Traveller, who is quoted as saying:

> I'm forty now and I don't know how folks should live . . . If we had space we would flourish and we don't have space. Space is what's needed. I've seen a few bits of country, and I still think that the more space per square mile, the happier folk are (Lowe and Shaw 1993: 111).

Notes

1. Jeremy Tucker, personal communication, May 1996. In 1999, Jeremy Tucker, a research student at the University of St Andrews, tragically died before his thesis on Findhorn was complete.
2. This particular argument is inspired by Riches' analysis of the potlatch, the spectacular ceremonial festival held among the Indians of the west coast of Canada, in which guests from neighbouring groups receive, as gifts, large quantites of food and durable wealth. Riches emphasises the symbolic significance to Indian groups that their local economic and artistic prowess be witnessed, and suggests that the importance of the ceremonial distribution is precisely to encourage neighbouring groups to come and perform the respective role (Riches 1984).
3. People who do not live in Glastonbury also know it as a mystical place. But this knowledge, again, is constructed in relation to a particular social situation. New Agers in Bradford sustain certain images of Glastonbury, but they will construe them differently from people living in Glastonbury itself.

291

4. For example, Hess (1993: 174) declares that the New Age movement is for baby-boomers to rethink the monoculture of their patriarchal, Judeo-Christian and Eurocentric cultural heritage. See also Puttick (1997) for a recent reiteration of the predominantly middle class social composition and, on balance, female majority in many new religious movements.

5. For example, Hendershott on Findhorn (1989); see also Thompson and Heelas's case studies of those who joined Rajneeshee communes (1986).

6. This is more or less Hendershott's description of the Findhorn population (1989).

13

Local, not Global

Most social or religious movements express themselves as doctrines whose validity transcends the single community or society. Characterising themselves as Christian, New Age, Neo-Pagan, socialist, ecofeminist, and so on, their identity rests with world or national headquarters, internationally recognised charismatic leaders, and written texts potentially available on a worldwide basis. Most academic work on religious movements has fallen into line with this perspective. Religious movements are understood as 'global phenomena', or as present-day precipitates of historically long-standing intellectual trends. For example, though the New Age movement as such is not subject to worldwide organisational coordination, by labelling it a 'movement' one acknowledges its pan-Western presence.

This is quite different from the way that we conceive of religious movements. In this book, religious movements, seen as 'alternative communities', are understood in terms of local social aggregations, not as global or national processes. True, religious movements generally express themselves 'top-down': they declare themselves in the name of some internationally renowned guru and the doctrine he or she propounds. But the explanation that we give is bottom-up: a religious movement's social and cultural content rests on ordinary human individuals in local arenas experiencing particular constraints in space and time. In this chapter, by way of concluding the book, we should like to air our prejudices, and be brief.

Two types of empirical fact are germane here. Firstly, ideas similar to New Age ideas were expressed during earlier periods of Western history. Secondly, in present-day times, 'alternative' ideas that are similar to one another are voiced in various geographical localities. The issue is what to make of this. For our part we do not assume that similar ideas in different times or different places reflect direct connections, such that Glastonbury ideas are explained either as the product of history or else as reflecting contemporary transnational social forces. Our premise is that ideas exist in the form they do, and in the place they are, because of local exigencies. Particular ideas are voiced in local situations, and would not be so voiced if local situations did not invite this to be. People in local communities, especially in literate cultures, know about similar ideas existing in other places or times; they may well consider that such similar ideas are directly influencing them in what they say and do. But local exigencies determine in the first place *whether or not* these ideas are taken on board, and in the second place *how* they are taken on board – to harmonise with local understandings and meanings such ideas come to be altered, or 'domesticated'. To put it bluntly, ideas from elsewhere get taken up, and domesticated, only because local exigencies have separately produced similar local knowledge, in terms of which these ideas from elsewhere can come to make sense. Therefore a sufficient explanation of a specific idea, in the form it takes in a given time or place, is in relation to such local social processes. Also, if similar ideas seem to be present in different times or different places, then this must be understood in terms of similar local situations being present in these different times or different places. In short, the analyst's challenge, with respect to a specific idea, is to show that local social processes have certain characteristics such that this specific idea is required.

Academic narrative that directly links ideas from different times or from different places is the opposite of this approach. The historical or macro-forces that such narrative implies, which by-pass ordinary human individuals and normal local scenes, may well, in our opinion, be spurious. Globalisation theory and secularisation theory are the twin narratives that most normally explain Western religious movements in this way, especially the new religious movements. Globalisation theory refers to an 'inter-active order' of societies in the present-day world (Dawson 1998b) that exists because of international capitalism, the mass media and the widespread movement of populations around the world, as refugees, migrants and tourists. Secularisation refers to the decline of religion in the contemporary west, for example as reflected in the pervasive marginalisation of religious institutions with respect to the conduct of daily life. Such narratives typically see religious movements as arising in opposition to the social trends that globalisation and secularisation imply, but yet taking a form that globalising and secularising processes predetermine. Globalisation and secularisation are seen as historically unfolding trends that spawn, but then reincorporate, moments of opposition.

The framework in terms of which globalisation and secularisation theses address the new religious movements is in principle similar to Weber's concept of re-enchantment. Globalisation and secularisation amounts, in the contemporary Western world, to the human individual being 'de-institutionalised', 'disembedded' from traditional certainties, and losing the value of historical 'memory', such that, among other things, the individual is forced to confront for himself or herself the nature of humanity. New religious movements arise in this context in order to re-embed the individual, to restore the value of traditional and historical memory, and effect a reflexive thematisation of the self (e.g., Dawson 1998b, Beyer 1998, Hervieu-Leger 1998). But globalisation also amounts to people being sensitive to diverse ways of human social living, so religious movements, by exploring further designs for living, contribute to this diversity and enhance people's sensitivities.

Globalisation/secularisation theses of religious movements are, for us, unconvincing because they imply that all Westerners should be signing up to be New Agers, when patently this is not the case. Such theses posit religious movements as globalising trends thrown into reverse. Globalisation leads inexorably to social conditions that are incompatible with human social life and psychological well-being, whereupon religious movements emerge to come to the rescue. This is unconvincing because in the Western world these days the overwhelming majority of people seem perfectly content with their secular existence. Globalisation and secularisation theory implies social trends whereby people come to be bereft of a proper social life, and which impact equally on everyone, but this does not seem to correspond with the facts at all. People who do join religious movements of course represent their decision in terms of facts and feelings similar to those that the globalisation and secularisation theses advance. But there are going to be deeper (and quite different) social processes responsible for them joining; otherwise religious movements would not be a minority way of life.

The fact remains, however, that religious movements, especially the more prominent ones, invoke transnational doctrine, that is to say, beliefs and practices valid wherever and whenever. How do these square with the emphasis on religious movements advanced in this book, which explains them as local social phenomena? We suggest that 'transnational doctrine' be problematized as an idea that local communities invoke. The religious movement objectively should be conceived of as a large number of separate local communities that happen to have certain ideas in common. (Here the 'world headquarters', if there is one, would be construed as just another local community.) The religious movement's transnational doctrine will be understood in terms of such separate communities reaching out to one another. We suggest that its transnational doctrine amounts to movement members *representing* what they happen to have in common as being caused by something transcendent (for example, a world-famous guru's revelations).

This can be elucidated when one clarifies the bottom-up approach to religious movements. In this perspective, global or international factors (for example, charismatic texts relayed on the internet) do not cause local manifestations of a particular movement to exist. On the contrary, communitas – or, more exactly, contradictions relating to communitas – causes the local 'alternative community' to exist. The movement members' representations of their involvement in the movement (that transcendent factors are responsible) should be elucidated in terms of the local social processes that this implies. Here one recalls the way local alternative communities announce themselves to the world. In Chapter 11 we explained that this is through certain potent and compelling symbols (dark versus light, past versus future, male versus female, etc.) in terms of which local teachers articulate an 'alternative vision' and declare it good. The (local) idea of 'religious movement as a transnational phenomenon' rests on the possibility that local alternative communities, desiring to portray themselves as right, compare and contrast themselves with their understandings of other alternative communities in other places. The compelling symbols are a crucial resource to enable this to happen. In terms of such symbols, local groups both learn about and evaluate other alternative communities, and pronounce them 'similar to us' or 'different from us'.

Transnational doctrine relating to religious movements may be understood as *local discourse* in terms of which this is achieved. Such doctrine, implying both categorisation and transcendence, constitutes the means whereby local alternative communities that declare themselves to be similar justify this similarity, and correspondingly justify excluding all those other alternative communities that they consider to be different. Transnational doctrine connotes categorisation, because to delineate a particular doctrine requires comparing it with other different doctrines. Comparison implies evaluation, such that particular local alternative communities, by summoning the idea that they are aligned with a particular transnational doctrine, claim for themselves a certain moral superiority. Transnational doctrine implies transcendence because the idea of globality that it contains evokes the concept of power; through the discourse of globality, local alternative communities summon the idea that they are as they are thanks to currents and trends much greater than themselves – currents and trends that brook no challenge.

This puts a perspective on world headquarters, international gurus, and globally available written texts. As local communities engage in the above processes, these institutions, amounting to supplementary local communities, function to facilitate them. Gurus offer their ideas to the world as transcendentally relevant (Chapter 11). But the ideas that they promulgate properly exist only in so far as local communities, because of their local requirements, embrace them (ideas do not exist if they fall on deaf ears). Millionaire New Age gurus, like Bhagwan Shree Rajneesh, will have started their careers in ordinary non-mainstream local communities, incumbent in social positions that ordinary members had constructed. Now they secure their rewards thanks to the fact that they continue to fulfil non-mainstream requirements. The exalted standing comes not from the fact that, thanks to their inspirational powers, they have won people over from the mainstream in their droves. Their recognition comes from the fact that non-mainstream local social associations, often loosely organised and sometimes without their own local charismatic leaders, need to make contact in order to uphold their moral integrity.

New Age, Neo-Pagan . . . Christian, Buddhist: these, then, are labels that local communities invoke. For local communities, the claim that the practices and the cosmology that they have constructed are morally superior is the stronger to the extent that the means to justify this superiority is itself elaborate and compelling; these labels, connoting global doctrine, provide the means. Likewise, the idea of transnational institutions and processes has credence to the extent that such institutions and processes are, in a similar way, elaborate and compelling. World headquarters, globetrotting gurus, texts and creeds that require obeisance: these constitute the organisational trappings that fulfil this requirement. Based on the symbols with which local communities reach out to one another, the condition for their existence is the ordinary local community, such as the Alternative Community in Glastonbury. These trappings have sense precisely because they relate to what it means to live in a local community. In the fact that local communities, in relation to their local existence, uphold the idea of transnationality, the particular people involved in developing these trappings may proceed – couching what they do as New Age, Neo-Paganism, Buddhism, Christianity (or whatever). The root of all doctrine is where real (ordinary) people live out their real lives.

Bibliography

Albanese, C. 1990 *Nature Religion in America: from the American Indians to the New Age*, Chicago, University Press.

——— 1992 'The Magical Staff: Quantum Healing in the New Age'. From *Perspectives on the New Age*, edited by J. Lewis and G. Melton, Albany, SUNY Press.

Allaby, M. 1989 *Thinking Green*, London, Barrie and Jenkins.

Alexander, K. 1992 'Roots of the New Age'. From *Perspectives on the New Age*, edited by J. Lewis and G. Melton, Albany, SUNY Press.

Anderson, B. 1983 *Imagined Communities. Reflections on the Origin and Spread of Nationalism*, London, Verso.

Argüelles, J. 1987 *The Mayan Factor: Path Beyond Technology*, Sante Fe, Bear and Co.

Badone, E. 1991 'Ethnography, Fiction and the Meaning of the Past in Britanny', *American Ethnologist*, vol. 18(3): 518–45.

Bainbridge, W. 1997 *The Sociology of Religious Movements*, London, Routledge.

Barnard, A. 1992 *Hunters and Herders of Southern Africa*, Cambridge, University Press.

Barnes, J. 1962 'African Models in the New Guinea Highlands', *Man* (old series), vol. 62(1): 5–9.

Barth, F. 1987 *Cosmologies in the Making*. Cambridge, University Press.

Barth, F. 1969 (editor/introduction) *Ethnic Groups and Boundaries*. Boston, Little, Brown.

Baudrillard, J. 1988 *Selected Writings* (edited by Mark Poster), Oxford, Polity Press.

Balch, R. 1982 'Bo and Peep: a Case Study of the Origins of Messianic Leadership'. From *Millenialism and Charisma*, edited by R. Wallis, Belfast, Queen's University.

Baumann, Z. 1988 'Viewpoint: Sociology and Postmodernity', *Sociology* 13(4): 790–813.

Beckford, J. 1985 'Two Types of Sectarian Organisation'. From *Sectarianism*, edited by R. Wallis, London, Peter Owen.

Bennett, J. 1967 *Hutterite Brethren*, Stanford, University Press.

Beyer, P. 1998 'Globalisation: the Religion of Nature'. From *Nature Religion Today*, edited by J. Pearson et al., Edinburgh, University Press.

Bird-David, N. 1992 'Beyond the Original Affluent Society: a Culturalist Formulation', *Current Anthropology*, vol. 31(1): 25–38.

——— 1994 'Sociality and Immediacy, or, Past and Present Conversations on Bands', *Man*, vol. 29(3): 583–604.

Bloom, W. 1991 (editor/introduction), *The New Age. An Anthology of Essential Writings*, London, Channel 4 Books.

Bohannan, P. and L. Bohannan. 1968 *Tiv Economy*, London, Longmans.

Bosanquet, N. 1983 *After the New Right*, London, Heinemann.

Bourguignon, E. 1977 'Altered States of Consciousness, Myths and Rituals'. From *Drugs, Rituals and Altered States of Consciousness*, edited by B. du Toit, Rotterdam, A.A. Balkema.

Bowman, M. 1993 'Drawn to Glastonbury'. From *Pilgrimage in Popular Culture*, edited by I. Reader and T. Walter, London, Macmillan.

Bradley, M. 1984 *The Mists of Avalon*, London, Sphere Books.

Brunton, R. 1980 'Misconstrued Order in Melanesian Religion', *Man*, vol. 15(1): 112–28.

––––– 1989 'The Cultural Instability of Egalitarian Societies', *Man*, vol. 24(4): 673–81.

Buber, M. 1937 *I and Thou*, Edinburgh, Clark.

Burridge, K. 1969 *New Heaven, New Earth*, London, Blackwell.

Burrows, R. 1993 'Holistic Approaches to Health and Well-Being in Northern Ireland' (PhD thesis, Queen's University of Belfast).

Capra, F. 1976 *The Tao of Physics*, London, Fontana.

Carrier, J. 1992 'Occidentalism: the World Turned Upside Down', *American Ethnologist*, vol. 19(2): 195–207.

Carrithers, M., S. Collins and S. Lukes 1985 (editors), *The Category of the Person. Anthropology, Philosophy, History*, Cambridge, University Press.

Castaneda, C. 1968 *The Teachings of Don Juan*, Berkeley, University of California Press.

Clark, S. 1992 'Myth, Metaphor, and Manifestation: the Negotiation of Belief in a New Age Community'. From *Perspectives on the New Age*, edited by J. Lewis and G. Melton, Albany, SUNY Press.

Cohen, A. 1985 *The Symbolic Construction of Community*, London, Ellis Horwood Ltd.

Cohen, A. 1982 (editor/introduction) *Belonging. Identity and Social Organisation In British Rural Communities*, Manchester, University Press.

Coon, R. 1989 *Physical Immortality: History, Theory and Techniques*. Glastonbury, The Omega Point Foundation.

Coward, R. 1989 *The Whole Truth – The Myth of Alternative Health*, London, Faber.

Daner, F. 1975 'Conversion to Krishna Consciousness'. From *Sectarianism*, edited by R. Wallis, London, Peter Owen.

Danforth, L. 1989 *Firewalking and Religious Healing*, Princeton, University Press.

Dawson, L. 1998a 'Anti-modernism, Modernisn and Postmodernism: Struggling with the Cultural Significance of New Religious Movements', *Sociology of Religion*, vol. 59(2): 131–56.

––––– 1998b 'The Cultural Significance of New Religious Movements and Globalisation', *Journal for the Scientific Study of Religion*, vol. 37(4): 580–95.

Dawson, L. and J. Hennebry 1999 'New Religion and the Internet: Recruiting in a New Public Space', *Journal of Contemporary Religion*, vol. 14(1): 17–40.

Dentan, R. 1994 'Surrendered Men: Peaceable Enclaves in the Post-Enlightenment West.' From *The Anthropology of Peace and Non-Violence*, edited by L. Sponsel and T. Gregor, Boulder, Lyne Rienner.

Devall, B. and G. Sessions. 1985 *Deep Ecology – Living as if Nature Mattered*, Utah, Peregrine Smith Book.

Douglas, M. 1966 *Purity and Danger*, London, Pelican.

Draper, P. 1978 'The Learning Environment for Aggression and Anti-social Behaviour among the !Kung'. From *Learning Non-aggression*, edited by Ashley Montagu, New York, Oxford University Press.

Dumont, L. 1980 *Homo Hierarchicus*, Chicago, University Press.

——— 1986 *Essays on Individualsim. Modern Ideology in Anthropological Perspective*, Chicago, University Press.

Eder, K. 1990 'The Rise of the Counter-Culture Movements against Modernity', *Theory, Culture and Society*, vol. 7(1): 21–47.

Eliade, M. 1964 *Shamanism: Archaic Techniques of Ecstasy*, New York, Bollingen Foundation.

Ellen, R. 1986 'What Black Elk Left Unsaid: The Illusory Images of Green Primitivism', *Anthropology Today*, vol. 2.

Evans-Pritchard, E.E. 1937 *Witchcraft, Oracles and Magic among the Azande*, Oxford, Clarendon Press.

Eyerman, R. and A. Jamison. 1991 *Social Movements*, Oxford, Polity Press.

Fabian, J. 1983 *Time and the Other*, New York, Columbia University Press.

Ferguson, M. 1980 *The Aquarian Conspiracy*, New York, St Martin's Press.

Fienup-Riordan, A. 1994 *Boundaries and Passages: Rule and Ritual in Yup'ik Eskimo Oral Tradition*, Norman, University of Oklahoma Press.

Fitzgerald, F. 1987 *Cities on a Hill – A Journey Through Contemporary American Cultures*, London, Pan.

Ford, N. 1983 'Consciousness and Lifestyle: Alternative Developments in the Culture of Rural Dyfed' (PhD Thesis, University of Wales, Aberystwyth).

Fortune, D. 1986 *Glastonbury, Avalon of the Heart*. Wellingborough, The Aquarian Press.

Gardner, P. 1991 'Forager Pursuit of Individual Autonomy', *Current Anthropology*, vol. 32(3): 543–72.

Gibran, K. 1980 *The Prophet*. London, Pan Books.

Green, D. 1987 *The New Right*. Brighton, Wheatsheaf Books.

Greer, P. 1996 'The Aquarian Confusion: Conflicting Theologies of the New Age', *Journal of Contemporary Religion*, vol. 10(2): 151–66.

Guemple, L. 1988 'Teaching Social Relations to Inuit Children'. From *Hunters and Gatherers*, edited by T. Ingold, D. Riches, and J. Woodburn. Oxford, Berg.

Hanegraaff, W. 1996 *New Age Religion and Western Culture*, Leiden, Brill.

Hart, K. 1973 'Informal Income Opportunities and Urban Employment in Ghana', *Journal of Modern African Studies*, vol. 57(4): 61–89.

Harvey, G. 1997 *Listening People, Speaking Earth*, London, Hurst.

Heald, S. 1986 'The Ritual Use of Violence: Circumcision among the Gisu of Uganda'. From *The Anthropology of Violence*, edited by D. Riches, Oxford, Blackwell.

Heelas, P. 1993 'The New Age in Cultural Context: the Premodern, the Modern and the Postmodern', *Religion*, vol. 23(2): 103–16.

——— 1994 'The Limits of Consumption and the Postmodern "Religion" of the New Age'. From *The Authority of the Consumer*, edited by R. Keat, N. Whiteley and N. Abercrombie, London, Routledge.

——— 1996 *The New Age Movement*, Oxford, Blackwell.

Heelas, P., S. Lash, and P. Morris 1996 (editors) *Detraditionalisation*. Oxford, Blackwell.

Helliwell, C. 1995 'Autonomy as Natural Equality: Inequality in Egalitarian Societies', *Journal of the Royal Anthropological Institute*, vol. 1(2): 359–76.

Hendershott, C. 1989 'Stranger than Paradise: Host and Guests in a New Age Community' (PhD thesis, New School for Social Research).

Hervier-Leger, D. 1998 'Secularisation, Tradition and New Forms of Religiosity'. From *New Religions and Religiosity*, edited by E. Barker and M. Warburg, Aarhus, University Press.

Hess, D. 1993 *Science and the New Age*, Wisconsin, University Press.

Hobsbawm, E. and T. Ranger 1983 (editors)*The Invention of Tradition*, Cambridge, University Press.

Holy, L. 1979 'Changing Norms in Matrilineal Societies'. From *The Conceptualisation and Explanation of Processes of Social Change*, edited by D. Riches, Belfast, Queen's University.

——— 1984 'Theory, Methodology and the Research Process'. From *Ethnographic Research – A Guide to General Conduct*, edited by Roy Ellen, London, Academic Press.

Holy, L. and M. Stuchlik 1983 *Actions, Norms and Representations*, Cambridge, University Press.

Horton, R. 1967 'African Traditional Thought and Western Science', *Africa*, vol. 37 (1 and 2): 50–71, 155–87.

Hostetler, J. 1974 *Communitarian Societies*, New York, Holt, Rinehart and Winston.

Hostetler, J. and G.E. Huntingdon 1980 *The Hutterites in North America*, New York, Holt, Rhinehart and Winston.

Howell, J. 1997 'ASC Induction Techniques, Spiritual Experiences, and Commitment to New Religious Movements', *Sociology of Religion*, vol. 58(2): 141–64.

Ingold, T. 1990 'An Anthropologist Looks at Biology', *Man*, vol. 25(2): 208–29.

——— 1993 'Globes and Spheres: the Topology of Environmentalism'. From *Environmentalism: The View from Anthropology*, edited by K. Milton, London, Routledge.

Jakobsen, M. 1999 *Shamanism: Traditional and Contemporary Approaches to the Mastery of Spirits and Healing*, Oxford, Berghahn.

Jameson, F. 1991 *Postmodernism, or, The Cultural Logic of Late Capitalism*, Duke University Press

Jenkins, R. 1983 *Lads, Citizens and Ordinary Kids*, Cambridge, University Press.

Jones, K. 1990 *The Goddess In Glastonbury*. Glastonbury, Ariadne Publications.

Kanter, R. Moss. 1972 *Commitment and Community – Communes and Utopias In Sociological Perspective*, Cambridge, Mass., Harvard University Press.

Katz, R. 1976 'Education for Transcendence: !kia Healing and the Kalahari !Kung'. From *Kalahari Hunter–Gatherers*, edited by R. Lee and I. DeVore. Cambridge, Mass., Harvard University Press.

Kent, S. 1992 'The Current Forager Controversy: Real versus Ideal Views of Hunter–Gatherers', *Man*, vol. 27(1): 45–70.

Kent, S. 1996 (editor) *Cultural Diversity among Twentieth-Century Foragers*. Cambridge, University Press.

King, D. 1987 *The New Right*. London, Macmillan.

Koekel, U. 1991 'Immigrants – Entrepreneurs of The Future'. Unpublished paper.

Kübler-Ross, E. 1995 *Death is of Vital Importance*, Barrytown, New York, Station Hill Press.

La Barre, W. 1970 *The Ghost Dance: the Oedipal in Religion*, Garden City, Doubleday.

Lawrence, P. 1964 *Road Belong Cargo*, Manchester, University Press.

Lee, R. 1988 'Reflections on Primitive Communism'. From *Hunters and Gatherers*, edited by T. Ingold, D. Riches and J. Woodburn, Oxford, Berg.

Lee, R and I. DeVore 1968 (editors) *Man the Hunter*, Chicago, Aldine.

Levi-Strauss, C. 1966 *The Savage Mind*, London, Weidenfeld and Nicolson.

Lindholm, C. 1990 *Charisma*, Oxford, Blackwell.

Lovelock, J. 1979 *Gaia. A New Look at Life on Earth*, Oxford, University Press.

—— 1991 'Gaia'. From *The New Age. An Anthology of Essential Writings*, edited by W. Bloom, London, Channel 4 Books.

Lowe, R. and W. Shaw 1993 *Travellers: Voices of the New Age Nomads*, London, Fourth Estate.

Luhrmann, T. 1989 *Persuasions of a Witch's Craft. Ritual, Magic and Witchcraft in Present-day England*, Oxford, Blackwell.

Lukes, S. 1973 *Individualism*, Oxford, University Press.

Lyon, D. 1993 'A Bit of a "Circus": Notes on Postmodernity and New Age', *Religion*, vol. 23(2): 117–26.

MacCormack, C. 1980 'Nature, Culture and Gender: a Critique'. From *Nature, Culture and Gender*, edited by C. MacCormack and M. Strathern, Cambridge, University Press.

McFarlane, G. 1981 'Shetlanders and Incomers: Change, Conflict and Emphasis in Social Perspectives'. From *The Structure of Folk Models*, edited by L. Holy and M. Stuchlik, London, Academic Press.

MacLaine, S. 1985 *Dancing in the Light*, London, Bantam Books.

Macpherson, C. 1964 'Post-liberal Democracy', *Canadian Journal of Economics*, vol. 30(4): 485–98.

Malinowski, B. 1922 *Argonauts of the Western Pacific*, London, Routledge and Kegan Paul.

Mann, N. 1985 *The Cauldron and the Grail*, Glastonbury, Annenterprise.

Mascarenhas-Keyes, S. 1987 'The Native Anthropologist: Constraints and Strategies in Research'. From *Anthropology at Home*, edited by Anthony Jackson, London, Tavistock.

Mauss, M. 1985 'A Category of the Human Mind: the Notion of Person; the Notion of Self'. From *The Category of the Person*, edited by M. Carrithers et al., Cambridge, University Press.

Melton, J.G. (with J. Clark and A. Kelly) 1991. The *New Age Almanac*, New York, Visible Ink.

—— 1992 'Introduction'. From *Perspectives on the New Age*, edited by J. Lewis and J.G. Melton, Albany, SUNY Press.

Mestrovic, S. 1994 *The Balkanisation of the West: the Confluence of Postmodernism and Communism*, London, Routledge.

Milton, K. 1996 *Environmentalism*, London, Routledge.

Morris, B. 1976 'Whither the Savage Mind: Notes on the Natural Taxonomies of a Hunting and Gathering People', *Man*, vol. 11 (4): 542–57.

Myers, F. 1986 *Pintupi Country, Pintupi Self*, Berkeley, University of California Press.

Natale, F. 1990 'The Age of Consciousness', *Kindred Spirit*, vol. 1. no. 12.

Needham, R. 1975 'Polythetic Classification: Convergence and Consequences', *Man*, vol. 10(2): 349–69.

Niman, M. 1997 *People of the Rainbow: a Nomadic Utopia*, Knoxville, University of Tennessee Press.

Orr, L. and S. Ray 1991 'Rebirthing'. From *The New Age. An Anthology of Essential Writings*, edited by W. Bloom, London, Channel 4 Books.

Ortner, S. 1974 'Is Female to Male as Nature is to Culture?' From *Women, Culture and Society*, edited by R. Rosaldo and L. Lamphere, Stanford, University of California Press.

Overing, J. 1990 'The Shaman as Maker of Worlds: Nelson Goodman in the Amazon', *Man*, vol. 25(4): 602–19.

Paine, R. 1969 'In Search of Friendship: an Exploratory Analysis in 'middle-class' culture', *Man*, vol. 4(4): 505–24.

Pearson, J. 1998 'Assumed Affinity: Wicca and the New Age'. From *Nature Religion Today: Paganism in the Modern World*, edited by J. Pearson et al., Edinburgh, University Press.

Pepper, D. 1991 *Communes and the Green Vision: Counterculture, Lifestyle and the New Age*, London, Merlin Press.

Piercy, M. 1979 *Women on the Edge of Time*, London, The Women's Press.

Pomroy, A. 1998 'Between the Individual and the Cosmos: a Study of Concepts of Change, Power and Agency among New Agers in Glastonbury' (Masters Dissertation, University of St Andrews).

Porter, J. 1996 'Spiritualists, Aliens and UFOs: Extraterrestrials as Spirit Guides', *Journal of Contemporary Religion*, vol. 11(4): 337–53.

Prince, R. and D. Riches 1999a 'The Holistic Individual: Context as Political Process in the New Age Movement'. From *The Problem of Context*, edited by R. Dilley, Oxford, Berghahn.

——— 1999b 'Back to the Future: the New Age Movement and Hunter–Gatherers', *Anthropos*, vol. 94(1): 107–20.

Puttick, E. 1997 Women *in New Religions*, London, Macmillan.

Rapport, N. 1987 *Talking Violence. An Anthropological Interpretation of Conversation in the City*, St Johns, Newfoundland, Institute of Social and Economic Research, Memorial University.

Rasmussen, K. 1929 *Intellectual Culture of the Iglulik Eskimo*, Copenhagen, Glydendalske Borgenhandel.

Redgrove, P. 1987 *The Black Goddess and the Sixth Sense*, London, Bloomsbury.

Richardson, J. 1985 (editor) *Money and Power in the New Religions*, Lampeter, Edwin Meelen Press.

Riches, D. 1977 'An Eskimo Cooperative – the Contradiction. ' From *The White Arctic*, edited by R. Paine, St Johns, Newfoundland, Institute of Social and Economic Research, Memorial University.

Riches, D. 1979a (editor/introduction) *The Conceptualisation and Explanation of Processes of Social Change*. Belfast, Queen's University.

——— 1979b 'Ecological Variation on the Northwest Coast'. From *Social and Ecological Systems*, edited by P. Burnham and R. Ellen, London, Academic Press.

——— 1982 *Northern Nomadic Hunter–Gatherers*, London, Academic Press, 1982.

——— 1984 'Hunters, Herders and Potlatchers: Towards a Sociological Account of Prestige', *Man*, vol. 19(2): 234–51.

——— 1985 'Power as a Representational Model'. From *Power and Knowledge*, edited by R. Fardon, Washington, Smithsonian Institution.

——— 1991 'Aggression, War, Violence: Space–Time and Paradigm', *Man*, vol. 26(2): 281–98.

——— 1994 'Shamanism: the Key to Religion', *Man*, vol. 29(2): 381–405.

——— 1995 'Hunter-Gatherer Structural Transformations', *Journal of the Royal Anthropological Institute*, vol. 30(4): 679–701.

Roberts, R. 1994 'Power and Empowerment: New Age Managers and the Dialectics of Modernity/Postmodernity', *Religion Today*, vol. 9(1): 10–13.

Rose, S. 1998 'An Examination of the New Age Movement: Who is Involved and What Constitutes Spirituality', *Journal of Contemporary Religion*, vol. 13(1): 5–22.

Roth, G. 1990 *Maps to Ecstasy: Teachings of an Urban Shaman*, London, Mandala.

Rupert, G. 1992 'Employing the New Age: Training Seminars'. From *Perspectives on the New Age*, edited by J. Lewis and G. Melton, Albany, SUNY Press.

Sahlins, M. 1984 *Stone Age Economics*, London, Tavistock.

——— 1986 *Culture and Practical Reason*, Chicago, University Press.

Sahtouris, E. 1991 'Gaia's Dance'. From *The New Age. An Anthology of Essential Writings*, edited by W. Bloom, London, Channel 4 Books.

Said, E. 1978 *Orientalism*, London, Routledge and Kegan Paul.

Sallnow, M. 1981 'Communitas Reconsidered', *Man*, vol. 16(2): 281–98.

Satin, M. 1978 *New Age Politics*, New York, Dell Publishing Co.

Schumacher, E. 1974 *Small is Beautiful. A Study of Economics as if People Mattered*, London, Abacus.

Scott, A. 1990 *Ideology and the New Social Movements*, London, Unwin Hyman.

Sharma, U. 1992 *Complementary Medicine Today*, London, Macmillan.

Shenker, B. 1986 *Intentional Communities*, London, Routledge and Kegan Paul.

Silberbauer, G. 1982 'Political Processes in G/wi Bands'. From *Politics and History in Band Societies*, edited by E. Leacock and R. Lee, Cambridge, University Press.

Sjoo, M. 1992 *New Age and Armageddon*, London, The Women's Press.

——— 1994 'New Age and Patriarchy'. *Religion Today*, vol. 9(1): 22–28.

Sjoo, M. and B. Mor 1987 *The Great Cosmic Mother: Rediscovering the Religion of the Earth*, San Francisco, Harper.

Smith, M. 1956 'On Segmentary Lineage Systems', *Journal of the Royal Anthropological Institute* (old series), vol, 86(1): 39–79.

Smith, R. 1985 *Kinship and Class in the West Indies*, Cambridge, University Press.

Solway, J. and R. Lee 1990 'Foragers, Genuine or Spurious?', *Current Anthropology*, vol. 31(2): 109–46.

Sorenson, E.R. 1978 'Cooperation and Freedom among the Fore of New Guinea'. From *Learning Non-Aggression*, edited by Ashley Montagu, New York, Oxford University Press.

Southwold, M. 1978 'Buddhism and the Definition of Religion', *Man*, vol. 13(2): 362–79.

Spiro, M. 1963 *Kibbutz: Venture in Utopia*, New Haven, Harvard University Press.

——— 1972 *Children of the Kibbutz*, New Haven, Harvard University Press.

Starhawk 1989 The *Spiral Dance: A Rebirth of Ancient Religion of the Great Goddess*, San Francisco, Harper and Row.

Stark, R. 1996 'Why Religious Movements Succeed of Fail', *Journal of Contemporary Religion*, vol. 11(2): 133–46.

Stark, R. and L. Iannaccone 1997 'Why the Jehovah's Witnesses Grow so Rapidly', *Journal of Contemporary Religion*, vol. 12(1): 133–56.

Strathern, M. 1987a 'The Limits of Auto-Ethnography'. From *Anthropology at Home*, edited by A. Jackson, London, Tavistock.

——— 1987b (editor/introduction). *Dealing with Inequality*, Cambridge, University Press.

Taylor, B. 1991 'The Politics and Religion of Earth First!', *The Ecologist* vol. 21(6): 258–66.

Taylor, D. 1982 'Becoming New People: Recruitment of Young Americans in the Unitarian Church'. From *Millennialism and Charisma*, edited by R. Wallis, Belfast, Queen's University.

Teillard de Chardin, P. 1959 *The Phenomenon of Man*, London, Collins.

Thompson, J. and P. Heelas 1986 *The Way of the Heart: The Rajneesh Movement*, Wellingborough, The Aquarian Press.

Tipton, S. 1982 *Getting Saved from the Sixties*, Berkeley, University of California Press.

Trevelyan, G. 1986 *Summons to a High Crusade*, Forres, The Findhorn Press.

Turner, V. 1969 *The Ritual Process*, Harmondsworth, Penguin.

——— 1974 *Dramas, Fields and Metaphors*, Ithaca, Cornell University Press.

Turner, V. and E. Turner. 1978 *Image and Pilgrimage in Christian Culture: Anthropological Perspectives*. Oxford, Blackwell.

van Hove, H. 1996 'Higher Realities and the Inner Self', *Journal of Contemporary Religion*, vol. 11(2): 185–94.

Wadel, C. 1973 *Now Who's Fault is That: the Struggle for Esteem in the Face of Chronic Unemployment*, St Johns, Newfoundland, Institute of Social and Economic Research, Memorial University.

Wallis, R. 1975 (editor/introduction) *Sectarianism: Analyses of Religious and non-Religious Sects*, London, Peter Owen.

——— 1978 *The Rebirth of the Gods? Reflections on the New Religions in the West*, Belfast, Queen's University.

——— 1979 *Salvation and Protest – Studies of Social and Religious Movements*, London, Francis Pinter.

——— 1982 'Charisma, Commitment and Control in a New Religious Movement'. From *Millennialism and Charisma*, edited by R. Wallis, Belfast, Queen's University.

——— 1984 *The Elementary Forms of New Religious Life*, London, Routledge and Kegan Paul.

Walter, T. 'Death in the New Age', *Religion*, vol. 23(2): 127–45.

Weber, M. 1958 *The Protestant Work Ethic and the Spirit of Capitalism*, New York, Scribners.

——— 1947 *The Theory of Social and Economic Organisation*, New York, Free Press.

Wilmsen, E. and J. Denbow 1990 'Paradigmatic History of San-speaking Peoples and Current Attempts at Revision', *Current Anthropology*, vol. 31(4): 489–524.

Wilson, B. 1970 *Religious Sects: a Sociological Study*, London, Macmillan.

——— 1973 *Magic and the Millennium*, Cambridge, University Press.

Woodburn, J. 1988 'Hunter–Gatherer Social Organisation: Is It Best Understood as a Product of Encapsulation'. From T. Ingold, D. Riches, and J. Woodburn, editors, *Hunters and Gatherers*, Oxford, Berg.

Worsley, P. 1957 *The Trumpet Shall Sound*, London, MacGibbon and Kee.

York, M. 1994 'New Age in Britain: an Overview', *Religion Today*, vol 9(3): 14–21.

——— 1995 *The Emerging Network: a Sociology of the New Age and Neo-Pagan Movements*, Lanham, Maryland, Rowman and Littlefield.

——— 1996 'New Age and Paganism'. From *Paganism Today*, edited by G. Harvey and C. Hardman, London, Thorsons.

Zohar, E. and D. Marshall 1993 *The Quantum Society: Mind, Physics and a New Social Vision*, London, Bloomsbury.

Index